FROM MEMORY
TO HISTORY

FROM MEMORY TO HISTORY

TELEVISION VERSIONS OF THE TWENTIETH CENTURY

JIM CULLEN

RUTGERS UNIVERSITY PRESS

New Brunswick, Camden, and Newark, New Jersey, and London

Library of Congress Cataloging-in-Publication Data

Names: Cullen, Jim, author.
Title: From memory to history : television versions of the twentieth century /
   Jim Cullen.
Description: New Brunswick : Rutgers University Press, [2021] | Includes
   bibliographical references and index.
Identifiers: LCCN 2020031107 | ISBN 9781978813816 (paperback) |
   ISBN 9781978813823 (cloth) | ISBN 9781978813830 (epub) |
   ISBN 9781978813847 (mobi) | ISBN 9781978813854 (pdf)
Subjects: LCSH: Television programs—United States—History—20th century. |
   Television and history—United States. | National characteristics, American. |
   History on television. | Television—Social aspects—United States. |
   United States—Civilization—20th century.
Classification: LCC PN1992.3.U5 C845 2021 | DDC 791.45/750973—dc23
LC record available at https://lccn.loc.gov/2020031107

A British Cataloging-in-Publication record for this book is
available from the British Library.

♾ The paper used in this publication meets the requirements of the
American National Standard for Information Sciences—Permanence
of Paper for Printed Library Materials, ANSI Z39.48-1992.

www.rutgersuniversitypress.org

Manufactured in the United States of America

For
Andy Meyers
Friend, Colleague, Presence

CONTENTS

INTRODUCTION
Television's History   1

1   **LEFT TO THE RIGHT**
The Waltons as a 1970s Version of the 1930s   17

2   **CAMP HISTORY**
Hogan's Heroes as a 1960s Version of the 1940s   45

3   **A FUNNY WAR**
M*A*S*H as a 1970s Version of the 1950s   69

4   **DREAM ADVERTISEMENT**
Mad Men as a 2000s Version of the 1960s   95

5   **WE'RE ALL ALL RIGHT**
That '70s Show as a 1990s Version of the 1970s   123

6   **DOMESTIC FRONT**
The Americans as a 2010s Version of the 1980s   149

7   **PROGRAMMING HOPE**
Halt and Catch Fire as a 2010s Version of the 1990s   169

CONCLUSION
Visualizing the Future of the Past   185

ACKNOWLEDGMENTS   187

NOTES   189

INDEX   207

FROM MEMORY
TO HISTORY

EMPIRE BUILDER

Atlantic City treasurer Nucky Thompson (Steve Buscemi) addresses the city's Women's Temperance League chapter in the pilot episode of *Boardwalk Empire* (2010). The series reminds viewers about the strong ties between those who favored Prohibition (which virtually everybody now thinks was a mistake) and women's suffrage (which virtually everybody now considers common sense) in a show about the 1920s that was fundamentally about the nature of power—one with contemporary reverberations.

INTRODUCTION

Television's History

ECEMBER 31, 1919. On the boardwalk in Atlantic City, revelers have gathered in the legendary Babette's Supper Club to ring in a new year, a new decade—and, with a combination of disdain and derision, the Eighteenth Amendment to the U.S. Constitution. The new law, buttressed by the recently passed Volstead Act, makes the manufacture, transportation, and sale of alcohol illegal, a set of regulations collectively known as Prohibition. Earlier on New Year's Eve, there had been a mock funeral procession featuring a gigantic fake bottle of "John Barleycorn" whiskey in a coffin, led by a blackface band performing a jazz version of "Battle Hymn of the Republic." Now, at the stroke of midnight, black balloons fall and the ensemble at Babette's performs a version of "Taps" before launching into a raucous rendition of "Tiger Rag," an early jazz standard. It's far from clear what Prohibition will mean—except to a group of political and business leaders who met earlier that evening to prepare for the bonanza that will result once the only way to get a drink will be illegally.

Not everyone regards the arrival of Prohibition as a joke or a financial opportunity. Three nights earlier, the Atlantic City chapter of the Women's Temperance League held a meeting in Atlantic City to herald the dawn of a new era. "Liquor, thy name's delirium," intoned the leader of the chapter in a poem she had written in honor of the occasion. Behind her a sign read, "Lips that touch liquor shall never touch

1

mine." She then introduces a special guest: the city's treasurer, Enoch L. "Nucky" Thompson.

Thompson proceeds to relate a childhood anecdote from the infamous blizzard of 1888, when, because of his father's drunkenness, he was forced to forage in railroad yard for coal to heat his family's home and killed rats for his family's dinner. "Prohibition means progress," Thompson tells the women as the moral of his story. "Never again will families be robbed of their father, held hostage by alcohol. How proud I am to live in a nation which, God willing, this year will give women the right to vote." Thompson's prayers would be answered: in 1920, women did indeed get the right to vote thanks to the Nineteenth Amendment to the Constitution. And Thompson would preside over a vast urban crime empire made possible by the Prohibition he piously affirmed at the meeting. When his driver notes that the personal anecdote he had just narrated was false, he responds, "First rule of politics, kiddo. Never let the truth get in the way of a good story."

Watching this story unfold a century later on a television screen—Prohibition, Atlantic City, and Babette's are real, the rest of the scenario fictive—it all seems like a long time ago. (Nucky Thompson is modeled on the actual Enoch Johnson, who presided less colorfully over the boardwalk from the 1910s until he went to jail in 1941.) There's no one alive today who can remember the 1920s, and much of what transpires in this show's rendition of them seems remote. If there's one thing anybody who knows anything about American history knows, it's that Prohibition was a failure—and as far as most people are concerned it was a stupid idea. Women's suffrage, by contrast, seems like common sense—stupid that it hadn't happened sooner. Less well known is that the two movements proceeded in tandem, the strong supporters of one tending to be strong supporters of the other. But inconvenient facts are soon forgotten. You don't let the truth get in the way of a good story—or, in this case, stories that seem like they should be kept separate.

Other aspects of this pilot episode of *Boardwalk Empire*, which first ran on the premium cable TV channel HBO between 2010 and 2015, are less remote. They have to be. Whatever the ultimate source of their revenue (advertisers, direct sales, subscriptions), television shows depend on garnering viewers, and the only way to get people to watch even the most escapist entertainment is to make clear that the world it depicts has some relevance for the one in which we live. This may be less difficult when a show has a contemporary setting, because such shows are implicitly saying *this is how it is*. It's more difficult when a show has a historical setting, because such shows are explicitly saying *this is how it was*.

The appeal of entertainment with a historical setting is nevertheless dialectical: it says *both* that the world you're watching is gone *and* that it's relevant. In the case of television, the primary way the former idea gets conveyed is visually, especially in production design and costumes. *Boardwalk Empire* is exceptionally good at this. Its main set, a re-creation of the Atlantic City Boardwalk built in Greenpoint, Brooklyn, lovingly evokes the storefronts, signage, and waterfront of a vanished world (aided by modern technology).[1] The costumes, which are so clearly different from the suits and dresses people wear today, are dated and stylish at the same time. Like all good shows of its kind, *Boardwalk Empire* also uses sound to good effect, whether in language—who today would name their child Enoch?—or in song, which includes actors playing former pop stars like Sophie Tucker ("Some of these Days") and Eddie Cantor ("The Dumber They Come, the Better I Like 'Em"). Sometimes such songs, played on what we would regard as primitive sound recording technology, sound tinny and dated. Other times, especially performed live, they sound startlingly vivid, like black-and-white photos bursting into color.

Unlike showing that times were different, conveying relevance is a little trickier. Doing so too directly will sound clunky ("I hear there's to be a battle at a little town called Gettysburg"). Characters have to say and do things that seem true to the world in which they live while at the same time pointing toward unstated contemporary realities that viewers with varying levels of sophistication can grasp—and feel pleasure in connecting the dots for themselves. Ideally, you'll have multiple strands so that viewers of varying levels of acuity will be able to discern one or more.

This, too, is something at which *Boardwalk Empire* excels. The series was created by Terence Winter, who wrote dozens of episodes of *The Sopranos* (1999–2007), the now-classic HBO series about a contemporary New Jersey gangster family that carried within its DNA a century of cinematic tradition of crime stories. With *Boardwalk Empire*, Winter and his collaborators regularly offered their viewers scenarios that were specific to its time and yet resonated in ours. So, for example, in the 2010 episode "Anastasia," we have what to all appearances is an ordinary Ku Klux Klan meeting in Atlantic City, something not likely to happen today. "Filthy immigrants, Christ-killing Jews, anarchists of every stripe: dangerous though they may be, make no mistake, my brethren: it is the coon that is the true bane of this great nation," the Wizard tells the Klansmen in the diction and cadences of another century. "Up from the South they come like so many rats, feeding on jobs heretofore reserved for white men, veterans, patriots, true Americans all consigned to the bread lines." Much of this dialogue refers to people and situations, like the Great Migration of African Americans from the rural south to the urban north, that have long since ended. But the organization of hatreds expressed here, reaching an apex in black racism, is recognizable to any sentient adult in the twenty-first century. When Nucky (played by the great Steve Buscemi) learns that that Warren Harding has won the 1920 Republican presidential nomination, he declares, "That imbecile is going to be the next president of the United States"—a sentiment that ricochets through the elections of Ronald Reagan, George W. Bush, and Donald Trump, all of whom were regarded with comparable contempt.

The most successful historical stories also express truths that those who experience them recognize as timeless. In the case of *Boardwalk Empire*, such truths have a distinctly cynical air. "If we only had good men, we'd never have leaders," Nucky explains to his companion Margaret Schroeder (Kelly McDonald) on a quiet night at home. "Then what should they be?" she asks. "Useful to those who support them," Nucky replies, offering a sturdy theory of politics, American and otherwise. In the ensuing episode, "The Emerald Forest," Nucky again tries to explain political realities to her: "This isn't some fantasy world like one of those children's books," he tells Margaret. (She has been reading *The Wizard of Oz* to her children, a book which itself was a parable of the populist politics of the 1890s.) "It's a real place with real people. And sometimes, to make it run properly, we need to tell those people what they want to hear."

Of course, figuring out what people want to hear, much less figuring out how to express it, are not simple tasks. Success depends on who these people are—and *when* they are. Which brings us to yet one more layer of complexity involved in stories about the past, specifically those stories that are clearly from a moment that has passed and yet in the living memory of those still alive. In cases such as these, storytellers carry an extra burden. They need to capture shared understandings of a moment with sufficient credibility ("Yes! That's just how it was!"), while at the same time conveying something fresh—something more than mere nostalgia, which while often pleasurable, is rarely fully satisfying for artists or audiences.

This book looks at the way the recent past, defined here as roughly the last century, has been represented in television shows of roughly the past half-century. The oldest people now alive may have (dim) memories of the Great Depression, while the youngest likely to be reading these words may have (dim) memories of the early Internet— or be personally close to those who *do* remember such events. This porous frontier of lived and proximate experience constitutes what is known as collective memory: a repository of reference points by which living people situate themselves in time. Sometimes this is a matter of specific historical events (the Cold War); in others, it's more a form of cultural shorthand ("the sixties"). The frontiers of collective memory are ever-shifting; the demographic bulge of people once known as the Baby Boom, referring to those who were born between 1946 and 1964, is now geriatric. And the twentieth century, which until recently was a time in which virtually everyone alive had once lived, is in the process of becoming another time. Few people today have any real idea of who Sophie Tucker or Eddie Cantor were. And the day is coming when a child will ask about, and mispronounce,

Beyoncé, for whom a first name identification may not be sufficient. Our time is forever slipping through our fingers.

MAKING WAVES

Television has a special role to play in the making of U.S. history. The successor to radio and the precursor of the Internet, TV was once an emblem of modernity itself, its very existence a source of wonder for generations of Americans. The basic technology was available as early as the 1920s, but it wasn't until the 1950s that it became a marvel—*the* marvel—of everyday life. Television remained pervasive at century's end, though more taken for granted in a society that had moved on to collective fascination with the computer age. People today still offhandedly talk about watching television, but relatively few actually do so in the way it was originally invented—the term "television" is really little more than an increasingly inaccurate shorthand term for a kind of cultural document that resembles what TV was once understood to be but in fact appears in homes—and any number of other locations—in a different way than it once did.

This is more than a matter of the size and nature of a technological box. Different forms of mass communication reach people in different ways. The key to television is that it was a *broadcast* medium. A program—not a set of computer algorithms but rather a discrete piece of cultural content that may take one of any number of formats or genres—would originate at a single point (typically a live set in a studio) and then be transmitted by wired networks and picked up by antennae in millions of individual homes, reconstituted as sound and image on a receiver known as a television set. Later the mode of transmission would be augmented by the advent of cable and satellite networks, but the basic concept—one site, multiple points, simultaneous experience—was the essence of what broadcasting meant.

In the closing decades of the century, television was supplemented by new forms of delivery that fractured the cohesion of broadcasting while offering viewers an increasing sense of control over the content they chose to watch. Videotaping made it possible preserve live performances for later transmission, a technology that became available for television networks in the 1950s and an increasingly popular consumer option beginning in the 1970s. The age of the videocassette recorder (VCR) in the 1980s was followed by the advent of a higher-quality and more durable format, the digital video disc (DVD) beginning in the 1990s. The early Internet, which relied on telephone lines for transmission, gave way to integrated service digital lines at the turn of the twenty-first century, making it possible to carry a much larger amount of data than ever before, which meant it was now possible to watch television on a computer. The growing number, quality, and range of wireless communications—"wireless" a term that once referred to radio broadcasting, born again for the Internet age—became commonplace over the course of the first decade of the twenty-first century and allowed viewers to watch television on any number of devices (like a cell phone). While broadcasting could once be conceived as a signal radiating outward to cover a particular geographic area, the new communications model was understood as a web of nodes connected at multiple points. Television was now a term that referred to a kind of *content* rather than a form of *transmission*.

What kind of content? The answer, of course, varied. Some kinds of programming—news, sports, drama, comedy, and the like—were not specific to a medium; you could encounter them in forms that included newspapers, radio, and live theater. But as with other media, television developed distinctive accents and kinds of shows that were uniquely well suited to it. Soap operas, so named for the companies that sponsored them, were a variety of melodrama that began in radio and migrated to television. Certain kinds of sporting events—initially boxing because it was contained in a ring and thus easy to broadcast—flourished on television, which got increasingly good at capturing other games (like football) on camera. Some genres, notably the situation comedy, had roots in other forms of entertainment but became uniquely identified with TV. Television differed from radio because it was visual; it differed from film because it was recurrent. It was different from them all in the sheer scale of its reach. There had never been anything like it before. And in some respects, there hasn't been anything like it since.

IMPROVING HISTORIES

One thing TV was not especially good at for much of its history was history itself. To some extent, this was a reflection of the medium—a symbol of modernity, television was also besotted with modernity. Part of its excitement was its ability to capture real life in real time for everybody to see.

It's not hard to imagine why depicting the past would also have some appeal. Despite the medium's ability to portray events with a verisimilitude that would have startled previous generations, however, television had some distinct limitations, especially relative to the competing medium of film. Much more than movies, television shows were a perishable commodity—and a commodity that had to be produced under often intense time and cost pressures.

Consider the basic nature of moviemaking. A film is a project that is a one-time proposition (sequels notwithstanding) with a fixed budget and timeline (overruns notwithstanding). A major studio production can afford filmmakers sufficient time, means, and locations to re-create a historical moment in meticulous detail. But while a high-profile movie production is shot over a series of months, a successful television episode must typically be made in weeks—at which point the whole process has to be started all over again, in seasons that can stretch on for years. There isn't usually enough time or money to belabor details (that's how you get cardboard graves, "exterior" settings that are really murals, and the like). This difference between movies and TV shouldn't be overstated: there are movies that are made on a shoestring budget, and TV shows that have a robust production design apparatus in place (*The Waltons*, subject of the first chapter of this book, is a good example of this.) But on average, a typical Hollywood movie is going to be more meticulous than a typical TV network show, and in the second half of the twentieth century, movies on average attracted a higher caliber of writing and acting talent than TV shows did.

In the early years of television, the predominant form of historical television programming was the western. Westerns first appeared on the small screen in 1954 when Warner Brothers—which had previously regarded the TV business with competitive suspicion—agreed to produce a weekly show. In 1956, there were four more; by 1958, there were at least twenty-five westerns on the air, and they accounted for seven of the top ten shows. Two of the most popular and long-running were *Bonanza* (1959–1973) and *Gunsmoke* (1955–1975).[2] Compared to cinematic peers such as *Shane* (1953) and *The Searchers* (1956), the production values of these shows could seem downright crude. But they came to viewers free in their homes on a regular basis and were able to amass devoted followings.

At the midpoint of the twentieth century, westerns were shows set in a vanished world of cowboys, Indians, horses, and vast landscapes. But they offered viewers comforting messages about a durable strain of individualism, resilience, and freedom that could feel invigorating in a Cold War world of conformity, bureaucracy, and ideological conflict. In an important sense, westerns were mythic: less about trying to accurately depict what the West was like and more as a repository of story, symbol, and language that could reinforce the convictions of their audiences. One can argue that all forms of history are mythic—something usually clearer to those who don't buy into a given mythology than those who do—but many fans of westerns would probably agree that the feelings they elicited, not their factual accuracy, was the primary source of their appeal.

The western began to recede in prominence by the mid-1960s, in large part because the mythology on which it rested was under growing strain amid the challenges of the civil rights, women's, and anti-war movements of that decade. Tellingly, one of the few new westerns of the decade was *F Troop*, a satire that ran from 1965 to 1967 and had a long subsequent life in syndication—that is to say, running on local stations that bought the rights to broadcast it. This sense of irreverence also influenced other television shows from the era that had historical settings, notably *Hogan's Heroes* and *M*A*S*H*, discussions of which are included in this book.

Other demographic changes were also underway. Network TV has always been funded by advertising: viewers watch shows in exchange for being subjected to periodic commercials—an economic model that took shape in the radio era and has continued into the Internet era. Since advertisers paid for the shows, and since one important imperative was not to offend a potential customer, they could exert significant veto power over content they didn't like—or simply would be perceived as not liking. In the early years of the medium, advertisers thought in terms of raw numbers, when shows like *I Love Lucy* (1951–1957) could command a huge, even majority, share of a given audience. Over time, they became more receptive to targeting their ads to certain desirable demographics and were willing to subsidize programming with weaker ratings but the right kind of viewers (like golf tournaments). Such slicing and dicing has become the coin of the media realm in a society that grows ever more segmented—and divided.

Toward the end of the century, shifting technological winds began to have even more of an impact on the ways TV shows were made. With the advent of cable, which began as a means of improving reception but evolved into a platform for premium content, the relationship between creator and viewer became more direct as a subscription model challenged advertising as a funding mechanism. (Cable too became more specialized in tailoring content to specific demographics.) Moreover, the reduced need to fit a show into a fixed number of minutes per episode, or episodes per season, opened up new vistas in how to make a show. The result was a renaissance in the television industry that has been dubbed "Peak TV." *The Sopranos* was an early harbinger of this; the years that followed brought a wave of new shows of unusual quality, daring, and appeal—dramas such as *The Wire* (2002–2008) and *Breaking Bad* (2008–2013); sitcoms like *Curb Your Enthusiasm* (2000–ongoing) and *Veep* (2012–2019); hybrids such as *Girls* (2013–2017) and *Orange Is the New Black* (2013–2019).

This new sense of artistic freedom, combined with newly muscular budgets from content providers like Netflix that were flush with cash, also had implications for the portrayal of history on television shows. The western, for example, was reborn with gloriously mud-spackled realism in *Deadwood* (2004–2006), a series in which once-forbidden profanity could rise to the level of poetry. Strictly speaking, *Game of*

Thrones (2011–2019) was in the fantasy genre, but its essentially medieval setting was a marvel of on-location shooting in Europe and expensive high-tech imagery. Now, for the first time, television became a serious alternative for A-list writers, actors, and directors, as the Hollywood film entered a long, slow slide into artistic enervation (like endless sequels and remakes) and declining box office receipts. "American movie audiences now just don't seem to be very interested in any kind of ambiguity or any kind of real complexity of character or narrative," the esteemed film director Steven Soderbergh said of his decision to embark on the HBO series *Luck* (2011–2012), with actor legend Dustin Hoffman.[3] In this regard, it's significant that Martin Scorsese, a man widely regarded as the greatest living American filmmaker, chose to direct the pilot of *Boardwalk Empire* and to stay on as an executive producer of the show. Now, finally, history on small screens had become a serious business.

REVISING THE PAST

And what of the oldest medium of history, the kind that's recorded not on tape or digital files but on paper?

In an important sense, it's the act of the recording—via technologies of (stone) tablets, scrolls, and quills, followed by the recognizable format of the codex and the invention of the printing press—that constitutes the essence of what history *is*: a fixed account of events in the past. For a long time, history was a literally poetic form of storytelling, rendered orally. Over time, it became (again, literally) more prosaic, its elements of artistry and feeling—which never entirely disappeared—giving way to more straightforward narrative.

And then, beginning in the late nineteenth century, history began to change.[4] The rise of the modern research university and the growing prestige of science led many new disciplines, like sociology or psychology, to adopt or mimic the quantitative methodologies of the sciences. History, too, was pulled by such currents, its traditions of literary expression and storytelling increasingly giving way to terminology like "evidence," "hypothesis," and empirical measurement. To put it more simply, history became analytical. Its goal was less a matter of telling a good story than formulating an argument. To be sure, many arguments were implicitly a form of storytelling. But historians, like many of their colleagues in academe, were now communicating more with each other than with a broader public. While much lamented, this approach was logical: history had never really been a realistic way for anyone to earn a living (indeed, much of it had been done by rich men with the resources to travel), while impressing one's peers was a good way to gain financial security via a tenured professorship. There were always a few historians who managed to break out into a wide general readership—like Richard Hofstadter of Columbia University, whose books *The American Political Tradition* (1948) and *The Age of Reform* (1955) remain classics and in print—but they were often regarded with suspicion and disdain. (Hofstadter was sometimes dismissed as a mere essayist, because his work was more interpretive rather than grounded in primary source research.) Historians who write for the public at large are sometimes dubbed "popularizers." It's not a complimentary term.

In important ways, then, history was cut off from the public at large in the second half of the twentieth century. The goal of historical scholarship now involved articulating *reinterpretations* of past events—which is to say it involved a revision or rejection of the prevailing conventional wisdom as likely to be understood by the general public. In effect, the goal was to say something new about the old. There were two important consequences in this development.

The first is that historical reinterpretations began to proliferate, spawning the subfield of historiography: the study of how histories themselves change over time. Why did the Civil War happen? Was it the result of constitutional conflict over the scope of states' rights? An economic conflict in which a capitalist North triumphed over a feudal South? Was it the result of a generation of blundering politicians who miscalculated and triggered a conflict they didn't want? Was it inevitable? (The answer to this last question has tended to be no. Historians tend to emphasize contingency, a notion that things could always have been otherwise, which perhaps reflects a bias toward free will and a desire to tell readers that their choices matter, which may well amount to a form of flattery—another example of Nucky Thompson's maxim about telling people what they want to hear.)[5]

There's an important corollary to this point about multiple explanations of historical phenomena. While at any given time historians will always generate multiple explanations for any given historical phenomenon—their jobs depend on it—it's also the case that particular interpretations tend to be dominant at any given time. Variations on the states' rights hypothesis were common in the early twentieth century; economic arguments held sway for much of the 1920s and 1930s; the Blundering Generation school held sway during the Great Depression and World War II. Which is not surprising: historical interpretations are often efforts to understand the present in terms of the past. Sometimes even opposing arguments are products of their time in preoccupations that they share. Loving socialism or hating socialism rests on a common notion that economic forces are the ones that matter the most—a premise that may wax, wane, or disappear entirely.

The second point worth making here is that while academic historians and the public at large have increasingly lost contact with each other, they've never been entirely out of touch. Over time, academic arguments sometimes seep into public discourse and significantly reshape it. For example, professional historians began foregrounding the role of slavery in the coming of the Civil War as early as the 1950s, long before the public at large did. Nowadays, you'd be hard pressed to find people who would say it wasn't central to the conflict, and those who think otherwise usually do so aware that theirs is a minority view—and not one with much academic support. In this regard, professional scholarship can sometimes become the vanguard for cultural change. It's also the case that the press of current events, like the civil rights movement, will lead scholars no less than laypeople to reconsider the past in light of current circumstances.

Such historiographic considerations can thus be instructive in looking at the history of television. As any number of sources indicate, the Great Depression of the 1930s was both experienced as well as remembered as a serious economic crisis. And that's evident in watching any given episode of *The Waltons*. But because the show premiered in 1972, in the wake of significant social upheavals of the 1960s, there are a notable number of episodes that deal with race relations as well as the status of women—though not necessarily in the ways they would be a half-century later. When *Hogan's Heroes*, a slapstick comedy about a World War II prisoner-of-war camp, went on the air in 1965, the Vietnam War was relatively uncontroversial. As the series continued into the late 1960s and early 1970s, however, the show could be seen as a veiled commentary on the sheer stupidity of war, even as it continued to valorize the ingenuity of the Americans in their quest to best the feckless Germans. *Hogan's Heroes* finished its run in 1971; the following year, *M*A*S*H* premiered at a time when the Vietnam War was deeply unpopular and indeed widely understood to be lost. So its antiwar messages were much more evident and much less likely to be viewed as controversial. Many of the same people worked behind the scenes for both shows, which may seem surprising given how different they are in tone.

With the advent of Peak TV at the turn of this century, historical interpretation seemed to become markedly more sophisticated. Some of this, again, was a matter of improved production values. But it also reflected a change in pacing of episodes, which viewers could stream (or rewatch) in rapid succession, rather than waiting for weekly components that were often self-contained rather than a flowing narrative. The scripts of such shows also tended to be more attentive to capturing the past on its own terms as well as contemporary ones. Or in bending them in interesting ways. *Boardwalk Empire*, for example, is nominally a show about Prohibition. But what it's really about is the nature of power: how it's acquired, how it's used, how it's challenged, and how it's lost. It's also something of a morality play: "There's a kindness in you, I know it," a perplexed Margaret tells Nucky in the first season finale. (She's right.) This is why she's so dismayed by the violence and corruption in which he's enmeshed: "How can you do what you do?" Nucky's response: "We all have to decide how much sin we can live with." As we see over the course of five seasons, Nucky can live with a lot. But he also pays a price—and Margaret proves to be an apt pupil who lands more squarely on her feet than Nucky does.

It's also useful to compare how two different shows engage the same themes. The world of women in *Mad Men* is notably more complex and richer than *The Waltons* in capturing the possibilities and limits in women's everyday lives. That's partly because women in New York City in the 1960s had more choices than women in rural Virginia in the 1930s. It's also because women held more positions of power in making *Mad Men* than *The Waltons* (although *The Waltons* was notable for the relatively large role women writers and directors played relative to shows that had come before). That's not necessarily to say that one is better than the other, any more than a Picasso portrait is inherently better than a Rembrandt one. Evaluations, historical and otherwise, are best made in context.

In the pages that follow, then, you will find discussions of television shows that are rendered in three temporal dimensions: (1) the time a given show portrays, (2) the time the show was made, and (3) how the show and the times that shaped it look in the 2020s, a subject that will be revisited in the conclusion. (A fourth dimension will emerge if anyone cares to look at this book in the future and reconsiders its 2020s assessments in that later light.) The chapters proceed chronologically in terms of the decades portrayed, though not in terms of the time a given show was made. You'll see that the dating is a little imprecise: *The Waltons* is designated a show of the 1970s even though it ran into the early 1980s, and while it's discussed primarily in terms of its portrayal of the Great Depression, its (less satisfying) episodes run through World War II. Similarly, *That '70s Show* is a described here as document of the 1990s, when its sensibility was formed, even though it ran until 2006. *Halt and Catch Fire* opens in the 1980s but is notable for the way it in effect renders an early history of the Internet in the 1990s. If the fit is imperfect, the same might be said of any historical account: it seeks to impose order on times that are finally too rich and complicated to ever be fully captured in all their untamable complexity. Simplification is the price of comprehension, which is always finite and imperfect. And thus requires the historian to proceed in a spirit of humility.

So, shall we go ahead and remember?

ALL IN THE FAMILY

The cast of *The Waltons*, circa 1975. The show's political sensibility built a bridge between the legacies of the Old Left of the 1930s and the New Left of the 1960s. Shown from left (top row): Richard Thomas (John-Boy), Judy Norton (Mary Ellen Walton), Jon Walmsley (Jason Walton), Mary Elizabeth McDonough (Erin Walton), Ralph Waite (John Walton Sr.), Michael Learned (Olivia Walton), Will Geer (Zebulon Walton), and Ellen Corby (Esther Walton). Bottom: David W. Harper (Jim-Bob Walton), Kami Cotler (Elizabeth Walton), and Eric Scott (Ben Walton). The dog's name was Reckless.

CHAPTER 1

LEFT TO THE RIGHT

The Waltons as a 1970s Version of the 1930s

Key Cast Members
- Michael Learned as Olivia Walton
- Ralph Waite as John Walton
- Richard Thomas as John-Boy Walton
- Jason Walmsley at Jason Walton
- Judy Norton as Mary Ellen Walton
- Eric Scott as Ben Walton
- Mary Elizabeth McDonough as Erin Walton
- David W. Harper as Jim-Bob Walton
- Kami Cotler as Elizabeth Walton
- Ellen Corby as Esther "Grandma" Walton
- Will Geer as Zebulon "Grandpa" Walton

Key Episodes
- *The Homecoming: A Christmas Story* (prequel movie, 1971)
- "The Scholar" (1973)
- "The Bicycle" (1973)
- "The Cradle" (1974)
- "The Conflict" (1974)
- "The Quilting" (1976)
- "The Fire Storm" (1976)
- "The Stray" (1977)

· "The Obsession" (1978)
· "The Illusion" (1978)
· "The Innocents" (1979)
· "The Unthinkable" (1980)

*I*N THE COLLECTIVE American imagination, most of the nation's turning points have hinged on wars. Its very creation, of course, rested on a successful military insurrection. It was preserved at great cost in civil war. The United States gained global preeminence after two world wars; it began to lose it after defeat in Vietnam. The significance of these armed conflicts was not simply a matter of what was resolved on now-obscure battlefields but rather the way they generated, accelerated, or arrested developments in civil society. These wars changed the shape of domestic life in terms of sociopolitical trends, cultural tendencies, and economic realities.

About the only event that could compete with such wars in terms of its impact on everyday life was the Great Depression, which essentially occupied the decade of the 1930s. There had been other severe economic downturns in U.S. history—the so-called Panics of 1819 and 1837 were exceptionally severe, as was a major depression in 1893. But the Great Depression remains the gold standard, as it were, in terms of the breadth and depth of its impact on virtually all Americans, who experienced the contraction to one degree or another (or who could not help but be aware of it if they did not). The basic economic metrics are striking: the nation's gross national product fell by 30 percent between 1929 and 1933, by which point 23.6 percent of the nation's workforce was unemployed, with a comparable percentage underemployed. The thirties were the only decade between 1880 and 1980 that the United States experienced no net economic growth.[1]

Beyond its immediate impact, there are a number of reasons why the Great Depression would remain vivid in collective memory for the next century. The most obvious is its historical proximity; there are still people alive who were born during it, though their numbers are dwindling rapidly. Another was the intensity with which the event was documented—indeed, cultural historians still speak of a "documentary impulse" evident in photography (most famously in the photography of Dorothea Lange, whose work for the Farm Security Administration in the 1930s literally captured the face of poverty in images like her 1936 "Migrant Mother"). This impulse spilled into film, like the 1939 John Ford movie *The Grapes of Wrath,* based on the John Steinbeck novel of three years earlier, that was similarly focused on rendering the realities of poverty with crystalline detail.[2]

But there are two interconnected reasons why the Great Depression has occupied a prominent place in collective national memory. The first is that the crisis coincided with a noticeable upturn in interest in American history itself in the 1930s. This mood was by no means universal. After all, the thirties were also a time when the appeal of international communism—which promised a break with the past—was at high tide even in the United States. But the decade was nevertheless notable for a new wave of interest in Americana, evident everywhere from the Puritan revival in architecture to Carl Sandburg's hugely successful multivolume biography of Abraham Lincoln, and the paintings of Thomas Hart Benton and (the admittedly ironic) Grant Wood.

The second reason why the Depression would remain an important touchstone has to do with the cultural politics in the century since. In general, the Left has had the upper hand when it comes to cultural politics (as opposed to other kinds), though for the most part it subsequently rejected the patriotic appeal that characterized the thirties. While earlier generations of social reformers, among them abolitionists and progressives, stitched their objectives into the fabric of the American experiment, more recent ones have tended to view the national past as a series of obstacles, mistakes, and scars. Early civil rights advocates, notably Martin Luther King Jr., cast their call for racial equality in terms of a still-viable American Dream (a term that, it's worth noting, came into popular usage in the thirties).[3] By the late sixties, such an integrationist project had faded in terms of a more militant approach that focused on the nation's failures, a sensibility that also characterized opposition to the Vietnam War—and pretty much every social movement on the Left ever since.

This was the context in which the television show *The Waltons* (1972–1981) was born. It was a show set in the era of the Old Left of the thirties, as it came to be known, in contrast with New Left of the sixties. The ties between the two were those of a complex family relationship: close, tetchy, and marked by generational friction. In general, the thirties Left prized broad-based coalitions rooted in labor, while the sixties Left was grounded in social equality, principally in terms of civil rights and feminism. *The Waltons* sought to bridge these sensibilities, even as it appealed to a silent majority whose outlook was temperamentally conservative. In short, *The Waltons* was a show about the thirties/forties that bore a clear consciousness of the sixties/seventies. Viewing it through such bifocal lenses can help one appreciate why it was able to capture and maintain such a large audience in its heyday, and why it is now little more than a curio on the cusp of disappearing from the national imagination. Such bifocals can also help one see why it deserves to be remembered.

FAMILY CONSIDERATIONS

That cultural event known in shorthand as the sixties was a time of transformation in many sectors of American society, not the least of which was the nation's popular culture. The music and film industries in particular underwent a renaissance. In the case of the former, innovators such as Bob Dylan and the Beatles were able to seize upon new technologies like FM radio and the emergence of 33-rpm album as a recording format. In the case of the latter, the collapse of the studio system that had governed Hollywood for a half century created an opening for a new generation of mavericks like Martin Scorsese and George Lucas. For the medium of television, however, the cultural upheaval of the sixties in some ways posed a bigger challenge to would-be rebels. The essence of the sixties was a collapse of cultural consensus, which had been the very foundation of television broadcasting up to that point. It was the most expensive of the mass media to produce and sustain—that fact alone gave it a conservative character in economic and political terms—and its financing depended on the goodwill of advertisers fearful of antagonizing any segment of the population. The result of this constellation of forces was a media order premised on what network executive termed "least objectionable programming," or LOP, the governing logic of the industry from its origins in the mid-1940s to the mid-1960s. Thus it was that the airwaves were dominated by a string of largely innocuous, lowest-common denominator fare such as *The Andy Griffith Show* (sitcom about small-town America), *The Lucy Show* (second-generation fare from the comic actor whose work in *I Love Lucy* in the fifties was once trailblazing but now reassuringly familiar), and *Bonanza* (one of a number of perennially popular westerns), all of which were among the top ten shows of 1968 according to the bellwether Nielsen ratings.[4]

By the end of the sixties, however, two forces challenged this conventional wisdom. One was external, in the form of increasingly dramatic events from the outside world—assassinations, protests, and a protracted war overseas—that made such conventional fare seem out of touch, if not outright jarring, especially when juxtaposed against dramatic news coverage. The other was internal, in the emergence (and, not coincidentally, the profitability) of a more segmented approach to audience research that targeted especially economically desirable demographic segments with disposable incomes, such as the Baby Boom generation, just coming of age in the late sixties and early seventies. The result was a renaissance in the sitcom in particular, led by shows such as the politically charged *All in the Family* (1971–1979) and its many spinoffs; the protofeminist *The Mary Tyler Moore Show* (1970–1977); and the thinly veiled antiwar manifesto *M*A*S*H* (1972–1983). These shows collectively changed the face of television, not only in paving the way for new topics and new faces but also in the sweeping away of more traditional fare, notably still-successful comedies such as *The Beverly Hillbillies* (1962–1971) *Green Acres* (1965–1971), and the *Andy Griffith* spinoff *Mayberry R.F.D.* (1968–1971), a development in the industry dubbed "the rural purge."

Such shifts in the broadcasting landscape, however, still required calibration. Older viewers hardly disappeared, and indeed were the demographic segment most likely to be loyal to shows they liked.

Young adults, while highly desirable, were also among the most likely to abandon the medium entirely amid their pursuit of education, careers, and more bracing cultural options. Broadcasting that could bridge generations—especially with children, who spent multiple hours a day watching TV—could still fill a potentially valuable programming niche, especially after the election of Richard Nixon in 1968 suggested the limited appeal of cultural revolution in the nation at large.

A middle-aged southerner named Earl Hamner Jr. was especially well positioned to exploit this set of circumstances. Hamner, born in 1923, the oldest of eight children, hailed from Schuyler, Virginia, a hamlet on the edge of the Blue Ridge Mountains that furnished the basis of a string of novels he wrote about rural life in the Great Depression in the vein of Harper Lee of *To Kill a Mockingbird* (1960) fame. His second book, *Spencer's Mountain* (1961), was selected by President John F. Kennedy for inclusion in a list of significant American books and was published in condensed form by *Reader's Digest*—an important index of middlebrow appeal at the time.[5] *Spencer's Mountain* was also made into a 1963 film starring Henry Fonda and Maureen O'Hara, though its setting was shifted from Appalachia to the Grand Tetons and from the thirties to the sixties. As a young man who came of age at the dawn of broadcasting, Hamner also made forays into radio and television, writing a series of scripts that included eight episodes of *The Twilight Zone* at the behest of his old friend and series creator Rod Serling.[6] In 1970, Hamner published *The Homecoming*, a sequel to *Spencer's Mountain* that focused on the events of a single day—Christmas Eve, 1933—and the struggle of the narrator's father to make it home to his family in a snowstorm. Hamner's agent sent the galleys of the novel to a new production company, Lorimar, which in turn pitched the project to CBS as a television movie. Ironically, it was executive Fred Silverman, the broadcasting wunderkind responsible for new, edgier programming, who greenlighted the wholesome *Homecoming*, which landed to strong ratings when it was broadcast on Christmas Eve of 1971. Network founder William Paley, who was still on the scene and had some weight he could discreetly throw around, urged that the movie be developed into a series, which laid the foundation for *The Waltons*, which debuted in September 1972.[7] It was a piece of counterprogramming to the new wave in television—and a return to rural-themed shows, this time with a new level of sensitivity and depth rather than the broad comic stereotypes of *The Beverly Hillbillies* and its ilk.

The Waltons was both similar to and different from its previous iterations. Whatever the setting, the episodes center on a large rural family, the immediate community of which it is a part, and the various struggles it faced—and overcame. The names and characters changed, whether to protect the identities of Hamner's own family members, contractual considerations (the Spencers were given another Hamner family name, Walton, to satisfy Warner Brothers, which still held the rights to *Spencer's Mountain*), or to streamline the cast.[8] The eleven children of the original novel—which included newborns Franklin Delano and Eleanor Walton—became nine in the movie and slimmed to seven for the TV show, which telescoped the characters of two Hamner real-life brothers. But they all feature a pious mother, a more pragmatic father, a pair of paternal grandparents, and the aforementioned offspring, which includes a scion who aspires to be a writer.

The overall evolution of the story from its origins to the arrival of *The Waltons* involved a sanding down of the characters' edges. The mother, always named Olivia, remains religious, though becomes less rigidly pious. In *The Homecoming*, she's played by the prodigiously talented Patricia Neal, though Neal seems too old to preside over the large brood of children. In *The Waltons* she's replaced by ("Miss," as she's listed for the first few seasons) Michael Learned, who seems a bit young. The father, who begins as Henry Fonda's Clay Spencer and morphs into John Walton—the brawny Andy Duggan in *The Homecoming* giving way to the compact Ralph Waite in *The Waltons*—becomes less randy, profane, or prone to pick up a bottle, though a running joke in the saga involves a pair of elderly spinster sisters (eventually called Mamie and Emily Baldwin), who dub the whiskey they illegally distill and circulate as "Papa's recipe," much to Olivia's dismay. The storekeeper, Ike Godsey, presides over a general store that becomes more genteel; the local sheriff, who becomes Ep Bridges, gets kinder but no less firm in upholding the law. The really pivotal adjustment, though, involved the casting of the adolescent Richard Thomas as John-Boy (formerly Clay-Boy) in both *The Homecoming* and *The Waltons*. Henry Fonda turned down the role of John Walton in the series because he correctly believed the show would be a John-Boy vehicle.[9] Thomas, who inhabited that part with charm and delicacy, carried the show for the first five seasons, and his character's voiceover narration that bookends each episode (actually the voice of Hamner, looking back as an older John-Boy) gave the show its essential framework for its entire run, including a half-dozen reunion movies periodically released in the sixteen years after it finished its nine-year lifespan in 1981.

Everything about *The Waltons* in its television iteration—the quality of the writing and performances; the production values and extensive sets; the gorgeous outdoor (Southern California) locations that were prominently featured, especially in the show's opening sequences—reflected a significant investment on the part of CBS. Nevertheless, *The Waltons* faced an uphill battle from the moment of its debut in September 1972. It's not hard to see why. Earnest family fare was no easy sell in the shifting cultural climate of the early seventies, and even splashy new shows that did try and seize the moment, like *All in the Family*, struggled initially to find their footing. Amid poor ratings—*The Waltons* debuted on a Thursday night pitted against the hip *The Mod Squad* on ABC and black comedian Flip Wilson's variety show on NBC—there were widespread concerns among members of the *Waltons* team and the network that it might not survive the first season ("Insiders are already calling this entry a probable loser in the all-important ratings game," noted one critic). But the show also had high-placed fans who rallied to its defense, among them a television critic from the *Detroit News* who urged viewers to write letters to CBS, which took out a full-page ad in major newspapers around the country with the banner headline "This Program Is Too Beautiful to Die!"[10]

The countercurrents swirling around *The Waltons* were apparent in the critical climate surrounding the show. It garnered a number of important—and unreservedly positive—reviews, notably from *New York Times* house TV critic John J. O'Connor, who praised it for the "disarming simplicity that carefully avoids becoming simple-minded."[11] Most elite critics got there too—even when it violated their deepest instincts. John Leonard, regarded by many as the dean of the nation's cultural critics, reviewed the show for *Life* magazine, where he wrote under the pen name of Cyclops. "Confronted with wholesomeness, a critic wants to stab it to death with a 19-cent Bic ball point," he said, referring to cheap pens omnipresent at the time. But, he finally conceded, "I like *The Waltons*. Only a churl would not."[12] Writing the following year, feminist writer Ann Roiphe grappled with her ambivalence in a long essay in the Sunday *Times*. "What keeps us watching this obviously corny, totally unreal family?" she wondered. Her answer: that the show time traveled to an idealized past, which however sentimental, was too valuable to relinquish. "It's a journey worth taking."[13]

In the end, it didn't take long for *The Waltons* to find a durable audience. The process was largely a word-of-mouth one where children lured their parents, churches advised their congregations, and the like. By the end of 1972, the show had climbed to the top of the ratings and won a bevy of honors at that year's Emmy Awards. Over the course of the ensuing decade, *The Waltons* would routinely draw audiences of 50 million on Thursday nights—numbers no broadcast other than the Super Bowl can match today. The show also had a significant global reach.[14]

"Wholesome" was the word John Leonard used to describe *The Waltons*. That's the way the show was understood at the time and ever since. Part of what wholesome meant in this context was timeless— an affirmation of traditional family values, a term with strong conservative accents (Earl Hamner biographer James Person notes that Hamner's family was described as exhibiting problematic "familialism," a sociological term referring to a dysfunctional degree of tribalism).[15] Another term associated with the show with a negative connotation is nostalgia—"a device that removes the ruts and potholes from memory lane," in the words of midcentury newspaper columnist

Doug Larson.[16] But—and this is very much the point of this discussion—*The Waltons* was never a mere exercise in antiquarianism. It was always a show at least as much about the seventies as it was the thirties.

LIBERAL ALLOWANCES

It's worth developing this point about the historical consciousness of *The Waltons* by returning again to the setting of the show: the Great Depression. This was a crisis that reached into households in ways evident from the value of stock portfolios to the food (or lack thereof) on people's plates. Not surprisingly, it figured prominently in a great many episodes of *The Waltons*. This ranged from repeated reminders in Hamner's John-Boy opening remarks about the scourge that the Depression represented for the family and its neighbors, to plot lines that involved struggles over cold, hard cash. One memorable 1974 episode involves a traveling salesman's efforts to swindle the Waltons by selling them a subscription to "The Five-Foot Shelf," a famous set of books popularized by Harvard president Charles Eliot, and pocketing the down payment to buy a doll for his daughter. He's exposed and forgiven—but however compassionate, young Elizabeth Walton (Kami Cotler) is not willing to part with her own doll so that the salesman's daughter can have one.

In terms of class, some effort was made to situate the Waltons in a kind of middle Appalachian landscape, sandwiched between the city folk of nearby towns like Charlottesville—notably the students and faculty of Boatwright University, modeled on the University of Richmond, which John-Boy will ultimately attend—and the rural poverty of hillbilly folk who live deeper in the mountains. For all their difficulties, the Waltons own their home, and it's a substantial one. They don't feel buffeted by the forces of modernity as much as their kin and neighbors do. In one memorable two-part 1974 episode, "The Conflict," another branch of the family tries to defy the construction of the Blue Ridge Parkway—funded by the Public Works Administration, part of President Franklin Roosevelt's New Deal—leading to a standoff in which John-Boy gets shot (nonfatally) in the process of mediating. The defiant family matriarch Corinne Walton (played by the great Beulah Bondi) capitulates to the government, and the family disperses with the help of John and Olivia. In a later episode, she makes a final visit to the Walton home, where she goes to die.

That said, the main branch of the Waltons are ardent New Dealers—a framed photo of FDR adorns the wall of the living room, as it does in Godsey's general store—with one exception: Grandma, played by Ellen Corby, who appeared in the 1946 Frank Capra classic *It's a Wonderful Life* along with Bondi. At the start of the series prequel movie *The Homecoming*, Grandma's character scolds John-Boy for mocking FDR's accent in his radio fireside chats—"He's your president!" she admonishes him. But in the show she's a consistent skeptic if not downright critic not just of Roosevelt but pretty much any new historical development since about 1925. It should be noted, however, that neither the Waltons nor anyone else around them typically engage in the kind of political shoptalk that characterized the intelligentsia in the thirties and ever since. This was by design; as Hamner noted in a production memo, "When they speak of 'the depression,' they only know its effects."[17]

Nevertheless, a distinctly leftist sensibility of both the thirties and the seventies animated *The Waltons*. Some of this was evident at face value in the character of Grandpa Zebulon Walton, performed by the stage legend Will Geer. Geer wasn't simply playing a man of the Left in the 1930s—he actually *was* one, a bisexual compatriot of Woody Guthrie and a card-carrying member of the Communist Party of the United States, blacklisted by the House Un-American Activities Committee (HUAC) in the 1950s for his unwillingness to name names. (He was angry at Bondi, who cooperated with HUAC and who played Grandpa's sister-in-law Corinne in a few episodes of *The Waltons*, but their relationship remained professional.)[18] Geer was an environmentalist who tossed seeds on location and plied a botanical avocation on the set, a man who embodied the fusion of leftist politics and American patriotism so characteristic of the thirties. As such he was a living link between the Old Left and the New Left that endowed the show with a subtle sense of authenticity, as those on the production noted in the countless testimonials they made after his death in 1978. Geer's passing, which occurred between seasons in 1978, prompted the inaugural episode of 1978–1979 to focus on the grieving process for Grandpa Walton.

There were other indirect but nevertheless palpable ways in which the show displayed a culturally progressive vision within its thirties milieu. One of these was sexual. Though this was a society that was portrayed as highly traditional when it came to rituals of courtship and mating, sexual urges were often depicted and discussed. The most potent illustration of them was the relationship between Olivia and John, which was charged with erotic overtones that hid in plain sight. "That show was innovative in many ways," Michael Learned reflected forty years later. "To have us sleeping in the same bed. . . . You just had the feeling they had a good sex life." (Apparently their chemistry was more than mere artistry; Learned revealed in 2019 that she and Waite were in love but never consummated their relationship.) The Waltons also dealt with the topic of sexual assault in the 1979 episode "The Violated," which portrays a woman reluctant to file charges against her rapist given the notoriety it will bring down on her. (John ultimately runs him out of town.)

Learned noted additional unassuming ways in which the show pushed the envelope. This included having shots of little Elizabeth sitting on a toilet or the matter-of-fact way the show handled Ellen Corby's 1978 stroke, which resulted in an extended hiatus. Corby eventually returned as a disabled actor playing a disabled, dignified Grandma Walton, who had also been afflicted by a stroke in what became a running plotline as Zeb tried to deal with his wife's extended in-patient recuperation. One episode ends with a moving variation on its "good night" dialogue (discussed below) with him bidding her good night in the dark outside the hospital.[19]

But one need not rely on such admittedly oblique indications of the show's ideological vision. In fact, the plots of many episodes are unabashed in their embrace of a robust post-sixties liberalism in which tolerance and a sympathetic stance toward minority perspectives are gently but repeatedly affirmed as the highest family values. Dozens of them rested on the arrival of representatives of the outside world wandering their way onto Walton's Mountain, where hospitality was a family specialty, whether for the deaf child who is abandoned there in the series' debut episode (she's eventually reunited with her parents) or the harsh new minister Reverend Matthew Fordwick (John Ritter, later to star in the notoriously raunchy sitcom *Three's Company*) who gradually comes to understand that his severe moralism was not going to move his flock. Before the first season was over, the Waltons would overcome mutual confusion and suspicion in hosting members of a carnival troupe, a family of wandering Gypsies, and Jewish refugees fleeing the Nazi regime.

Over the course of its run, *The Waltons* also engaged a series of social issues that were relevant in the thirties and the seventies—and ever since. One of these is addiction, addressed in a pair of 1978 episodes. In "The Obsession," eldest daughter Mary Ellen (Judy Norton Taylor) begins taking amphetamines to power through preparing for nursing exams, which soon gives way to barbiturates to balance the effects of the stimulants. The episode is resolved tidily with Olivia aiding her exhausted daughter to sleep by reading aloud a biography of Florence Nightingale, but the arc of her descent seems all too vivid in its inexorability. Similarly, "The Captive," which aired a few weeks later, deals with the alcoholism of Ike Godsey's wife Corabeth (played by Ronnie Claire Edwards, who steals many a scene as a woman struggling with her quotidian lot in life), culminating in John Walton telling her a story about an old World War I army buddy's drinking problem—which Corabeth, and just about anybody else hearing it soon realizes is in fact a personal confession about himself. The writers try to avoid tying up the loose ends too tightly; the episode—directed by Ralph Waite, himself a recovering alcoholic who stopped drinking after taking the role of John Walton[20]—ends with Hamner's voiceover stating that Corabeth's struggles with liquor would continue for many years.

There's probably no issue on *The Waltons* that is engaged more frequently or systematically than feminism—which is never formally invoked as such but suffuses a great many episodes as a principal or secondary plot line. In part, this may reflect the participation of a substantial number of women in the production, not only influential figures like Learned's Olivia or Corby's Esther Walton (both of whom received story credits on episodes) but also a stable of women writers and directors. Of the approximately seventy-five people listed as writers on the show, about twenty were women, including Kathleen Hite and Claire Petersen, who wrote forty-six episodes between them, ranking second and third respectively after Hamner himself. There were three women among the thirty-one who directed episodes, including Gwen Arner, who ranks fifth in terms of the number she directed (thirteen) and who had a distinguished career helming female-centered shows such as *Dr. Quinn, Medicine Woman* (1993–1998) and *Dynasty* (1981–1989). Claylene Jones, who started out as a production coordinator on *The Waltons*, was later promoted to producer of the show, a title she held for the six subsequent reunion movies made between 1982 and 1997.[21]

Women were not only important behind the camera; they also figured prominently in storylines in the series. One of the more intriguing episodes when it came to seventies issues hovering over thirties realities was the way the show dealt with reproductive concerns and the unspoken specter of abortion. In the 1974 episode "The Cradle," Olivia discovers she is pregnant with her eighth child, a discovery that occurs just as she is embarking on a successful bid as a liquid soap and bubble bath saleswoman at a time when the family could really use the extra income. Any joy she might feel by this development is shadowed by medical concerns that accompany what is considered a geriatric pregnancy. Those concerns are shared by her children. "They teach you in Sunday School that every new life is sacred, but sometimes you have to wonder about that," John-Boy tells Grandpa in an episode that aired almost exactly a year after the 1973 Supreme Court decision *Roe v. Wade* affirmed a woman's right to an abortion. "You really wonder if another mouth to feed is really a blessing after all." The septuagenarian Zeb replies, "I don't believe I've lived long enough to answer that question," prompting John-Boy to say, "You want to know somethin' else? I betcha I'm not the only one who's asking."

He's not. Later in that episode, Mary Ellen—who begins reading the book about Florence Nightingale that Olivia will read to her when she's recovering from her addiction—tells Grandma and her sister Erin (Mary Elizabeth McDonough) about another role model of hers, dancer Isadora Duncan. "I'm pondering my destiny as a woman," she tells them as they sew. Noting that "the laws are made by the men for the men," she notes that Duncan "kept her two babies because she wanted to," and asks, "Suppose you had a baby and you didn't want it? Is there any law that says you have to keep it?" They react negatively. "Of course there is," Erin replies. "There is man's law and God's law," Esther says firmly. But the audience as likely as not will side with Mary Ellen, who will eventually have a child of her own and become a doctor. The issue at hand is rendered moot when Olivia has a miscarriage. She undergoes a grieving process, but it's Zeb who has the last word. "Blaming yourself is the easy way out," he gently admonishes her. "It's much harder to think what happened happened for the best." Olivia rises from the chair in which she's sitting and begins observing her playing passel of children, a silent smile gradually taking shape on her face.

The struggles of the Walton women are generally less morally fraught but are experienced no less acutely. In the season 1 episode "The Bicycle," a frustrated Olivia finally snaps when John-Boy fails to do an errand for her and blows off steam by making the necessary walk to Godsey's store herself. Once there, she discovers a used bicycle: an extravagance, but one she ultimately can't resist buying, and its effect—literally a newfound sense of mobility—is emancipating. As often as not, however, Liv is a stoic when it comes to the gendered burdens of domesticity. "Maybe something's wrong with me, but I don't think I want to be a cook or even a wife," Mary Ellen tells her mother in the 1972 episode "The Scholar."

"Every woman feels that way sometimes," Liv responds.

"Even you?"

"About three times a day. But there's always something that needs tending to, and we do it, and there's something to be said for that."

"Why does it always have to be us?" the frustrated Mary Ellen asks in the 1974 episode "The Fulfillment" when confronted with the task of cleaning dinner dishes. "Because you are used and mistreated," her mother responds sarcastically. "Now clear [the table]!"

In later years of the series, when the arrival of the Second World War generates a voracious need for labor, the locus of issues surrounding women's work shifts to the off-site settings. The key character here is Erin, who becomes an increasingly indispensable manager at a metal products factory with a series of wartime government contracts for a firm owned by the cartoonishly sexist J. D. Pickett (the fine character actor Lewis Arquette, father of actors Roseanna, Patricia, and David Arquette), who repeatedly has to beg Erin to take her job back after she quits in disgust over his boorishness. Erin isn't his only challenger. "The last time I came back from a business trip she had all my lady workers wearing slacks like that Rosie the Riveter," he complains of Mary Ellen. But it turns out that Pickett's most implacable opponent is Olivia, who in the 1979 episode "The Innocents" is appalled by the lack of childcare arrangements at the plant and maneuvers him into partially converting a bar into a daycare center. "I'd rather deal with the whole German army than have to bargain with you," he finally concedes.

The final episode of *The Waltons* is set in 1946, but the subsequent reunion movies follow the family for another twenty-three years, a span over which the Walton women continue to evolve in a feminist direction. They all marry, though while the series was still running Mary Ellen becomes a widow when her husband dies at Pearl Harbor. In an unlikely plot twist, he later resurfaces as a changed man with whom she no longer has anything in common, and so she ends up as the only person in the family—or, it would appear, Walton's Mountain—who ever gets a divorce (something only mentioned in passing much later). She has a few romances, notably with a man named Jonesy, whom she eventually marries and with whom she has two additional children. She also realizes her aspiration to become a physician. Erin marries, has children, and becomes a schoolteacher; Elizabeth travels the world for years before finally returning home to marry the childhood sweetheart who carried a torch for her. And in the final film, *A Walton Easter* (1997), set in 1969, we watch Olivia read Betty Friedan's *The Feminist Mystique* and pursue a college degree at Boatwright University, where she puts a sexist professor to shame in the ease with which she demonstrates her knowledge of American history. She too has become a teacher, successfully recognizing the untapped talents of one of her pupils and persuading his recalcitrant father to allow him to continue to attend her school. A circle has closed.

About the only theme comparably prominent to the role and status of women in *The Waltons* is race relations. By the standards of the twenty-first century Left, many of the storylines here are cringeworthy in the way they dodge irreconcilable conflict, indulge white savior complexes, and offer limited racial representation. Actually, it would not be anachronistic to assert the show's limitations even in the context of 1970s, when the landmark television miniseries *Roots* explored the history and legacy of slavery from a black point of view and the Norman Lear sitcom *The Jeffersons* (1975–1985) gleefully shattered stereotypes. In this regard, *The Waltons* was not a paragon of enlightenment, then or ever since. Yet the legacy of the civil rights movement was nevertheless woven in the fabric of its DNA in a sustained way, and its creators tried to be progressive by the lights of its time. This includes behind the camera: the African American director Ivan Dixon (who starred in *Hogan's Heroes*, to be discussed in the next chapter) directed seven episodes of *The Waltons*.

There were limits to how far the show could credibly go. A big part of the reason is geographic: the Waltons are white southerners. More specifically, they're Appalachian white Virginians who inhabit what was once a liminal space during the Civil War. To the nearby east was Richmond, capital of the Confederacy, and the Tidewater elite that had a major financial stake in slavery. To the nearby west were the Blue Hill Mountains and the neighboring state of West Virginia, which seceded from Virginia in 1863 precisely because its overwhelmingly white majority, while no less racist, nevertheless resented the overweening dominance of that elite. The transitional quality of this border zone is reflected in the Walton family history. In "The Conflict" episode discussed above, we learn that Grandpa Zeb Walton's older brother fought alongside Stonewall Jackson and Jubal Early for the Confederacy (Zeb himself is a veteran of the Spanish-American War prone to exaggerating his exploits). His wife, Esther, has what she regards as skeletons in her closet that John-Boy unearths during the 1995 reunion movie *A Walton Wedding*, when he announces to her chagrin that her father was opposed to slavery and fought for the Union, to the shame of his family. In the 1975 episode "The Boondoggle," John-Boy alarms the Baldwin sisters—who are members of the Daughters of the American Revolution as well as Daughters of the Confederacy—with his investigations into their family history, fearing that their revered late father (curiously, they never refer to their mother) had a similarly shameful Unionist past, though it turns out he merely tended wounded Northern soldiers in his home.[22] Images of Confederate flags occasionally surfaced on the show, but no character makes any effort to justify the Lost Cause as anything beyond a matter of duty for fathers and sons to protect home and hearth. The most direct comment on the war actually comes from a minor black character, Hawthorne Dooley, in an early 1972 episode, "The Hunt," who puckishly notes that in contrast to other pioneer immigrants who settled the area, his people would have been happy enough to take the boat back. John Sr. expresses surprise at Dooley making a joke about a painful history, leading him to respond "You know, my folks had to laugh to keep from cryin'." (The role of Dooley in this episode was played by Teddy Wilson; Dooley was first portrayed by the charismatic Cleavon Little in *The Homecoming*, who would return to *The Waltons* as a boxer with aspirations for becoming a minister in the evocative 1975 episode "The Fighter." Little was one of a number of rising or actual stars—among them Sissy Spacek, Ron Howard, and country singer Merle Haggard, who would appear on *The Waltons* over the course of its long run.)

Befitting the general demographics of the area at the time, African Americans are a relatively small but unmistakable presence on Walton's Mountain, appearing in a variety of roles and episodes over the course of the series. The most important such character is Verdie

Grant (Lynn Hamilton), who figures in a series of continuing story-lines. We see her visage at one point in "The Bicycle" as an implicit counterpoint to a rebel flag; later, she boards a bus where, notably, she does not sit in the back, a kind of visual pun alluding to the later activism of Rosa Parks.

One of the more moving episodes in the entire series, "The Scholar," occurs at the end of the first season. Verdie is excited about her daughter's pending graduation from college up north, but dreads making a trip and being unable to sign her name or read a menu. Embarrassed by her deficiency—and all too understandably suspicious of the motives and assumptions of her white neighbors—Verdie gingerly accepts the help of John-Boy, who helps her achieve literacy, an effort almost foiled at one point over her anger at her incorrect belief that he has divulged her secret. "This was a story I long wanted to tell," writer John McGreevey later explained. "There would be an adult who can't read or write and finds himself/herself in a situation where the secret will be an excruciating embarrassment." It was only later, McGreevey said, that he made the character African American. He won an Emmy Award for his work on the episode.[23]

Verdie's character arc takes an important turn when she meets Harley Foster, an itinerant laborer who wanders into Walton's Mountain with his son, Jody, in the 1973 episode "The Roots." Harley is inclined to move on from a gig picking peaches, but Verdie takes a shine to the boy and strongly advocates that Harley stick around so that Jody can get a proper education, which she is eager to supervise. Verdie and Harley fall in love and marry, both remaining recurring characters in the series. Jody will ultimately serve in the navy in World War II (the grown-up version of the character played by Charles R. Penland), and upon his return will team up with Walton third son Jim-Bob (David W. Harper) to buy an auto mechanic shop across from Godsey's general store, the focus of the 1981 episode "The Hot Rod." Their relationship is important in that it's grounded in shared restlessness after the war, a love of racing cars, and a desire to make money, suggesting the possibility of bonds independent of racial considerations. However, while Jim-Bob demonstrates no obvious bias, Harley must nevertheless contend with a steady stream of prejudice that Jim-Bob witnesses, just as Jody did when he was in the navy.

Indeed, for all its obvious sentimentality in matters related to race, *The Waltons* did occasionally demonstrate a hard-headed realism. Perhaps the most remarkable instance of this involves the arrival of yet another waif (Todd Bridges), a charming orphan named Josh, who walks his way from a "home for colored children" in North Carolina to the Walton homestead in the 1977 episode "The Stray." Olivia is especially enchanted by Josh and in a bedtime conversation tells John she wants to adopt him. "In this day and age, you know what that would do," her husband responds her, reminding her of the realities of racial segregation. "We couldn't take him to some of the places we normally go."

"We just wouldn't go to those places," she replies.

"Like the church?" (This hits home for the pious Liv; interestingly, the very final image of the Waltons saga involves the family attending an interracial outdoor church service on Easter Sunday at the invitation of Verdie.) "He couldn't go to school like the other kids. He'd suffer, and they'd suffer." A false equivalency there, but John's larger logic is hard to refute.

Ultimately, it's Verdie who comes to the rescue and adopts Josh. Not that it's easy for John to relinquish him, as indicated by some of the most wrenching dialogue of the series. "Why can't I belong to you?" Josh asks the surrogate father he calls "Mister John."

"Just wouldn't work, son."

"Would it work if I was white?"

"That'd make it some easier."

"You wouldn't have to be proud of me. You wouldn't even have to call me son if you didn't feel like it."

"Josh, I'd be proud to call you son. . . . I can't do it. Maybe in ten years, maybe in a hundred years. But not here, not now. It'd be a hurtful thing for you, even if we tried."

The two part sadly as Josh remains with Verdie. "I want you," she tells the boy.

"I want him," he replies, indicating John.

"But you don't belong with him. You belong with Harley and Jody and me. . . . The Waltons are kind people. But they don't know much about us folks.[24] I'm going to raise you to be a man. A fine black man. And proud."

The Waltons would also occasionally depict some compelling intraracial—and intergenerational—black relationships as well. Once again, Verdie (whose quest to discover her roots is the focus of the 1978 episode "The Family Tree") is pivotal. "They figure you black you don't know much," Jody tells his mother in the 1978 episode "The Illusion."

"Colored," she corrects him.

"Esther [his stepsister] says black."

"That's New York talk."

"Black. Colored. They don't give us no books."

"Be glad you're learning as a kid; I only did as an adult."

Later in that episode Verdie has an intense conversation with the visiting Esther, who bitterly describes herself as "an overeducated nigra." She goes on to explain the source of her unhappiness. "You see, it's the dream," she says. "The false hopes. The illusions that cause pain. Telling ourselves that being black makes no difference. Makes all the difference." Having spoken this hard truth, the episode undercuts it when Erin facilitates a job at the J. D. Pickett plant for Esther. He initially resists hiring her, but as always, gives in.

Not all the racial depictions in The Waltons are a matter of black and white. In the 1980 episode "The Medal," Eddie Ramirez (Enrique Castillo), a Chicano soldier, comes to Walton's Mountain to give Mary Ellen a citation earned by her presumably dead husband Curt at Pearl Harbor. "Spic and span—mostly spic," one GI notes as Ramirez gets off the bus. "I bet his mamma's still flippin' frijoles all day long," another sneers; when he then mocks the combat decorations on his chest Ramirez slugs him. The soldiers later settle their differences, and Mary Ellen and Ramirez will have an intense interracial romance before he returns to duty; we're told in the final voiceover that he participates in the D-Day invasion.

There are also episodes involving Native Americans. In "The Conflict," Corinne Walton tells the Walton boys that Shawnees, Delawares, and Catawbas once lived where she does, correctly predicting they'll find arrowheads in nearby fields. In the 1977 episode "The Warrior," an aged Cherokee warrior (Jerado Decordovier) who experienced the Trail of Tears comes to Walton's Mountain with his grandson (Ernest Esparza III). John genially hosts them until the centenarian claims the land the family barn sits on is a sacred burial ground and tries to burn it down. A potentially sticky situation is averted when the old warrior dies while on trial for his transgression. John, Zeb, and Elizabeth help the grandson bury him near a holy site on the mountain. "Who owns the land?" the older John-Boy asks in the final voiceover. "Only the land knows. We mortals are passersby and our lives are but a brief moment in the great span of time." The Waltons, whose claim to the land, we're told in the 1979 episode "The Tailspin," extends back to 1765, are metaphorical tenants (albeit with legal rights). One production detail worth noting here: there were tensions on the set because Will Geer insisted that an indigenous actor be hired for the part of the old Cherokee warrior over the objections of director Ralph Senensky, who felt Decordovier was an insufficiently experienced actor. The two overcame their differences; Geer was a man who in many ways was ahead of his time.[25]

There is one other demographic minority that's a factor in the Waltons saga: Jews. We first encounter them in season 1 as refugees from the newly installed Nazi regime, where they understandably interpret an accident—Jim-Bob and middle Walton son Ben (Eric Scott) breaking a window in their new home with a slingshot—as a hate crime. The mishap is of course eventually worked out and the Waltons host a bar mitzvah. In the 1976 episode "The Fire Storm," John-Boy encounters significant opposition when he plans to publish excerpts from Adolf Hitler's manifesto *Mein Kampf* in his local newspaper so that the residents of Walton's Mountain can see for themselves how hateful it is. The effort costs him dearly: a loss of advertising; Ike won't stock the paper in his store; a rock is hurled at the family's window; Erin blames John-Boy for losing a beauty pageant. But when Reverend Fordwick hosts a book burning, John-Boy acts to stop it, and the first book pulled from the flames turns out to be a German-language edition of the Bible. A few years later in the 1980 episode "The Unthinkable," Jason, who is training troops at an army camp, experiences ambivalence about how hard he should be on an incompetent Jewish New Yorker named Ted Lapinsky (Todd Susman), eventually concluding that the biggest favor he can do is be tough to prepare Lapinsky for the challenges ahead. The two eventually become friends, and Jason brings him home, where amid a lively dance to "Hava Nagila," Lapinsky breaks down remembering his grandfather, who perished in a concentration camp. Lapinsky is subjected to typical anti-Semitism—"He just doesn't have the mettle to be a sergeant," says one commanding officer. "That's what I don't like about you people: pushy and hot-headed," says another when Lapinsky challenges his bias—but Jason continues to support him. Jason also ultimately marries Toni Hazelton (Lisa Harrison), inartfully described as a "Jewess" by Corabeth Godsey. The two actors were actually married in real life by Ralph Waite, an ordained minister with a degree from Yale Divinity School.[26]

A major part of the argument here involves the ways *The Waltons* projected seventies concerns onto the thirties, but some of the most interesting aspects of the show involved the way it captured historical realities that would soon recede almost entirely from collective memory. Religion is a good example of this. In the twenty-first century, denominational differences have been bleached beyond recognition; one typically hears references to "Christians" as an undifferentiated mass, or "believers"—Catholics/Muslims/Jews perceived as having more in common *as* believers than those who consider themselves unaffiliated, or "nones." But in the world of the show, it's significant (maybe even inevitable) that the wealthy Baldwin sisters are Episcopalians, for example. An important credential the Waltons have as salt-of-the-earth working people is that they're Southern Baptists, though John keeps the church at arm's length, much to the chagrin of Olivia, a true believer.

An important index of this piety is her temperance. One of the more amusing frictions on *The Waltons* is Liv's opposition to the Baldwin sister's "recipe." Though they never acknowledged it, apparently even to themselves, Baldwins were in fact distilling moonshine whiskey, which would eventually get them in trouble with the U.S. government in the 1981 episode "The Carousel," notwithstanding the unimpeachable kindness and integrity of the spinsters. Like all the major characters on the show, Liv is imperfect, in this case for her rigid abstemiousness, but neither her nor anybody else's foibles compromise our affection for them.

One inside joke on *The Waltons* is a historical artifact in its own right. For most of the series, the family lacks a telephone, relying on Ike Godsey, who has one in his store and often delivers messages in person. But in the 1978 episode "The Anniversary," Liv decides to celebrate twenty-five years of marriage by having a phone installed for her husband. What ends up happening is that a house full of Walton teenagers monopolize it to the irritation of their parents, as often happened in the 1970s (and long after). The mass proliferation of cell phones at the end of the twentieth century has erased this once common family experience; it is effectively preserved in amber on the show.

CONSERVATIVE APPROACH

Amid the forays undertaken here—exploring the ways *The Waltons* was a document of the seventies as well as a document of the vanishing world of the thirties and forties—one should not lose sight of its narrative core: a family story centered on a boy's coming of age as a writer and as the bearer of a legacy to the wider world who experience it as a television show. The saga was in many ways a traditional story, but Richard Thomas also believed his character of John-Boy represented an innovation as well. "This is a kid who was different in his native soil," he noted of his character decades later. "A new kind of male, a kid who was quoting Gerard Manley Hopkins to his mother" (as indeed he did in the 1973 episode "The Courtship").[27] Thomas held the starring role for the first five seasons of *The Waltons*, but even after he left—John-Boy's novel gets accepted by a New York publisher, and he moves to Manhattan to continue his writing career—his character effectively presided over the series in the opening and closing monologues that framed each installment.

After his departure, there were still many good episodes, but the air slowly went out of the series. Will Geer's death cost the cast Zeb Walton, and Ellen Corby's stroke drastically reduced the scope of her character Esther Walton. The producers brought in a new actor, Robert Wightman, to play the part of John-Boy, who returned home periodically, but this proved unsatisfying—Michael Learned cited it as a factor in her own decision to leave the show.[28] In later episodes we're told she's spending time in Washington tending to an injured John-Boy, whose plane was shot down during the war. Olivia later comes down with tuberculosis and relocates to Arizona, occasionally resurfacing. But it was often unclear where she was or why she was absent in the show's final seasons. The final two, which rushed through World War II and its immediate aftermath, were particularly weak, especially scenes set in the Pacific, where Ben was a prisoner of war held by some painfully caricatured Japanese captors. The six reunion movies (three in 1982 and then three more in 1993, 1995, and 1997 respectively) were especially unsatisfying, untethered to the device of memory or any wider social issues.[29]

After Thomas's departure as John-Boy, Richard Waite's John Sr. became the anchor of the show. He is in many ways a remarkable character: scrupulous not to impose on his children but expecting them to take responsibility for their mistakes, proud and protective of his independence. He could be ornery, and his aversion to churchgoing and occasional resort to the bottle were indicative of his imperfections. While his younger sons Ben and Jim-Bob were understandable to him in their entrepreneurial and mechanical ability, his older ones John-Boy and Jason (one a writer and the other a musician) were more opaque. But he was never threatened or disappointed by them, and his steadfast support clearly empowered them to strike out on their own. John was more protective of his daughters, but here too he could absorb the incipient feminism of Mary Ellen, the career aspirations of Erin, and the wanderlust of the adult Elizabeth. In an important respect, he represented the final—and most credible and compelling—iteration of the effective father figures who had dominated the early decades of television. Henceforth, beginning with Archie Bunker, the new ethos would be father knows least (unless, like Cliff Huxtable of *The Cosby Show*, they were nonwhite).[30]

The idealized, but nevertheless plausible and compelling, vision of an intact, productive and loving nuclear family proved compelling for even the most instinctively skeptical viewers, who recognized its importance, even necessity, in a culture subject to powerful centrifugal forces. This was something Anne Roiphe recognized in her searching assessment of the Walton myth of the happy family in her 1973 *New York Times* essay:

> The myth is indeed beautiful and anyone who scoffs has forgotten how to hope. It could be said that these myths torment us, describing role fulfillments that aren't there, promising marital peace that never arrives and forcing us to stare at the pitiful discrepancy between what is and what we would want. If that were the only function of this kind of myth, we would manage somehow to do away with it. The TV ratings would fall and that would be the end of it all. However, another function of the myth is to portray the ideal, the goal—it's not good enough to be always realistic about what the world offers. There must be some kind of image to strive for, some kind of positive cultural thought that serves to heal wounds and to point to the future.[31]

This mythic vision of the American family was distilled into is purest form in the way each episode of *The Waltons* ended: with an aerial shot of the house in the dark illuminated by bedroom windows and the characters saying good night to each other. In collective memory this is represented in shorthand as "Good night, John-Boy," though there were many variations on it. "After the drama of the episode, it was the making whole again," Thomas explained. "It's sort of an iconic thing."[32]

The power of this affirmation of the nuclear family may be why, despite the show's determined efforts to portray rural life with a distinctly rural vision, despite the fact that rural voters for most of

American history have been Democrats, *The Waltons* was gradually claimed by the Republican right, a process that was largely complete in the years following the series' run. The most famous such appropriation came from President George H. W. Bush, who while running for reelection in 1992 declared, "We need a nation closer to the Waltons than the Simpsons."[33] (The fictive Bart Simpson's reply on his show two days later: "Hey, we're just like the Waltons. We're praying for an end to the depression too," referring to the deep recession of the early 1990s.)[34]

In the twenty-first century, this perception of *The Waltons* as conservative has strengthened. In part, that's because the movies are a fixture of the Hallmark cable channel, which has unofficial but strong connotations with the right.[35] The show's devotees, though dwindling, are still relatively numerous, but they're aging and overwhelmingly white, reflecting a receding demographic in American life. There are websites devoted to the show, and a museum devoted to the fictional family opened in Schuyler, Virginia, in 1992. There have also been periodic reunions of the cast and fans, some of which are available on video. But few people born after about 1980 have any knowledge of the Walton family.[36]

Which, of course, never existed as such in the first place. But the fact that we're in the process of forgetting them doesn't mean they don't matter. We just have to remember differently, maybe better, so that the family can be reconstituted.

MIXED NUTS

The prisoners of Stalag 13 and their German overseers in characteristic poses in *Hogan's Heroes*. Shown from left: Richard Dawson (Cpl. Newkirk), Bob Crane (Col. Robert Hogan), Robert Clary (Cpl. LeBeau), John Banner (Sgt. Schultz), and Werner Klemperer (Col. Klink). In retrospect, it seems amazing that a comedy about a prisoner-of-war camp could have ever made it to television. (It did at the time, too.)

CHAPTER 2

CAMP HISTORY

Hogan's Heroes as a 1960s Version of the 1940s

Fellow-citizens, we cannot escape history.
—Abraham Lincoln, Annual Message
to Congress, December 1, 1862

Key Cast Members
- Bob Crane as Colonel Robert Hogan
- Werner Klemperer as Colonel Wilhelm Klink
- John Banner as Sergeant Hans Schultz
- Robert Clary as Corporal Louis LeBeau
- Richard Dawson as Corporal Peter Newkirk
- Ivan Dixon as Staff Sergeant James Kinchloe
- Larry Hovis as Technical Sergeant Andrew Carter

Key Episodes
- "The Informer" (pilot, 1965)
- "The Prince of the Phone Company" (1966)
- "Is General Hammerschlag Burning?" (1967)
- "The Witness" (1969)
- "The Softer They Fall" (1970)

*I*T WAS, AND REMAINS, arguably the most bizarre concept for a sitcom ever to hit the airwaves: an antic comedy about prisoners of war in Germany during World War II. Then and since, there were those who considered it a terrible idea. "There's something a little sick about *Hogan's Heroes*, an insensitive and misguided extension of Hollywood's belief that anything and everything can be converted into cheap slapstick," *New York Times* reviewer Jack Gould asserted when the show debuted in September 1965. Five years later, with the show coming to the end of its run, a professor of sociology at Rutgers was similarly despairing. "It is apparently true, as a few cynics have observed, that the Nazis won the war," he wrote of watching an episode at his children's bedtime. Three decades later, with Hollywood in the grip of reboot fever, there was talk of a *Hogan's Heroes* movie to star Mel Gibson, which reportedly foundered when he turned his attention to other projects (talk of a film version continued well into the 2010s). "Call this political correctness if you like, but under no circumstances should a film of *Hogan's Heroes* be made," *Boston Globe* writer Renee Hamilton wrote in 1998. "Let's be clear here: Nazis are never, ever funny."[1]

Others were a good deal less sure about that. This list included members of the *Hogan's Heroes* cast—a number of whom, as to be discussed, were Jewish refugees and/or incarcerated in Nazi concentration camps. It also included Mel Brooks, whose classic 1968 film *The Producers*, which involved a financial scheme to create an offensive Nazi musical, premiered in the middle of *Hogan's Heroes'* run and was revived in Broadway and film versions in the twenty-first century. And, of course, it included the sitcom's audiences, which sustained the show for six seasons on CBS and then for decades in syndication.

Still, even its champions recognized that *Hogan's Heroes* had to be handled with care. "Shall we say, 'If you liked World War II, you'll love *Hogan's Heroes*?'" humorist Stan Freberg asked series star Bob Crane in a promotional radio interview in 1965. "No, let's not say that," Crane responded, realizing how bad this could sound. The spot was yanked. Conscious choices also marked the way the show was presented to audiences. "We did an experiment with *Hogan's Heroes* where they played it without a laugh track—and it was kind of a failure. Nobody liked it much, and it was kind of weird," CBS executive Perry Lafferty later reported. "We put a laugh track on it, and it just went through the roof." The use of such an artificial device was regarded as a nuisance by the makers of *M*A*S*H*, another wartime sitcom (to be discussed in the next chapter). But it was questionable whether *Hogan's Heroes* could have survived without it.[2]

The issue at hand, however, is not whether *Hogan's Heroes* should have ever aired. Nor is it whether or not the show was any good. Nor can we entirely plumb the motives of those who made the show even when they're reasonably clear (a desire for fame and wealth prominent among them). Instead, the question here is what statements *Hogan's Heroes* made about World War II, its relevance in its time, and in ours. These are surprisingly difficult questions to answer.

And that's no accident.

RERUNNING HISTORY

To watch *Hogan's Heroes* is to experience oneself on a far side of a historical divide: it feels like a very old show. The pilot was shot in black and white, and subsequent episodes begin with a promotional assertion by CBS that the show is being broadcast in color—a novelty in 1965, and as such a sign of confidence that the network had in its prospects. Many viewers in any case would lack more expensive color televisions for years to come. But the sensibility of the episodes themselves is also different. We've become habituated to shows, even the most unpretentious of sitcoms, that strive for an element of verisimilitude in their sets—no stock footage of explosions, no obviously fake backdrops for characters driving in a car—and some degree of narrative trajectory within and between seasons. While the characters don't change much, their circumstances can. We expect that as a matter of sustaining interest in a show, of keeping it fresh, and giving prospective viewers an incentive to embark on the show the way one might a long novel. (This is especially true since the advent of DVD sets at the turn of this century—which were packaged to look like books—and streaming). Such an approach was explored as early as *I Love Lucy* (1951–1957), when the Ricardo family relocated from Manhattan to the Connecticut suburbs. But this was more the exception than the rule in the first few decades of the medium, which was partly a function of that show's unmatched success: virtually everybody watched *Lucy*.

The expectations were a little different for most sitcoms back then. Since episodes were only broadcast twice a year—once in the fall, a rerun in the spring, and no opportunity for most viewers to see them in between—they tended to be modular, self-contained in a way that made it easy to drop in at any time and get the gist of what was happening. This approach was especially pronounced in the case of *Hogan's Heroes*, which adhered to a fairly rigid formula in each of its 168 episodes: an opening challenge (the arrival of a prisoner or agent in the prison camp; a new weapon or munitions plant nearby; disruptive conflict between German officials); a plan to overcome it; an unexpected complication; and an ingenious solution that depended at least as much on psychological manipulation as technical prowess. In every case, American-led ingenuity (sometimes with allies) triumphs over German ineptitude. And yet, every week, the pins were set up again for "the Heroes," as they were colloquially known, to knock them down again. This sense of temporal repetition extended to the boundaries of the series: it effectively began *in medias res* with the setting and principal characters already established, and ended six years later with a final episode that made no attempt to offer any resolution. It's as if the show was freeze-dried.

Which is exactly the way the series creators wanted it. One reason for this was strictly commercial. The goal for producers was to generate enough episodes (typically five or more seasons) whereby a show could go into syndication to be rerun in local markets, "stripped" the same time in Monday to Friday slots. The profits for anyone cut in on such a deal could be enormous, so the incentives to make a show attractive for syndication were powerful. In such a scenario, sitcoms with too strong a chronological or sequential thread would be harder to spool continuously through a station schedule. In the early years of television, syndication didn't happen until the show went off the air, enhancing the drive to make the jump as quickly and seamlessly as possible. This could make for some abrupt endings in the life of a show while part of a network schedule, but serve as programming comfort food for generations of viewers, whether retirees whiling away their days or kids coming home after school, for whom television was a primary form of leisure. As such, *Hogan's Heroes* would prosper for the remainder of the twentieth century.[3]

There was an important issue of content no less than form here. It was not simply a matter of avoiding controversial topics that would make advertisers skittish, though that imperative always loomed large. It was also a matter of avoiding references that could make a show seem prematurely dated. This is something Jack Gould of the *New York Times* noted in 1967. "The idea of making sport of the Nazis as clownish oafs originally struck this corner as a wily improbable premise," he noted of his review two years earlier. But, he acknowledged, the fact of the show's ongoing run, then in its third season, "speaks for itself" (Gould did praise its use of plot and setting). He nevertheless understood that the real metric of the series' success for its creators was in syndication. "Because of the importance of replays over several years after a show's initial presentation, the situation comedy is confined to themes that will not become dated. All possibility of topicality is thereby instantly lost and the situation-comedy must operate in the never-never land of enduring blandness and irrelevance to today's immediate world."[4]

This imperative for avoidance held for the past no less than the present. In his acute study of *Hogan's Heroes*, Robert Shandley, a scholar of German and film studies, put the matter succinctly: "Comedy is not used to understand history; history is used to create more effective comedy."[5]

But the fingerprints of history are always present. This is because any attempt to render a middle-of-the-road rendering of any past can never elude the important truth that the middle of the road shifts: today's common sense is tomorrow's tired myth—or forgotten lesson. It's also because the present moment of any cultural creation is inevitably time-stamped, betraying the moment of its birth in any number of ways. *Hogan's Heroes* tried to depict history and elide history at the same time. For a few years, it appeared to do both. In retrospect, it appears to have done neither.

THE GOOD WAR

When *Hogan's Heroes* first aired in 1965, the Second World War had been over for twenty years. This is a significant segment of time: long enough to feel like a while but recent enough to be remembered by a large slice of the population—those who fought in the war, those who did not, and many who were young at the time but now established adults whose tastes could set a national tone. As with previous wars, works of popular culture about the war began appearing immediately. But a critical mass crested in the mid-1960s, especially on TV, where, as the *Chicago Tribune* noted in a 1966 headline, there was "a military invasion of television."[6]

The first major World War II stories emerged at the movies, where films such as *Casablanca* (1942) and *Bataan* (1943) dramatized current events. In the years that followed, the war went through a series of interpretive phases. The first postwar films captured the toll the war exacted on those who fought it, typified by the Academy Award–winning Best Picture of 1946, *The Best Years of Our Lives*. It was followed by a more existential set of movies that focused on a struggle to survive outside the grand human objectives of the conflict, such as *Battleground* (1949). The release of *The Longest Day* (1962), a multifaceted dramatization of D-Day, marked the return to the more unvarnished heroic approach of the war years.[7]

The immediate roots of *Hogan's Heroes*, however, is in a set of films that focus on a specific aspect of the Second World War: prisoner-of-war camps. These films were not common in the war years, perhaps for the obvious reason that they were sobering stories of setback and privation at a time when maintaining morale was paramount. The first major such film to surface, in that existential phase cited above, was a movie that had a major influence on *Hogan's Heroes*: 1953's *Stalag 17*, directed by the legendary Billy Wilder. "I don't know about you, but it always makes me sore when I see those war pictures all about flying leathernecks and submarine patrols and frogmen and guerillas in the Philippines," says a voiceover narrator at the start of the film. "What gets me is that there was never a movie about POWs."

This one stars William Holden as a cynical prisoner, whose skepticism about his fellow prisoners' escape prospects and sharp trading practices engender suspicions that he's a German operative subverting his barracks from within. The movie is a kind of detective story whereby Holden's character identifies and exposes the real enemy on the way to making his own escape. *Hogan's Heroes*, which is set in a camp known as Stalag 13, borrowed a series of elements from *Stalag 17*, among them the plot device of enemies within, a vein of humor in somewhat stereotyped characters (the prolix Jew; the patrician Yankee) and a German prison guard named Johann Schultz, whose personality and last name would be shared by a similar character, Hans Schultz, played by John Banner in *Hogan's Heroes*.[8]

Two other films are worth mentioning here. Perhaps the most famous POW film of all time was the Academy Award–winning Best Picture of 1957, David Lean's *The Bridge on the River Kwai*, which depicts the brutal experience of British prisoners in a Japanese camp (and the high-minded idealism of an officer played by Alec Guinness). But *Hogan's* owes relatively little to the film other than an American character, again played by William Holden, who exhibits bracing realism in contrast to the Brits around him, along with a sense of humor that would later be aspects of the title character of *Hogan's Heroes*. Much more directly influential was yet another classic film, John Sturges's *The Great Escape* (1963), which recounts the true-life story of seventy-six Allied prisoners who escaped from a German POW prison in 1944. *Hogan's* star Bob Crane cited James Garner's performance in that film as a model for his embodiment of Colonel Robert Hogan.[9] One also senses the cynical charm of Steve McQueen in that movie as an influence on Crane.

All these movies were linked by what might be termed a gender project. If, as was widely believed at the time and ever since, the essence of manhood is a sense of agency—one tested and proved most vividly in wartime—then the experience of becoming a prisoner can be perceived as an emasculating loss of autonomy and purpose. By showing men who endure and/or overcome such privation with their dignity intact—and, especially, like the characters portrayed by Holden and McQueen, do so with insouciance—these films offer viewers an experience of vicarious triumph, a kind of ideological jiu-jitsu where the liability of imprisonment makes the process of escaping it all the more impressive and satisfying.

Which brings us to another pop culture genre that was a major vector in the emergence of *Hogan's Heroes*: the spy thriller. While not necessarily about the experience of imprisonment (though its characters are sometimes captives in some form for any given stretch of storyline) these stories usually involve an individual or team involved in a long-shot enterprise against powerful enemies, requiring a literal and figurative ability to think on one's feet. The relevant prototype here is the first James Bond movie, *Dr. No* (1962), followed in rapid order by *From Russia with Love* (1963) and *Goldfinger* (1964). Ian Fleming, who authored the novels that became the basis of these movies, was involved in launching a television version of the spy thriller, *The Man from U.N.C.L.E.*, which ran on NBC from 1964 to 1968.

Hogan's Heroes also emerged in a television ecology of prior World War II sitcoms. These included *The Phil Silvers Show* (1955–1959), notable for Silver's iconic portrayal of Master Sergeant Ernest G. Bilko, a calculating soldier at a U.S. Army post in Kansas. There was also *McHale's Navy* (1962–1966) and a cluster of related movie and TV shows; this one starred Ernest Borgnine as the commander of a patrol torpedo (PT) boat in the Pacific. Another was *Gomer Pyle, U.S.M.C.* (1964–1969), a spin-off of *The Andy Griffith Show*, starring Jim Nabors as the guileless title character who repeatedly stymies the scheming Gunnery Sergeant Vince Carter (Frank Sutton) at a California Marine Corps base.

All these cultural strands converged as *Hogan's* creators Albert S. Ruddy (an architect looking for career change) and Bernard Fein (an actor looking to move into producing) came together to develop a TV show about a group of convicts at a minimum-security prison who are actually running the place. But they couldn't sell it. A turning point reportedly occurred after Fein was on a plane and saw someone reading *Von Ryan's Express*, a 1963 novel that became a 1965 Frank Sinatra film about a group of Allied war prisoners who blow up a train. Fein and Ruddy retooled their project, which at this point was in a race against time against a rival show, *Campo 44*, that NBC was developing about an Italian prisoner-of-war camp (it was launched in 1967 but quickly canceled). Drawing on what had by then become a series of familiar conventions, the two developed a show that featured a motley cast of characters, in this case a puckish pickpocket Brit named Peter Newkirk (the role went to Richard Dawson), an urbane French cook-tailor named Louis LeBeau (Robert Clary), an earnest, ingenuous North Dakotan explosives expert, Andrew Carter (Larry Hovis), and a black communications technician (Ivan Dixon, who would go on to become a distinguished director whose work included a number of Blaxploitation pictures as well as episodes of *The Waltons*, among other shows). They were led by the charming, clever, and secretly manipulative Robert Hogan (Bob Crane), a pilot from Bridgeport, Connecticut. In another nod to a familiar trope—one evident in *The Great Escape*, among other movies, Hogan enjoyed relatively friendly relations with his German counterpart, Colonel Wilhelm Klink (Werner Klemperer, playing against type as a vain fool).

Fein and Ruddy's first pitch for the revamped show went to NBC, which turned them down. CBS chairman William Paley was initially skeptical—"I find the idea of doing a comedy set in a Nazi prisoner-of-war camp reprehensible," he said—but came around after hearing their pitch. Ruddy moved on to film production, and ownership of the project was brought under the banner of singer-impresario Bing Crosby's production company. The show's prospects brightened further when two major sponsors, Philip Morris and General Foods, agreed to buy advertising.[10]

A major reason the project could get off the ground was a form of ideological inoculation that probably proved crucial: many of the people involved in the show (beginning with Fein and Ruddy) were Jewish. This was true of all the actors playing major Nazi characters, many of whom had experienced the war personally. Klemperer, the son of famed orchestra conductor Otto Klemperer, came to the United States as a child fleeing Nazi persecution. John Banner, who played Sgt. Schultz, was an Austrian actor working in Switzerland when the Nazis came to power and he was fired. He came to the United States—appearing in a series of army recruiting posters[11]— and resumed his acting career before serving in the Army Air Corps (a forerunner of the Air Force). Leon Askin, a recurring member of the cast as German General Burkhalter, was, like Banner, an Austrian Jew who was arrested and beaten by the Gestapo as well as detained in France before making his way to the States. Robert Clary, probably the most experienced member of the cast, spent almost three years in concentration camps before being liberated from Buchenwald in 1945.[12]

Not everyone was willing to go along with the show's premise, however. Leonid Kinskey, best known for his role as the "crazy Russian" Sascha in *Casablanca*, appeared in the pilot as a Soviet prisoner and was to be a featured member of the cast. "The moment we had a dress rehearsal and I saw German SS uniforms, something very ugly rose in me," he told series chronicler Brenda Royce. "I visualized millions upon millions of bodies of innocent people murdered by the Nazis. One can hardly, in good taste, joke about it. So in the practical life of the TV industry, I lost thousands of dollars, but I was, am, at peace with myself." (His place was taken by Hovis, who went from what was a single appearance in the pilot to a regular member of the cast.) Another actor, Paul Lambert, who appeared in four episodes, was similarly uneasy. "I always felt a little queasy about doing this show about 'funny Nazis.' If it wasn't for the money, I wouldn't have done *Hogan's*."[13]

The typical response to these concerns by defenders of the show was to regard them as misplaced. Clary, who also performed in blackface in his career, emphasized that he was playing a character and that the scenario was not a concentration camp, but rather a prisoner-of-war camp, which operated under different rules. Banner emphasized the subversive quality of the show: "We will always be able to laugh at someone flaunting authority." Klemperer, who also took a role as a Nazi in *Judgement at Nuremberg* and played the notorious Adolf Eichmann in *Operation Eichmann* (both 1961) was determined that his character, Col. Klink (whose name evokes a slang synonym for prison—clink) would always be shown in the wrong, while at the same time giving him a human dimension, much in the way Carroll O'Connor would with his role as Archie Bunker in *All in the Family*. "My role is satisfying because it challenges me to develop new facets of the character," he said in a 1966 interview. "Here and there I can extend his pomposity while never forgetting that he is, basically, a scared little man."[14] In the 1967 episode "Casanova Klink," one of many where Hogan saves Klink's foundering career as a matter of self-interest—after all, the clueless Kommandant you know is better than the prospect of a dangerously competent one—Klink indulges in a periodic moment of sentiment. "Hogan, it's at moments like these when I'm sorry you and I are not on the same side," he tells his prisoner. Hogan's typically ambiguous reply: "Thank you, Colonel. A great many moments I'm glad you are." Klemperer would win two Emmy Awards for his portrayal of Klink.

Ultimately, the success of *Hogan's Heroes* as a viable economic and cultural proposition would rest on what might be termed two historical subtractions. The first was the actual history of American POWs in German prison camps, which were alternately more brutal and numbing than anything shown on the show. Indeed, the relatively cushy standard of living the characters enjoyed, and their ease in coming and going as part of their sabotage operations, was a running joke. It's established in the show's pilot, when Hogan decides to show a German agent (Noam Pitlik, who would play a string of Allies and Germans over the course of the series) the whole underground apparatus—one that included forgery operations, a barber shop, steam room, and multiple tunnels—correctly guessing that Klink and Burkhalter will find the informer crazy when he tries to explain. This was nothing like what was experienced by the 115,000 U.S. POWs, over 90,000 of them in Germany, who endured any combination of hostility from locals, food shortages, severe discipline, and sheer boredom. And these were generally the lucky ones: the situation in Germany was far better than in Japan, where numbers were lower because survival rates were lower owing to the climate, a Japanese reluctance to take prisoners at all, and the use of prisoners for slave labor. (So-called hell ships, where prisoners were transported to such sites, had conditions resembling the Middle Passage of African slaves across the Atlantic in the seventeenth and eighteenth centuries.) Americans were also treated far better by the Germans than the Soviets were, as the war was far more savage in Eastern Europe. On the western front, Germany generally honored the Geneva Conventions, which built on those of The Hague at the turn of the twentieth century and codified in 1929. Hogan routinely refers to the Geneva Conventions over the course of the show, and frequent mention was made of the much-coveted (by Germans no less than Americans) Red Cross packages sent to prisoners.[15]

The other, more serious, omission is any mention of the Holocaust. Indeed, we never see a Jewish character, hear about any atrocities against Jews, or even the word "Jew" itself at any point in the series. Few viewers at the time could be unaware of this history; as Shandley notes in his study of *Hogan's Heroes*, "The Holocaust is a bit like an apparition that haunts the series without ever allowing itself to be seen."[16] However striking or appalling, this silence was not peculiar to *Hogan's Heroes* itself. The Holocaust was only making its way into the center of explicit World War II mainstream discourse in the mid-sixties. Elie Wiesel's famed concentration camp memoir, *Night*, was published in the United States in 1960, and he was among those who urged diffidence in handling such a difficult topic. The Holocaust was a particularly difficult subject for television to handle with any sensitivity. The first real effort to do so, the 1978 miniseries *Holocaust*, which came out in the wake of the spectacularly successful *Roots* the previous year, was criticized for its portrayal of the subject as well as the context in which it was depicted. *New York Times* reviewer John J. O'Connor labeled *Holocaust* "presumptuous," lamenting its "sterile collection of wooden characters and ridiculous coincidences." He was especially critical of the way commercials routinely intruded into the most grave moments. Not hard to see, then, why a sitcom that aired a decade earlier would avoid the subject entirely, however problematic it was to do so.[17]

So what, then, remains? Is the show devoid of any interpretive statement about World War II, nothing more than an ideologically evasive burlesque performed in Nazi uniforms? Not quite. The logic of the show suggests two arguments that are clear, if contestable.

The first, common at the time but less so since, was to make an evident, if generally unspoken, distinction between the *Germans* and the *Nazis*.[18] We certainly see a gallery of villains on the sitcom, notably Major Wolfgang Hochstetter (played by Howard Caine, another Jew), who's much sharper than Klink and suspicious of Hogan but nevertheless always foiled by him. "What is this man *doing here*?" he regularly asks in exasperation whenever Hogan shows up where he isn't supposed to. Although Klink has few redeeming qualities, his childlike vanity, which Hogan continually plays upon, makes it hard to really hate him, and he himself has a repeated line about Hochstetter, who ranks below Klink but as a member of the Gestapo routinely bullies him: "I *despise* that man." In the 1968 episode "Will the Real Col. Klink Please Stand Up?" Hogan gives a mock-serious speech about how his fellow POWs ended up in their benighted state: "They're here because they're men who believe in freeing the world from the yoke of tyranny and oppression." He tries to continue, but Klink cuts him off. "When I want to hear a long-winded speech, I listen to the Fuhrer."

The pivotal figure in this regard is Banner's portrayal of Sgt. Schultz, a lovable buffoon. The POWs often hatch their schemes right in front of him, knowing that he won't report anything that will make him look bad or complicate his relatively simple life. (The single most important running joke of the series, uttered by Klink in every episode, that there has never been an escape from Stalag 13, which is true as far as he knows, which of course isn't very much. In the 1970 episode "Klink's Escape," Hogan notes his operation has aided 519 escapees to freedom.) Schultz's refrain—"I see *nothing*," "I know *nothing*," or some variation on both—became a signature line of the series, what we would today call a meme, and one dubbed "the Sgt. Schultz defense" used by tight-lipped witnesses in congressional hearings at the turn of this century.[19] Easily bribed by the prospect of food (especially candy bars), Schultz is often slow to process what he hears, reacting belatedly in alarm. It is fitting to learn that before the war Schultz was the owner of a toy company and that a surprised Klink, who was a bookkeeper, angles for a postwar job with him. He was also a Social Democrat before the war—a German political party that opposed the Nazis.[20]

The actors playing these parts were aware of the German/Nazi issue question and addressed it directly. Clary, as a concentration camp survivor, is someone who might plausibly regard the distinction as without a difference, but nevertheless insisted on it. "Really, with the students it's the first question: 'How could you have done *Hogan's Heroes*, which dealt with Nazism?' And I say, not all Germans were Nazis, and not all Nazis were Germans, and we did not deal, really, with Nazism, we left that apart. As comedy you cannot do that." Banner was similarly emphatic. "I see Schultz as representative of some kind of good in any generation," he said. He also noted that his character may not be as dumb as he seems. "You think Schultz is stupid?" he once asked rhetorically. "Notice that he survives."[21]

Banner's emphasis on the dignity and decency of a given individual points toward the other major interpretative statement of *Hogan's Heroes*: the role of the little guy (and, occasionally, gal) as an agent of history. Robert Shandley has shrewdly unraveled one of the most perplexing mysteries of the show as a vehicle of advancing this argument: its seemingly perverse scrambling of chronology. We all understand that *Hogan's Heroes* takes place between 1942 (a title card indicating this is the first thing we see when the pilot begins) and 1945, when the war ends. But even that's a little strange: given that Americans didn't begin arriving on the western front until late 1942, there were relatively few opportunities for someone like Hogan to be captured—or "captured," if one assumes his operation was pre-planned so that he could be a mole reporting on German operations. At different points in the next six seasons, we hear references to— even have episodes built around—D-Day, the race to build the atomic bomb, and German development of V-1 and V-2 rockets, in no particular order. As Shandley notes, the effect of "this history without time is a sense of war as a permanent condition"—especially since we never get any depiction of any characters' lives before or after it.

But this permanent condition is also cyclical: "By the end of each episode, the task has been accomplished and the Germans have been defeated for the day." The result, Shandley notes, is a "'little guy' theory of history: Every time an episode claimed that the outcome of the war will turn on the prisoners' ability to pull off a stunt [steal plans; blow up a factory; help a defector escape] the show suggests that history is not made in the halls of power but in the sphere of influence occupied by common people."[22] Here it's worth noting that while Hogan is an officer—albeit one who commands with a light touch—his teammates are corporals and sergeants; in real life, officers and enlisted men were typically separated in prison camps. The fact that the world at large may never know the role Hogan and his compatriots had in saving the world may be all the more satisfying to audiences who are effectively in on the secret. There's also a subtle element of metatextual flattery involved at times, given that many viewers were likely to be World War II buffs. "I warn you: we have ways of making you talk," Klink tells Hogan in the 1967 episode "Praise the Fuhrer and Pass the Ammunition." Hogan's reply: "Sir, you've been seeing too many war movies."

Somewhat paradoxically, this emphasis on the local and individual had important geopolitical implications, and one that served U.S. interests. As Shandley notes, "*Hogan's Heroes* went on the air ten years after the Federal Republic of Germany was admitted into the North Atlantic Treaty Organization [NATO]. The construction of the Berlin Wall in 1961 created even more solidarity between the United States and its vanquished former enemy; it quite literally cemented West Germany as a reliable ally in the Cold War." In the words of a common joke at the time, NATO was designed "to keep the Americans in, the Russians out—and the Germans down." In this regard, *Hogan's Heroes* served a larger political project of consensus, foreign and domestic, at the zenith of the American Century.[23]

But this consensus began to break down in the second half of the 1960s. It would prove to be a challenge for the people running the U.S. government. It would also be one for those running a sitcom that tried to sidestep that breakdown while keeping the laughs, and the profits, coming.

SIDESTEPPING THE QUAGMIRE

The run of *Hogan's Heroes* between 1965 and 1971 corresponded to one of the most divisive periods in U.S. history, a time of war, racial conflict, and a generational challenge to deep-seated cultural norms in American society. All sitcoms present a stylized version of reality—escapism is central to their appeal—but there was a peculiarly jarring quality to the juxtaposition between TV and real life in the late sixties, when footage of combat and protest jostled with light comedies and commercials. (The top ten TV shows in 1968 included the literally magical *Bewitched*, the fish-out of-water *Beverly Hillbillies*, and the nostalgic small-town *Andy Griffith Show*.)[24] Many sitcoms of the era battened down the hatches in offering their viewers alternatives to, and retreats from, social conflict. But the tension was increasingly hard to manage, and would ultimately lead to a new television order grounded in a greater sense of realism. But that would take a while. And *Hogan's Heroes* made the most of this interregnum—even as, inevitably, it refracted the 1940s through the world of the 1960s.

Some of this was trivial, offhand stuff. A good example comes from the pilot, when Hogan is showing the German agent part of the team's operation to produce fake guns that are actually cigarette lighters. "Of course the Japanese will copy us and undersell us, but that's free enterprise," he says—an allusion to the fact that Japanese manufacturers were flooding into the electronics business in the sixties, an early step in that nation's rise as a global economic superpower. This theme gets picked up again a few years later. "I don't mean to knock your ally, Kommandant, but these Japanese radios," he says, holding up a device with a broken wire in the 1968 episode "The Ultimate Weapon." (Hogan was actually the one to snap it.)

But there were two relatively substantial contemporary streams threading through the series as it ran in the second half of the sixties. One was the civil rights movement, and the key vehicle for addressing it was the character of Kinchloe ("Kinch" for short), played by Ivan Dixon. Dixon was one of very few African American actors to appear as a series regular in any TV show in the mid-sixties—two others were

Bill Cosby in *I Spy* (1965–1968) and Greg Morris in *Mission: Impossible* (1966–1973)—and he is consistently portrayed in a mild-mannered light, which was something of a mixed blessing. "Kinch is the one person on either side of the war to whom Hogan does not condescend," Shandley notes. "While this made the character respectable, it often caused him to disappear among the comedic actions of the other members of the ensemble."[25] Dixon, for his part, maintained a clear-eyed realism about his own objectives: "I needed the money," he said of his participation in the show, which he left as his directing career began to take off.[26] One flashpoint occurred when Robert Butler, who directed five episodes between 1965 and 1955, supervised a scene in which the men ogle a female member of the French resistance when she enters the camp. Butler wondered if Dixon should as well—it seemed easier to avoid the fraught issue of black men's sexual interest in white women—a suggestion to which Dixon strongly objected. Producer Feldman weighed in on Dixon's side and Butler said he readily acquiesced.[27]

There were a number of installments that did focus on racial issues. In the 1966 episode "The Prince of the Phone Company," Dixon plays a double role: his usual one as well as the prince of an unnamed African nation where the Germans wish to build an air base. (Such masquerading, particularly by Carter/Hovis, who impersonated Hitler among other Nazis, was common on the show.) The fake prince's negotiations with a German count (Lee Bergere) are tetchy:

PRINCE: I just don't know if we can do business.
COUNT: Why not?
PRINCE: Herr Hitler has made some pretty nasty remarks about my people.
COUNT: He was misquoted, sir. He loves your people.
KLINK: Oh, yes. Always singing and dancing. He loves your people.
COUNT: Klink, stay out of this!
KLINK: What did I say?

Note that the most egregious racism is attributed to Hitler and Klink; Hogan is firmly allied with Kinch as one of the good guys.

Another pivotal figure is the Prince's wife Yawanda (Isabel Cooley), who upon discovering the ruse casts her lot with Kinch. He's a former telephone operator from Detroit—hence the title of the episode—while she's from Cleveland. "We'll meet in Toledo," she tells him as romance kindles between them. The actual Prince is portrayed as a haughty opportunist. "My subjects will take their revenge," he tells Hogan at the end of the episode, after he's been boxed out of a deal. Hogan's typically flippant reply: "If you can find any, yes."

But as time went on, it would not be credible to portray U.S. race relations in quite so chummy a manner. In "Is General Hammerschlag Burning?" first broadcast in November 1967, Kinch is again a pivotal figure, this time as someone Hogan brings to Paris to procure secret military plans from a German general (Paul Lambert, who, as noted earlier, expressed misgivings about his participation). Once again we have subterfuge, as the only person he trusts is a black clairvoyant named Kumasa (Barbara McNair), who's actually Carol Dukes, an old high school classmate of Kinch's. But she's not so quick to jump on board. "You cats amaze me," she says, incredulous of their scheme to steal the plans. "Keep the faith, baby," he replies. (Note here that the dialogue, while not entirely anachronistic, seems more redolent of the sixties than the forties.) Kumasa/Dukes actively challenges what she regards as Kinch's false consciousness: "What's in it for you? Money? Medals? Oh, they gonna give you the key to the city if you get back to Detroit?" Kinch replies as an integrationist liberal: "Most people go through life semi-involved. I dunno, maybe they like it. But you're in a spot now where you've got to take a position. Either you turn us in, or join up." Given the constellation of forces outlined here, it's a foregone conclusion that she'll come around. The really interesting thing is that she posed her challenges in the first place, a sign of how U.S. racial politics were penetrating the fairly thick ideological wall the makers of the show constructed. They nevertheless sought to maintain their sense of humor by inverting racist tropes. When Kinch presents Hogan, who's impersonating General Hammerschlag as a mute who can nevertheless channel the great Prussian leader Otto von Bismarck, Kinch describes his boss dismissively.

"Look at him," he says of Hogan/Hammerschlag. "Obviously a man of limited intelligence. Observe the eyes, how close together."

By 1970, with Richard Nixon in office, the show tacked slightly back to the right. In "The Softer They Fall," an episode that takes place against the backdrop of Muhammad Ali's larger than life presence in American culture, Kinch is portrayed as a former Golden Gloves boxer who's recruited as a sparring partner for Bruno (Chuck Hicks), a German fighter. It quickly becomes clear Kinch is the better athlete, which concerns General Burkhalter, who recites the history of the black American track athlete Jesse Owens at the 1936 Berlin Olympics. He arranges for a well-publicized match in which Bruno will cheat by packing metal in his boxing gloves. Kinch's charge was originally to have the match last long enough for Hogan's crew to pull off a heist, but now it's a matter of hanging in there. He nevertheless manages to gain the upper hand—and throws the fight once the objective is achieved. Newkirk is appalled: "Hogan's Cowards," he says disgustedly. But Kinch and Hogan have their eyes on the prize of their mission, not racial bragging rights. Geopolitics matters more than identity politics.

These episodes are being discussed in relative detail because they're revealing of the way a present-day issue, in this case race relations, leached into *Hogan's Heroes*. But they're not really representative of the show as a whole, which largely avoided references to the civil rights movement. One issue that did, obliquely but durably, loom over the show was the Vietnam War. Vietnam is never referred to directly nor is U.S. policy there. But the perception that the war was increasingly becoming a quagmire—especially for young Americans expected to fight there and the loved ones who worried about them—becomes allegorically captured in the repeated threat that any German character who makes an error will be sent to the Russian front. By all informed reckonings, the German/Soviet conflict in World War II was truly horrible and something to be avoided at all costs, which is how being drafted to fight in Vietnam was widely seen in the United States by the late sixties. In the 1968 episode "Clearance Sale at the Black Market," which kicked off the fourth season, Klink informs

Schultz that he's to be shipped east. Schultz's reaction is suggestive of the way many American men felt about going to Vietnam:

KLINK: Schultz, I have the pleasure to tell you that you are being transferred to the eastern front. Isn't that thrilling?

SCHULTZ: Thrilling? I'm out of my mind. What happened, Herr Kommandant? Did I do something wrong?

KLINK (*disingenuously*): Of course not! You are just being asked to use your knowledge and experience in the service of the Third Reich.

SCHULTZ: Yeah?

KLINK: You want Germany to win the war, don't you?

SCHULTZ: Yeah.

KLINK: Being transferred to the eastern front, you can make that possible.

SCHULTZ: Would it be so bad if we lost the war?

"Anybody who had watched the evening news an hour before *Hogan's Heroes* came on would have no trouble assimilating Schultz's query about losing the war with discussions of Vietnam in the news," Shandley observes of this exchange, noting the vein of cynicism that lurks under Klink's dialogue. "Wanting to win a war that was understood as unwinnable was the joke of this exchange."[28] When, in the 1970 episode "Get Fit or Go Fight," a panicked Klink is himself to be transferred to the eastern front, he's rescued by Hogan's crew, which arranges to have him fail his physical, just as many draft-dodging Americans sought to do at the time.

A related, but more ambiguous, corollary issue was the Cold War with the Soviet Union, a major reason why the Vietnam War was being fought in the sixties. This topic is complicated by the fact that the United States and the Soviets were allies, however uncomfortably, during the Second World War. The matter is finessed on the show through the inclusion of one of the few significant recurring female characters in the series: Marya, amusingly played by Nita Talbot. Marya, though introduced in 1966 as a White Russian, nevertheless proves to be an effective (Red) Soviet agent over seven episodes in using her sexuality, improvisational skills, and concealed planning to achieve her objectives. Though full of good cheer, routinely referring to Hogan as "darling," he distrusts her, and she's the only person in the series whose moves he can neither anticipate nor control (nor apparently can he resist her charms, though Hogan typically romances most of the gallery of female civilians and operatives who pass through the show in ways that seem far-fetched at best and appallingly sexist at worst from a contemporary standpoint). But although she can make his life difficult, Marya never actually betrays Hogan and his allies, even if it's always clear Soviet interests come first. In the 1969 episode "The Witness," she exposes an operation Hogan was working on and manipulates him into getting involved in a propaganda project as part of a larger scheme to get a Russian defector working on rocket technology back to the USSR.

It's worth noting in this regard that Richard Powell, who wrote dozens of episodes of the show over its six-year run, was blacklisted during the Red Scare of the 1950s. This fact, and the Left valances described above, complicate a view of *Hogan's Heroes* as politically neutral or de facto conservative in trying to avoid controversy. As Paul Buhle, the preeminent scholar of left-wing Hollywood has noted of the show, "One of the industry's inside jokes was the antiwar, liberal, and left wing character of the writing staff and most of its actors." (The only Republican in the cast was Bob Crane.)[29] History may be impossible to escape. But it can be surprisingly useful.

DURABLE PLASTIC

The ethos of *Hogan's Heroes* was always more factory than boutique: compared with many of its cinematic counterparts and sitcom successors, it was a fairly simple operation built on cheap sets, recycled plots, and stock characters. It was nevertheless constructed with a kind of sturdiness in mind, and the fact that it lasted for six years in a crowded prime-time television schedule and into the next century in syndication demonstrates a certain kind of success, even if the sitcom's limitations, aesthetic and political, are clear. The show walked through a minefield and survived. By the turn of the new century it was fondly viewed as a nostalgic rendition of World War II as well as an artifact of the sixties—that version of the sixties before the sixties went crazy.

But *Hogan's Heroes* was not, of course, immune from the ravages of time. As noted, there was some impatience even to get the show off the broadcast schedule on the part of Bing Crosby Productions. It was bumped from its prime Friday night slot on the CBS schedule, an experience that tends to weaken even successful programs. But the real turning point was the arrival of another sitcom: *All in the Family* debuted as a midseason replacement on CBS in 1971. Its launch, which engaged social and political issues with sometimes brutal candor, was undertaken with some trepidation on the part of the network, and early audience indications were uncertain. But as it became increasingly clear that *All in the Family* was indeed the harbinger of a new television order, CBS executed its so-called rural purge and axed an array of shows—*Green Acres, Petticoat Junction, The Beverly Hillbillies*—that included *Hogan's Heroes*. The final episode, an unremarkable installment named "Rockets or Romance," aired on April 4, 1971. The following year, CBS unveiled a new sitcom about the Korean War, *M*A*S*H*, that was widely seen as a more sophisticated successor, part of a new wave of quality television that would define the 1970s. *Hogan's Heroes* became a relic.[30]

The cast and crew moved on to other projects, few surpassing the notoriety they achieved in Stalag 13. Gene Reynolds, who directed thirty-four episodes of *Hogan's Heroes*, went on to cocreate *M*A*S*H* (see next chapter). As noted, Dixon enjoyed a long directing career. Richard Dawson enjoyed a successful run as a game show host. The tragic figure here is Bob Crane, who could not reproduce his success on the show and descended into a sex addiction that he chronicled as an early adopter of home video technology. His decline and his murder, which was never resolved, is chronicled in the 2002 Paul Schrader film *Auto Focus*, where he is portrayed by Greg Kinnear as a man who doesn't seem to grasp just how dysfunctional he's become. *Hogan's Heroes* would linger in collective memory—popular in Germany in the 1990s; the subject of occasional speculation for a film version; an influence in the encyclopedic mental closet of Quentin Tarantino, whose 2009 film *Inglourious Basterds* owes a debt to *Hogan's* sensibility—as its cultural half-life grows ever weaker.

As Robert Shandley suggests, however, the show may deserve a little more credit than it typically gets. He notes that unlike *M*A*S*H*, which arrived after consensus against the Vietnam War had already formed, *Hogan's Heroes* had to walk a more difficult path and did so with real finesse. "Throughout the series, *Hogan's Heroes* suggests that, in warfare, the line between what is justified and what is criminal is not easily ascertained." Moreover, "it offer[ed] a level of skepticism that was generally aligned with American attitudes as they developed throughout the six years of the series' run."[31]

Articulating common sense, however perishable, is no mean feat. Especially when it's outrageously funny.

WARRING COMRADES

First iteration of *M*A*S*H* cast, 1972–1975, in a genial moment. The sitcom turned the Korean War into a virtual allegory of the Vietnam War. Shown from front left: Larry Linville (Maj. Frank Burns), Alan Alda (Capt. "Hawkeye" Pierce), Wayne Rogers (Capt. "Trapper John" McIntyre), Gary Burghoff (Cpl. "Radar" O'Reilly), and Jamie Farr (Cpl. Klinger). Back row: Loretta Swit (Maj. Margaret "Hot Lips" Houlihan), McLean Stevenson (Lt. Col. Henry Blake), and William Christopher (Fr. Mulcahy).

A FUNNY WAR

*M*A*S*H* as a 1970s Version of the 1950s

> Goddamn war.
> That is all.
> —final two lines, *M*A*S*H* (1970 movie)

> We could leave something behind that says
> who we were and why we were here.
> —Major Margaret Houlihan, final
> episode of *M*A*S*H* (TV series, 1983)[1]

Key Cast Members

- Alan Alda as Captain Benjamin Franklin ("Hawkeye") Pierce
- Loretta Swit as Major Margaret ("Hot Lips") Houlihan
- Wayne Rogers as Captain ("Trapper John") John McIntyre
- McLean Stevenson as Lieutenant Colonel Henry Blake
- Larry Linville as Major Frank Burns
- Gary Burghoff as Corporal Walter ("Radar") O'Reilly
- Jamie Farr as Corporal Maxwell Q. Klinger
- Warren Christopher as Father Francis Mulcahy
- Mike Farrell as Captain B. J. Hunnicutt
- Harry Morgan as Colonel Sherman T. Potter
- David Ogden Stiers as Major Charles Emerson Winchester III

Key Episodes
- "Sometimes You Hear the Bullet" (1973)
- "Abyssinia, Henry" (1975)
- "The Interview" (1976)
- "The Nurses" (1976)
- "Preventative Medicine" (1979)
- "Goodbye, Farewell and Amen" (1983)

*T*ELEVISION RATINGS RECORDS, like professional sports records, are made to be broken. (Actually, the most watched shows of all time have long been Super Bowl broadcasts.) In TV, the passage of time has meant more chances for a program to achieve landmark status—most, longest, best—and a steadily growing population creates a larger base from which to work. But just as some sports records (Joe DiMaggio's 56-game hitting streak for the New York Yankees in 1956; Wilt Chamberlain's 100-point game for the Philadelphia Warriors in 1962) seem unlikely to be surpassed, some television achievements are products of environments that are long gone. Well over 100 million watched the finale of *M*A*S*H*,[2] a long-running sitcom about an army hospital in the Korean War, when it aired on February 28, 1983, breaking the record for the most watched television show of all time. (It also prompted congratulatory telegrams from three U.S. presidents who served while the show was on the air—Ford, Carter, and Reagan.)[3] That viewership figure was eclipsed three years later by a Super Bowl, but as of this writing *M*A*S*H* is only non-football championship game in the top ten and is notable in that it was an episodic weekly series, not a one-time event. Given the fragmentation of television audiences that has occurred since the advent of cable and streaming, when numbers that were once considered anemic are now considered astonishing, *M*A*S*H*'s distinction seems secure for some time to come.[4]

And yet, considered in the context of its time, there's something a little surprising about this. Clearly, *M*A*S*H* was a beloved show, reflected by the fact that it lasted for eleven seasons in a highly competitive network schedule. But the sitcom never finished at the top of the annual Nielsen ratings, and only 9 of its 256 episodes won a given week. At its peak, it was seen by 30 million viewers weekly—an enormous figure by contemporary standards. But its CBS peer *All in the Family* (1971–1979) reached 50 million weekly and was the top-rated show in television five years in a row. Actually, in an important respect, *All in the Family* saved *M*A*S*H*. At the end of its first season in 1972–1973, it languished in the ratings, finishing forty-sixth. But in 1973–1974 CBS moved the show to its now legendary Saturday night schedule, where it was nestled between *AITF* and another thoroughbred, *The Mary Tyler Moore Show* (1970–1977). *M*A*S*H* got its sea legs after that, and indeed became a programming anchor its own right on Monday and Tuesday nights in the latter half of its run, generating steadily enormous profits for the network.[5]

At some fundamental level, the reason why *M*A*S*H* existed—the basis of broadcasting in the United States from its inception—was to sell advertising. But television shows also sell a vision of life that's implicitly or explicitly political as they go about the business of entertainment. In the case of *M*A*S*H*, this message was filtered through a historical lens in depicting a war that had ended a generation before the show went on the air. As a number of observers have noted, *M*A*S*H* was a sitcom about the Korean War that was *really* about the Vietnam War, which was winding down when the show debuted in 1972. As we've seen, *Hogan's Heroes*, which was far more celebratory of U.S. involvement in World War II than *M*A*S*H* was of Korea, also commented on Vietnam, albeit in a much more oblique way. But one could forget about Vietnam while watching *Hogan's Heroes*—for some viewers, that may well have been the point—in a way that was never really possible with *M*A*S*H*, whatever its creators may have intended (which, as we'll see, was not necessarily meant as a direct allegory).

Actually, *M*A*S*H* functioned as an indirect commentary on U.S. civilian life as much as it did the nation's foreign policy. In essence, it was a seventies show about the fifties that was at heart about the sixties—a critique of a conservative fifties, an affirmation of a liberal sixties. More specifically, the sitcom affirmed one of the key features of its era: a skepticism, even hostility, toward institutions, whether public ones like government and the military, or private ones like religion or the family. *M*A*S*H* tapped a deep libertarian sensibility that had long been a feature of American culture. But it affirmed that sensibility in a distinctive way at the very moment it was beginning to recede in national life, giving way to a libertarian ethos of a decidedly different sort, embodied by a figure many of the characters and actors from the show would have considered a joke: Ronald Reagan. By the time *M*A*S*H* ended in 1983, it represented the end of an era not only in American television but in the nation's political culture more generally.

MASHUP

Before *M*A*S*H* was a TV show, it was a 1970 movie, and before that, it was a 1968 novel. That novel was authored by "Richard Hooker," a collaborative pen name for real-life surgeon Richard Hornberger and writer W. C. Heinz. Hornberger went to Korea as a young doctor in 1951, and his experiences there formed the core of a saga that would take multiple forms in the fifteen years that followed.

Military medical care in the U.S. army had evolved rapidly since the First World War, when the first mobile hospital (MH) had opened in 1918. In both World Wars, wounded soldiers were transported to medical units near the front by ambulance. The name changed from surgical hospital (SH) to portable surgical hospital (PSH) before being designated mobile army surgical hospital (MASH) by the time the Korean War broke out. At war's end, these hospitals were saving 98 percent of the wounded who were brought there—a fact frequently cited in the TV series in valorizing the excellence of the characters who worked in one. They had become facilities that were a long way from the improvised tents where medical care was dispensed without lighting, plumbing, and other utilities. One key innovation: the wounded were now evacuated from the battlefield by helicopter, an iconic visual in *M*A*S*H* lore.[6]

Hornberger was assigned to the 8055th MASH unit, near the 38th parallel that separated North and South Korea. It was the site of a major battle at the war's outbreak in 1950, when Communist North Korean forces swept south and almost swallowed the entire peninsula before a counterattack by General Douglas MacArthur, leading an American-led United Nations coalition, pushed the North Koreans all the way to the Chinese border. But in more ways than one, MacArthur went too far, at which point the Red Army entered the conflict and the front moved rapidly southward again. MacArthur was removed by President Harry Truman, a controversial decision in what was now universally considered a wearisome war, its designation as a "police action" notwithstanding. The conflict stabilized near where it started, though bloody encounters occurred regularly in three years of fighting before the new president, Dwight Eisenhower, backed negotiations that culminated in the Truce of Panmunjom. Technically, the United States remains at war with North Korea to this day, though the truce is widely considered a de facto treaty. The conflict it receded rapidly in collective memory, which is why the pilot opens with the subtitle "Korea, 1950"—followed by an ironically inaccurate but comically apt "a hundred years ago."

Hornberger returned from Korea and practiced medicine in Bremen, Maine (soon to be fictionalized as Crabapple Cove). In 1956, he began writing a novel about his experiences that he tried to get published without success. It's at this point that another figure, sportswriter W. C. Heinz, who had also written a novel about a surgeon, entered the picture. Heinz, who had worked as a war correspondent in Europe during World War II, revised the novel with Hornberger and created the pseudonym of Richard Hooker. The revised manuscript was published by William Morrow in 1968 as *MASH: A Novel about Three Army Doctors*.

In an important sense, *MASH* isn't really a novel at all. It's more like a set of vignettes involving a trio of draftee surgeons: New Englander Benjamin Franklin "Hawkeye" Pierce, midwesterner John McIntyre, and southerner Duke Forrest, who cohabit a barracks they dub the Swamp. The various high jinks of these surgeons culminate in a football game against a competing unit in which a lot of money changes hands (Heinz's football expertise helped here). The characters are vivid, the humor is broad, and the cynicism is rampant. "Most of these Regular Army types are insecure," Hawkeye asserts at one point, with a contempt for social convention that reflects his namesake (the protagonist of James Fenimore Cooper's *The Last of the Mohicans*). "If they weren't, they'd take their chances out in the big free world. Their only security is based on the efficiency of their outfits."[7] Hornberger would turn *MASH* into a franchise that included a sequel and a series of subsequent novels, not all written by him, that proceeded in parallel to the TV series, for which he had little use beyond regular royalty checks. "I know more about war than a bunch of under-educated actors who go around blithering those sanctimonious self-righteous noises," he complained.[8] The anarchic individualism of *MASH* did not necessarily translate into a left-wing antiwar message.

But that possibility nevertheless lurked in the story's DNA. The novel found its way into the hands of Ring Lardner Jr., a key figure in the American culture wars of the mid-twentieth century. Lardner, son of the famous short story writer of the same name, enjoyed a highly successful career as a Hollywood screenwriter before he was ordered to appear before the House Un-American Activities Committee in 1947. Refusing to answer questions about his or others' political commitments, Lardner spent a year in jail and was blacklisted in Hollywood for the next eighteen years, writing a series of screenplays under pseudonyms. He began getting credited in his own name again in 1965, and three years later embarked on the task of adapting *MASH* into a movie. Fifteen directors turned down Lardner's script before 20th Century Fox, which was producing the film, gave the job to Robert Altman, a young director with an iconoclastic reputation for both the content and execution of his movies. (He was fond, for example, of having his actors recite their often improvised lines over each other to create an air of conversational verisimilitude.) Altman put together a cast of young and upcoming actors that included Donald Sutherland as Hawkeye, Elliott Gould as McIntyre—now nicknamed "Trapper

John"—and Tom Skerritt as Duke. Released in March 1970 as a black-comedy satire, M*A*S*H (as its title was marketed) rode a wave of anti-war sentiment with a public that had turned decisively against U.S. involvement in Vietnam.

The characters of the MASH novel, largely written in the fifties, were rebels without a cause. Those of the film, which premiered as American defeat in Vietnam was imminent, had a cause—more like an anti-cause—too obvious to be missed. There were other elements in the movie, some carried over from the novel, that were designed to offend establishment sensibilities as well: a steady stream of profanity, nude shots of Margaret "Hot Lips" Houlihan, played by Sally Kellerman, and a black surgeon with the highly charged nickname of Spearchucker Jones (played by former professional football player Fred Williamson). Such elements are indicative of the undercurrent of misanthropy that runs through Altman's work. Like Hornberger, he too was dismissive of the subsequent television show, falsely claiming "the guys with the slanted eyes are the bad guys," complaining that the creators of the TV show "don't make you pay for the laugh." The movie in any case captured the zeitgeist, grossing $36 million at the box office and seen by approximately 14 million people.[9] It got a jump on Mike Nichols's World War II satire Catch-22, which was released three months later and fared poorly at the box office. While it's Joseph Heller's 1961 novel for which most people remember Catch-22, Altman's version of M*A*S*H is better known than the book(s). Though of course M*A*S*H the TV show is better remembered than any of them.

M*A*S*H was not exactly an obvious candidate for television—it appeared too dark and too expensive to work as mainstream TV. But the industry was changing in the early seventies. All in the Family had pioneered comedy that stretched boundaries in terms of its language and topics. There was an opportunity when it came to cost too—the head of 20th Century Fox television, William Self, was aware that the studio had kept the M*A*S*H film's outdoor set intact in nearby Malibu. When plans for a sequel to the movie fell through, Self acted quickly and worked his industry contacts to develop the show, getting a commitment, sight unseen, from CBS, which was highly unusual.[10]

Self next turned to veteran producer Gene Reynolds, a former child actor whose directorial credits included *Hogan's Heroes*, for which he directed thirty-four episodes. In the early seventies, Reynolds was producing the ABC series *Room 222*, a path-breaking show about a Los Angeles high school that combined elements of comedy and drama—what we would today call a dramedy. Frustrated with network interference and ABC's ambivalence about this evolving approach to the form, Reynolds accepted Self's offer to produce *M*A*S*H* and sought to land Lardner as the primary writer for the fledgling series. Failing that, he turned to an old acquaintance, Larry Gelbart, who was living in London at the time.

Gelbart, like Reynolds, was an entertainment industry veteran whose career stretched back to his childhood, when he wrote jokes for comedian Danny Thomas for radio. After writing for Jack Paar and Bob Hope in the 1940s, and serving in the military at the end of World War II, where he worked for the Armed Forces Radio Network, Gelbart entered the nascent television business, rubbing shoulders with the likes of comedy pioneers Sid Caesar, Mel Brooks, and Woody Allen. He later joined forces with Stephen Sondheim and Burt Shevelove to create *A Funny Thing Happened on the Way to the Forum* (1963), a musical comedy based on the farces of the ancient Roman playwright Plautus. Gelbart moved to England to work on a production of the show there, as well as others.[11]

As he made clear multiple times in the decades that followed, Gelbart was cautious when Reynolds approached him about *M*A*S*H* a few days after he happened to see, and like, the film. "If we can capture that anarchic flavor, and the spirit of it, yes," Gelbart, who had toured Korea with Bob Hope, told Reynolds. "But if they want another *Hogan's Heroes*—which was one *Hogan's Heroes* too many for me—or *McHale's Navy*, then no."[12] Reynolds made clear he shared Gelbart's vision, and their partnership was augmented by the addition of associate producer Burt Metcalfe, who focused on casting the show while Gelbart wrote the pilot.

Beyond its script and setting, M*A*S*H would be innovative in its production values as well. Unlike most sitcoms that were shot with three cameras on a soundstage, M*A*S*H would rely on a single camera, giving it a visual feel closer to a movie rather than a television show. The producers would experiment with compelling techniques. These included the 1978 episode "Point of View," shot entirely from the perspective of a wounded soldier; the 1979 episode "Life Time," in which a clock is posted on the television screen to depict the struggle to save a patient in real time; and, perhaps most famously, the 1976 episode "The Interview," a faux documentary shot in black and white, featuring the actual TV wartime journalist Clete Roberts, who interviewed the characters, many of whose answers were improvised on camera.

The first major recruit for the M*A*S*H ensemble was Gary Burghoff as the ingenuous Corporal Walter "Radar" O'Reilly, so named for his uncanny ability to anticipate what others were about to say or do. Burghoff was the only actor with a major part to carry over from the film to the TV show. Other roles, like that of Trapper John McIntyre, were cast by audition; that part went to soap opera star Wayne Rogers. McLean Stevenson, who was hoping for the lead part of Hawkeye Pierce, was instead cast as his superior officer, Lieutenant Colonel Henry Blake. Larry Linville (Major Frank Burns) and Loretta Swit (Major Margaret Houlihan) got their parts because Metcalfe was familiar with their previous work.

That left the lead part of Hawkeye. "I needed an articulate intelligent guy, a guy with passion, a guy who could do light comedy and yet intelligent enough to be the editorial voice of the show," Reynolds explained to an interviewer decades later.[13] That quest went down to the wire. The producers had their eye on Alan Alda, the son of an Italian-American film actor who had made a name for himself on Broadway. Like Gelbart, Alda was chary of a sitcom that played war broadly for laughs, and he was a committed New Jerseyan reluctant to move to Hollywood (he ended up commuting there weekly). "I told them I was afraid the show might become nothing more than high jinks at the front, that under the pressure to entertain, it might make war look like a fun place to be," he said in his 2005 memoir, *Never Have Your Dog Stuffed*. But reassured by Gelbart and Reynolds, he accepted the part the night before rehearsals were to begin.[14]

M*A*S*H the TV show adopted many elements from *M*A*S*H* the movie. One, as already indicated, was the set. Another was the device of a loudspeaker that delivered sardonic—and occasionally metatextual—messages at regular intervals, among them ones that called attention to the artifice of the saga by reciting the credits of the actors. A third was the theme song, "Suicide Is Painless," written by the well-known film and television composer Johnny Mandel. (A set of lyrics, written by director Robert Altman's adolescent son Michael, are sung in the film. "I'm gonna lose it anyway/The losing card I'll someday lay/So this is all I have to say/That suicide is painless," croons a chorus of honey-voiced singers.) Both movie and TV show begin with the main characters playing golf on an improvised driving range adjacent to a minefield. The image captures the spirit of *M*A*S*H* as a whole: in wartime, zaniness is the only way to stay sane.

But there were differences too. In the movie as well as the book, the primary characters are a trio of Hawkeye, Trapper John, and Duke. But Duke—a southerner who's named after the notorious Confederate Nathan Bedford Forrest—was written out of the TV show, and it became increasingly clear that Trapper John is secondary to Hawkeye (which is why Rogers would leave the show after its third season). Other minor characters made the transition but subsequently disappeared, among them Captain "Ugly John" Black and First Lieutenant Maria "Dish" Schneider. The most notable withdrawal was that of Spearchucker Jones, who continued to be played by Timothy Brown in early episodes of the series. The Spearchucker moniker would likely have proved increasingly problematic—actually, it's a little surprising it got by network sponsors in the first place—but according to Gelbart, his disappearance from the show was a matter of historical verisimilitude. "The research just didn't bear us up," he later explained. "There were lots of black soldiers but no black surgeons." This isn't entirely convincing, in part because there are not lots—some, but not lots—of black soldiers in the series. More plausible, perhaps, is Gelbart's assertion that the series needed to streamline the cast of characters, especially as it became clear that Alda's Hawkeye would be the locus of the show. "He acted like a magnet," Gelbart remembered of his writing process.[15]

Reflecting its specific setting and its time, M*A*S*H was a sitcom whose cast was comprised mostly of white men. But there were a number of Asian characters, notably nurse Kellye Yamato (Kellye Nakahara), who appeared in well over 150 episodes; her prominence increased in the later years of the show. Veteran actors Jack Soo and Richard Lee-Sung appeared a number of times in different roles, as indeed did a number of white actors. Rosalind Chao, whose career remains prominent and active, was featured in the final installments of the series. Many of these performers were of Japanese ancestry, though there were some, like Lee-Sung, who were actually Korean. By contemporary standards, this casting would be found wanting. But it was relatively progressive for its time.[16]

THIS SEVENTIES SHOW

In its early seasons, the basic architecture of M*A*S*H came down to two sides: the admirable Hawkeye and Trapper John against the priggish Burns and Houlihan (who were not-so-secretly lovers; Burns was the only one of the four who was married and thus the only adulterer, another departure from the movie that Gelbart engineered under pressure from CBS).[17] Colonel Blake was the umpire who leaned toward Hawkeye/Trapper John. Radar was essentially the team mascot who was treated affectionately by them and dismissively by Burns/Houlihan. The sensibility of the show is established in the pilot, in which Hawkeye learns he has been successful in a plan to get the Korean houseboy of their quarters, Ho-Jon (Patrick Adiarte), a scholarship at his alma mater. But Ho-Jon will need about $2,000 to cover transportation and expenses. Hawkeye comes up with a plan to hold a raffle for a weekend's leave in Tokyo with Lt. Dish (Karen Philipp), whom he convinces to play along by promising she won't actually have to bed the winner. Burns and Houlihan are disgusted by the ruse, and in a subsequent argument, Hawkeye slugs him, which is problematic because Burns is Hawkeye's superior officer. The arrival of the wounded at the unit short-circuits plans for a court-martial, and after a series of complications, the raffle raises most of the needed money. The winner of the weekend with Dish is announced: it's the unit's chaplain, Father Francis Mulcahy (George Morgan, soon to be replaced by Warren Christopher), who as a priest will not consummate his prize. The plot encapsulates much of what will follow: shady means enlisted in the service of sterling ends, all done in good humor without anyone, even the bad guy, ending up seriously hurt. It was a winning formula, and variations on it would sustain the series for the next decade.

The reason why shady means could be funny and satisfying is that our heroes were literally operating in an environment that was fundamentally corrupt. Their job was to save lives so that their charges could go back into combat. Hawkeye and Trapper John, who hold the rank of captain, are draftee surgeons, not career officers. ("Pierce, you're the most unmilitary man in this man's army," Burns sneers at him at one point. "Thank you," he replies.) This situation is particularly problematic given that the Korean War is itself problematic even for those who *are* committed to it. "This war is different. It seems like the reasons we're here aren't as clear," Colonel Sherman Potter (Harry Morgan), who has fought in both World Wars and will later replace Blake at the 4077th, muses in the 1979 episode "Dear Uncle Abdul." Fr. Mulcahy agrees. "Quite true, colonel. There's no feeling of unity. No brave slogans to rally around, like 'Remember Pearl Harbor.'"

It's at moments like this where the ghosts of Vietnam, who hovered closely in the 1970s, loom large over *M*A*S*H*. In one revealing slip, Hawkeye in the second episode of the series negotiates with a Korean black market trader and refers to *south*east Asia, when of course Korea is in *north*east Asia. That said, one looks in vain in the discourse among the creators of *M*A*S*H* for a sustained discussion of the Vietnam War; the principals were reluctant, then or since, to consider *M*A*S*H* a direct allegory of the conflict. (Gelbart repeatedly cites fights with the network over censoring bloodshed or referring to sex rather than politics, which was not a problem.) "It was in my mind *not* about the Vietnam War," Alda has said. Reynolds and Gelbart have acknowledged the Vietnam critique, but more as something they would concede as true—in part.[18] More commonly, they referred to the show as an antiwar document, one reason why they never sought out military consultants for their scripts. Perhaps the most compelling explanation of what they understood themselves to be doing comes from Reynolds, who described the show as "existential"—a philosophical concept that was widely prevalent and compelling in the postwar decades, where totalizing ideologies like communism, fascism, and, increasingly, capitalism were regarded as enemies of an authentic experience of autonomous individualism. "I say it was existential in that here were some doctors who were not here by choice—they were drafted—and they could not leave, which is another existential element of the theater of the absurd . . . their efforts were futile in a way, in that their project, their duty, their obligation, is to heal, and to put people back together in an overall effort that is to destroy life," he told the Archive of American Television in 2000. "That's *M*A*S*H* in a nutshell."

Existentialism as a philosophy emphasizes the power of personal choice in the face of indifferent or hostile forces in a given society. While not necessarily opposed to large institutions, the existentialist regards them with skepticism and emphasizes a need for vigilance against the inevitable compromises they impose. It does not, however, rule out a sense of humor about this, reflected in its often sardonic tendencies. Such a worldview crystallized in *M*A*S*H* over the course of its run, in which impersonating officers, playing practical jokes, and heavy drinking—one key feature of the Swamp was the still from which the doctors drank bad gin—were all staples of its storytelling amid a backdrop of sustained and senseless violence.

The show's anti-institutionalism suffuses its storylines. Government (in the form of the military), business, organized religion, the family: all are regarded with distant respect at best and outright scorn at worst. The domestic life of the United States in 1950s is almost never depicted on the screen. We occasionally see home movies from the characters, which are rendered in a key of tenderness, but the

overall impression of American society as a whole is one of conformity and complacency. In the classic 1974 episode "O.R.," which is
shot entirely in the operating room—and entirely without a laugh
track, a source of struggle between the makers of the show and the
network that was never entirely resolved—an exhausted Hawkeye
expresses his bitterness about life back at home. "I don't know why
they're shooting at us," he says of the North Koreans (and, possibly,
Chinese). "All we want to do is bring them democracy and white
bread. Transplant the American Dream. Freedom, achievement,
hyper-acidity. Affluence, flatulence, technology, tension, the inalien-
able right to an early coronary sitting at your desk while plotting to
stab your boss in the back. That's entertainment."

Even Col. Potter, who's far less caustic than Hawkeye, laments the
insularity of the folks back home in the 1976 episode "Hawk's Nightmare." "I call the States and they're watching Milton Berle," he
laments to Major Sidney Freedman (Allan Arbus), an army psychiatrist who appears in many episodes. "The dream is peaceful,"
Dr. Freedman tells Potter. "Reality is the nightmare."

In the first half of the show's run, Frank Burns functions as the foil
for our heroes—"a technical contrivance," in the words of Larry Linville, who played him for five seasons.[19] Frank is a man whose
veniality and stupidity correlates directly with his credulity for
grand collective pieties. "Now listen to me, soldier," he tells an ailing
Radar in the 1972 episode "Love Story." "We're all in this together
with a common goal: to serve our country and repel the godless horde
from the north that would engulf our way of life—" Hawkeye cuts
him off. "You're making *me* sick," he tells his fellow doctor. When, in
"The Interview," reporter Clete Roberts asks Frank if the war has
changed him in any way, Burns is taken aback by the question. "Certainly not," he says, damningly.

"I think there's a misconception on the part of lots of people in this
country that Frank Burns is unusual," Linville explained to journalist
David Reiss a few years after he left the show, having felt he had done
as much as he could with the character. "My hope is that they see he's
not unusual. He is fairly ordinary. He comes in sleeker packages, God

knows. I hope that when people think about who they are going to vote for, or who they're going to work for, or whatever, they cast an eye toward Frank Burns and say, 'Now does this person behave the same way? Am I dealing with this kind of monster?'"[20] The show's creators did not necessarily assume they would get their preferred answer. Gelbart later remembered a letter he got from a fan. "God, I love your show," the young man wrote. "I can't wait to join the army."[21] In the world of art, the audience always gets a vote.

The most direct expression of the conflict in outlooks that sparks the show occurs in the 1974 episode "George," which is notable for its sympathetic portrayal of a gay man in the military. Naturally, Frank finds him repugnant, leading to this clarifying exchange:

> FRANK: The man is not normal.
> HAWKEYE: What's normal, Frank?
> FRANK: Normal is everybody doing the same thing.
> TRAPPER JOHN: What about individuality?
> FRANK: Individuality is fine. As long as we all do it together.

"Don't you object to anything?" Frank asks them as they press him on his prejudices. "We have you, Frank," Trapper John replies. "We don't need anything else."

M*A*S*H's mission was to challenge such mindless conformity. This was possible in that the culture of the 1970s was considerably more open than that of the 1950s, where any depiction of a homosexual character on TV, let alone a sympathetic one, would have been inconceivable. Such a project was nevertheless challenging given that M*A*S*H was a sitcom built for mass consumption and still subject to corporate supervision and control, because advertisers wary of controversy paid the show's bills. Its creators nevertheless stretched the boundaries of the television medium and sitcom form in often impressive ways.

Sometimes this was a matter of depicting aspects of widely shared human experience, like unexpected death, with a degree of frankness that could be shocking. One early foray into this approach was the first season episode "Sometimes You Hear the Bullet," in which Hawkeye greets an old friend, only to encounter him again on the operating table, where Hawkeye fails to save him. At some level, this is not sup-posed to happen—even at this early juncture in the series, we viewers are not accustomed to see Hawkeye fail—and neither is he, as his tears at episode's end attest—nor do we expect to see a character we have met and come to know a bit meet a jarringly tragic end. This experience was ratcheted up to a much higher degree in the finale of season three, "Abyssinia, Henry," which was understood by every-one—including the actors working on the episode—as a fond fare-well to Henry Blake, who was going back to the States. Instead, his plane home crashes in the Sea of Japan, cutting his life short. In this age before *Game of Thrones* (2011–2019), viewers were shocked, and more than a few were appalled, by the summary death of a major character. Gelbart recalls writing hundreds of letters to indignant fans, though many if not most surely understood the larger point: this is what war does to people.[22]

Other challenges to conventional wisdom were more lighthearted—and ambiguous. Perhaps the best example is a character invented by Gelbart who started out as minor and ended up a fixture of the cast: Corporal Max Q. Klinger (Jamie Farr). Klinger sees himself as caught in a Catch-22: you can get out of the army if you're crazy, but a desire to get of the army proves that you're not. He tries to square this circle by donning women's clothing in the hope that it will lead to a Section 8 discharge on the basis of mental illness. A notion of (nonsatirical) cross-dressing as self-evident insanity would be regarded by many people today as offensive, though it was regarded as such in the psychi-atric manuals of the time. (The American Psychological Association declassified homosexuality as a disorder in 1973, a landmark decision in the normalization of queer culture in the United States.) Klinger, for his part, is simply playing the hand he's dealt and working with army regulations as he finds them at a time few men would dare to do so for any reason. Not that it does him any good. No one except star-tled outsiders takes him seriously, but one of the jokes of the series is that Klinger turns into something of a clothes horse who begins to derive real pleasure from his couture and that of the women he encoun-ters. In short, he subverts what we would today call the gender binary.

He abandons the effort after a few seasons, trading his now-impressive wardrobe to Korean prostitutes so that the temporarily displaced 4077th can use a school building the women are occupying. But his good-natured pragmatism and refusal to stigmatize himself and others represents what can be seen a discrete step forward in the history of gender. Gelbart, whose creation of Klinger was reportedly inspired by a similar ruse undertaken by comedian Lenny Bruce during World War II, would go on to be one of the screenwriters of the 1982 film *Tootsie*, another culturally ambiguous document.[23]

In other ways, *M*A*S*H* could be relentlessly—and to many modern viewers, appallingly—retrograde. It's ironic that Alan Alda, a staunch supporter of the Equal Rights Amendment who was lionized at the time in countless media stories as "feminism's poster boy,"[24] played a man who routinely played the field, refused to commit, and indulged in sexist behavior. Worse still, it's clear that unlike Frank Burns, we were supposed to *like* him when he did so—all in good fun, like when he plants an unsolicited sardonic kiss on the uptight Houlihan in the 1974 episode "Nothing Like a Nurse." Depicting such liberties in the fifties was meant to be understood as representing the opening rounds of what would become the sexual revolution of the seventies. But that's not necessarily as it would have been seen then or since. Swit, however, rejected such an analysis when asked about it in 2018. "There was no predation," she told the *New Yorker*. "The nurses were using the doctors too—they had needs of their own," she said. (Perhaps so, but such needs were never as evident as male lust was.) Alda, for his part, was more circumspect. "Every show reflects its time," he said.[25]

Still, one of the more striking things about *M*A*S*H*—and one of the typical things about midcentury liberalism, something it made it attractive to so many people at the time—was its capacity for self-criticism and reform. *M*A*S*H* was a largely male show in outlook, but its creators did take steps to recognize and incorporate the talents of women in front of and behind the camera. A good example of this is the 1976 episode "The Nurses," written by Linda Bloodworth (who would go on to have a distinguished career as a television impresario) and directed by Joan Darling, whose credits included *The Mary Tyler Moore*

Show. "The Nurses" focuses on intragender relations between the female nurses at the 4077th and their tetchy relations with their commanding officer, Major Houlihan, who, while unquestionably competent, is someone they regard as a martinet. The episode climaxes with Houlihan deciding not to press charges against an errant nurse, and a frank conversation that leads to them sharing fudge (made against regulation). "I was allowed to continue to grow," Swit said of her character in regard to this episode.[26]

Indeed, Swit's Houlihan undergoes a more thorough transformation than any other character on *M*A*S*H*. She gradually but unmistakably becomes disenchanted in her extramarital affair with Frank, which leads to a marriage and eventual divorce from Lieutenant Donald Penobscot, a largely off-screen presence during their relationship (played by Beeson Carroll and Mike Henry in seasons 6 and 7). Houlihan and Hawkeye have a tryst when they find themselves trapped beyond enemy lines in the two-part 1977 episode "Comrades in Arms," a moment that does not lead to a long-term romance but seems to deepen the respect and affection they have for each other. Their final moment together in the finale is marked by what may well be the longest kiss in the history of television, leaving the other characters who witness it to stand around awkwardly waiting for it to end.

By virtue of her position and the tremendous authority with which she wields it, Houlihan could have well been considered a feminist icon from the very start of the show. But her gender consciousness and assertiveness deepen even as her personality softens over the course of *M*A*S*H*'s trajectory. In the process, she gives Hawkeye an education as well. Exhibit A in this regard may well be the 1977 episode "Hepatitis," in which Hawkeye leeringly savors the prospect of administering an inoculation to her buttock (notably, there's no laugh track here):

HOULIHAN: How dare you come in here on the pretext of giving me a shot and then stand there ogling me as if I were a sideshow attraction?

HAWKEYE: Boy, I show you a little appreciation and you hit the roof. What do you want from me?

HOULIHAN: Respect. Simple respect. I expect nothing more, and I'll accept nothing less.

HAWKEYE *(looks down, nods)*: Hey, that's pretty good. You got me with that.

HOULIHAN: Good.

One other indication of changing mores in this regard: Houlihan's "Hot Lips" nickname recedes; by the end of the show Hawkeye is routinely referring to her as "Margaret."

As with any long-running show, M*A*S*H was marked by cast and production changes. Stevenson and Rogers wanted out at the end of season 3; Gelbart moved on after season 4; Reynolds and Linville after season 5; and Burghoff early in season 8. There were also three new featured cast members who not only successfully plugged the holes but demonstrated the show's ability to adapt artistically and ideologically.

The first major replacement, B. J. Hunnicutt, played by Mike Farrell, comes aboard as a surgeon after the departure of Trapper John. Hunnicutt—note his last name—is a mild-mannered Bay Area surgeon who hates being taken away from his wife and daughter, recalibrating the show with family values that had been missing and giving it a much more feminist-friendly character than that of Trapper John. He and Hawkeye hit it off instantly, and Hunnicutt shows himself to be Hawkeye's equal when it comes to a sense of humor, as in the 1982 episode "The Joker Is Wild," in which he delivers on a promise to successfully pull off a practical joke on all his pals in the unit in the space of twenty-four hours. Hunnicutt is also the peer who can criticize Hawkeye credibly and sympathetically, in part because he's willing to look honestly at himself. "We sit around here in our Hawaiian shirts and our red suspenders, thumbing our nose at the army, drinking home-brewed gin and flouting authority at every turn and feeling oh-so superior to those military fools who kill each other and oh-so self-righteous as we clean up after them," Hunnicutt tells Hawkeye after receiving a Bronze Star he feels he doesn't deserve in the 1982 episode "Bombshells." He later pins it on a wounded patient.

Another form of recalibration comes in the form of Colonel Potter, who takes over as commanding officer after the death of Blake at the end of season 3. While Blake was something of a genial bumbler, Potter—played by veteran actor Harry Morgan, best known for playing the almost comically straight-arrow Los Angeles police officer Bill Gannon on *Dragnet* (1967–1970)—strikes an impressive balance, "giving the role equal doses of Harry Truman and sitcom papa," in the words of cultural historian David Marc.[27] It quickly becomes clear Potter genuinely loves his charges, but nevertheless maintains his authority—and his values. His firmness in the face of the piercing Pierce is illustrated in the 1981 episode "Your Retention Please," in which Klinger—of all people!—decides to reenlist after all those years of seeking a discharge. "Face it," Klinger tells a gently skeptical Potter. "I'm just a poor kid off the streets. The only real experience I have is hustling pool. But now I have a chance to rise in the army's ranks and make something of myself."

Hawkeye is incredulous—and disgusted. "C'mon, he's crazy," he tells Potter. "Nobody but an idiot would ever reenlist."

"I wonder if you can think of any exceptions to that rule," his commanding officer, an army man in his fourth decade of service, replies drily. Pierce concedes the point. "Olive drab and gray matter don't necessarily clash," he admits. Klinger, for his part, will be rewarded with a Korean bride played by Chao at the end of the series, remaining in the country.

The most politically interesting addition to the cast was Frank's replacement, Major Charles Emerson Winchester III—who, as his name suggests, was a stuffy Boston Brahmin sharply at odds with Hawkeye's more iconoclastic Down East sensibility—and for that matter, that of the plain-spoken midwestern accents provided by Missourian Potter, Iowan Radar, and Ohio by way of Lebanon Klinger. To enumerate such distinctions is to recover regional and ethnic shadings of whiteness have since been largely lost in a world where diversity is understood largely in racial and gender terms. David Ogden Stiers gave Winchester an accent and diction a few miles north of William F. Buckley, and endowed him with sufficient pomposity to make him an almost irresistible target for Hawkeye and Hunnicutt, particularly in light of backhanded compliments like, "Congratulations indeed, Klinger. I've always been envious of you swarthy types and your natural gift for demeaning labor." But Winchester, who describes himself as "a man who has endured four FDR elections," is no Frank Burns: he's a far more talented and intelligent surgeon who can give as good as he gets in jockeying for advantage or delivering pranks. We also learn he's got a heart, as when he fails in his quest to keep a large Christmas gift to a Korean orphanage secret or when he aggressively intervenes to protect a bullied GI with a stutter (we later learn his beloved sister had one). In many ways, Winchester is a representative of a WASP world that had already largely vanished by the time his character showed up on M*A*S*H in 1977. And yet his avowed libertarianism and cunning market instincts also made him the harbinger of a new conservative order that was taking shape even as M*A*S*H was at high tide. The character also served as a reminder of what the Left would regard as a more respectable conservatism than the grubby materialism associated with the New Right.

For the most part, however, M*A*S*H stuck to its liberal values. This was particularly true in its later years, when Alda increasingly asserted himself as a writer, director, and story consultant. In the first couple of seasons, M*A*S*H had a strong slapstick element; before the third season, Gelbart and Reynolds journeyed to Korea and came back with a trove of anecdotes they used in ensuing years (they also regularly consulted with physicians to maintain the verisimilitude of individual episodes). But in its later iterations, M*A*S*H could get preachy. "You're a dangerous man," Hawkeye tells a general who's callous about the casualty rate he generates in the 1979 episode "Preventative Medicine." "The stirring speeches, the strategy, the execution with a capital E. It's all one big bloody game to you. And then when they're carrying the wounded players off the field, you become the cheerleader. You make me sick." He's not the only one: a black soldier tells the general to keep the Purple Heart he's about to be awarded.

This particular episode is notable, however, for the ethical dilemma it posits—and the disagreement that results between the characters.

Hawkeye decides that the only way to stop more senseless deaths is to induce a case of appendicitis in the general so that he'll need an operation and won't be able to lead a planned assault. "You cut into a healthy body and you're going to hate yourself for the rest of your life," Hunnicutt tells him. "I hate myself now," Hawkeye responds. "I hate me, and I hate you, and I hate this whole life here. And if I can keep that maniac off the line with a simple appendectomy, I'll be able to hate myself with a clean conscience." Hunnicutt refuses to assist Hawkeye, who proceeds without him. "You treated a symptom. The disease goes merrily on," Hunnicutt tells him after Hawkeye completes the deed. The dispute between them goes unresolved.

Toward the end of its run, *M*A*S*H* focused ever more on the inner life of its characters, one of the ways it's a document of an era famously dubbed by Tom Wolfe as "the Me Decade."[28] A key indicator here is the prominence of the pointedly named Sidney Freedman, the psychiatrist who appeared in a dozen episodes when characters were having mental problems, including the good doctor himself in the 1976 episode "Dear Sigmund," another one of those epistolary installments where Freeman pages Dr. Freud and recovers his equilibrium at the good old 4077th by writing about it. Gentle Father Mulcahy is a paragon of decency in *M*A*S*H*, in large measure because he wears his Catholicism lightly. But it's Freedman whom the characters more frequently turn to when they're lost. This is particularly true for Hawkeye, which may reflect the fact that actor Alan Arbus (one-time husband of the famous fashion photographer Diane) and Alda were particularly close at a time when Alda a powerful force on the show. So it is that in "Hawk's Nightmare" we have Freedman straighten Hawkeye out when he begins sleepwalking (he's trying to go back to his less stressful childhood), and the 1981 episode "Bless You, Hawkeye," when he develops a case of uncontrollable sneezing brought on by a wounded soldier who has fallen into a ditch of muddy water (it triggers a childhood memory of when he was almost drowned by a beloved cousin). "I was so convinced that he was a psychiatrist I used to sit and talk with him between scenes," Alda later remembered.[29]

It is fitting, then, that a therapeutic setting is central to the show's finale. When it begins, Hawkeye has suffered a nervous breakdown and is being treated at a psychiatric hospital, where he's visited by Freedman. We learn in flashback that Hawkeye snapped when the unit was returning from a beach trip in a bus that was suddenly threatened by enemy ambush. A South Korean passenger was carrying a chicken she couldn't keep quiet at a time when this was imperative, and so she strangled it. Except we learn it wasn't a chicken: it was an infant (the script was based on a true story).[30] "You son of a bitch. Why did you make me remember that?" Hawkeye asks Freedman. "You needed to get it out in the open," the good doctor replies. "Now you're halfway home." Apparently cured of his posttraumatic stress syndrome, Hawkeye makes his way back to the 4077th just as the armistice is announced, partaking in a series of goodbyes among the characters that also functioned as a round of goodbyes for the actors—and, of course, the audience. On February 28, 1983, M*A*S*H became a show about history that passed into history, an event that was widely reported and witnessed.[31]

EQUALLY TOGETHER

The status of M*A*S*H as a historical artifact was established quickly. Four months after the broadcast finale, the Smithsonian Institution's National Museum of American History opened "M*A*S*H: Binding Up the Nation's Wounds," an exhibit featuring items from the real life 8055th MASH unit as well as props, costumes, and sets from the fictive 4077th. It ran until September 30, 1984.[32]

By that point, Ronald Reagan was about a month away from winning reelection in one of the most lopsided presidential campaigns in American history. His victory ratified conservatism as the dominant strain in American political culture of the time, so much so that in its wake the newly formed Democratic Leadership Council—whose members included the young governor of Arkansas, Bill Clinton— began plotting a new course for the party. A decade later, President Clinton would famously declare that "the era of big government is over,"[33] a statement that in theory Hawkeye Pierce may well have welcomed, but not in the way Clinton intended. It wasn't so much "You're free to pursue your bliss," but more like "You're on your own." Clinton knew the voters he courted would not want him to say something as brutally honest as that. Hawkeye would have heard him, though, loud and clear.

It's not like the vision of liberalism embodied by M*A*S*H disappeared instantly—indeed, the show would remain a television staple for decades to come. But it would do so increasingly as a source of nostalgia, its sensibility chipped away on the left by a rising tide of identity politics and on the right by a combination of economic libertarianism and unreconstructed patriotism. Its "harmony of self-interest and social consciousness," in the notably crisp formulation of David Marc, was a center that could not hold.[34]

Actually, M*A*S*H's vision of liberalism was not the only one available even in its heyday. The sitcom's run coincided with that of its CBS companion The Waltons, which also debuted in 1972 and ran until 1981. M*A*S*H had an essentially hostile relationship to the fifties, whose dominant mood was at odds with that of the countercultural seventies, which is precisely why there was a countercyclical revival of fifties culture in some quarters of American society in the seventies, typified by the two sitcoms that routinely beat M*A*S*H in the ratings: Happy Days (1974–1984) and Laverne & Shirley (1976–1983), both of which bathed the fifties in a deeply affectionate light. The Waltons, by contrast, was a seventies show about the thirties that looked to that era as a repository of New Deal values that were still resonant and relevant, notwithstanding the skepticism they encountered in the thirties as well as the seventies. The key to this affirmation was its stalwart institutionalist vision. The Waltons was a show that embraced God, country (which included the military), and family, while M*A*S*H regarded all three with suspicion at best. Both shows affirmed the dignity of the individual in an egalitarian spirit, and both had a reformist bent (which is how you could smuggle protofeminist plotlines into The Waltons). But they disagreed on how you got there.

In the early twenty-first century, this confidence in egalitarian individualism was lost. Both the Right and the Left considered the phrase a contradiction in terms, alternatively regarding inequality as the price of progress or turning to tribalism as a more reliable source of empowerment. It's hard to see how the underlying optimism of M*A*S*H—an optimism that however insane or inhumane the situation, decency and growth nevertheless remain possible—can again become the dominant chord in our national anthems.

The only reason to think so is that the chord has lingered for so long, suffusing Benjamin Franklin's gently satirical Poor Richard, Walt Whitman's songs of ourselves, and Bruce Springsteen's songs of the open road. History suggests we may yet wake up and remember that we still have a dream.

MAN POWER

Jon Hamm in a 2008 pose as 1960s ad man Don Draper at the offices of Sterling Cooper. The character embodied the American Dream of *Mad Men* in all its magnetic attraction—as well as its concealed tawdriness.

CHAPTER 4

DREAM ADVERTISEMENT

Mad Men as a 2000s Version of the 1960s

The average American experiences a level of luxury
that belongs only to kings in the rest of the world.
We're not chauvinists. We just have expectations.

—Don Draper to Conrad Hilton in
"Wee Small Hours," *Mad Men* (2009)

Key Cast Members

- Jon Hamm as Donald Draper
- January Jones as Betty Draper
- John Slattery as Roger Sterling
- Elisabeth Moss as Peggy Olson
- Vincent Kartheiser as Pete Campbell
- Alison Brie as Trudy Campbell
- Christina Hendricks as Joan Harris (née Holloway)
- Kiernan Shipka as Sally Draper
- Jessica Paré as Megan Draper (née Calvet)

Key Episodes

- "Smoke Gets in Your Eyes" (pilot, 2007)
- "The Wheel" (2007)
- "Maidenform" (2008)
- "Guy Walks into an Advertising Agency" (2009)
- "The Suitcase" (2010)
- "The Other Woman" (2012)
- "Person to Person" (2015)

*I*N 2015, just after its highly successful eight-year run ended, *Mad Men* creator Matthew Weiner sat down for an interview with the Academy of Television Arts and Sciences (known colloquially as Television Academy). Voluble and articulate, Weiner toggled between detailed analyses of plot points and sweeping interpretations of what he thought the series was all about. "The show is based on the premise that advertising does not make you do anything," he explained. "It reminds you to do what you already want to do."[1]

It is perhaps not surprising that a show about the advertising industry—as a title card announces in the series premiere, the name of the show is an affectionate inside reference to how the denizens of Madison Avenue advertising agencies referred to themselves in the industry's mid-twentieth-century heyday—would embrace its ethos.[2] Weiner has repeatedly referred to himself as, among other things, a businessman, and his recitation of facts about the show included advertising rates and his various efforts to procure sponsorship deals.[3]

But *Mad Men's* appeal is broader than that of a general paean to the advertising industry centered on Sterling Cooper, a fictive advertising agency based in midtown Manhattan.[4] The show has a specific historical focus on the decade of the 1960s: its first episode is set in 1960, its last in 1970. As such, it's presented as a series of snapshots from the middle of the American Century, offering an almost palpable experience of daily life from that moment when the nation reached the apex of its global power and began its long journey down from the mountaintop. The picture it offers is not uniformly positive, but it is nevertheless alluring. In this regard, it's just like the most potent advertisements, which never entirely displace the ugliness and anxieties they are designed to address in the process of promoting an alternative to make a sale.

As such, *Mad Men* itself functions as an advertisement for the American Dream—which is not simply a matter of reminding you of what you want but affirming that desire as legitimate, achievable, and a source of social cohesion all at once. Go ahead, you can have it: this, in essence, is what both advertising and the American Dream are all about—fables of abundance in which the acquisition of material goods takes on transcendent dimensions.[5] The show conveys this message not simply as a matter of the sleek fantasies of consumption conjured by its characters for products that range from Hershey bars to Jaguar cars but through the lives of those characters themselves, all engaged in their different ways to achieve an imagined destiny— to close the gap between "what I want, and what's expected of me," as Weiner put it in that interview. (The line is also uttered by Dr. Faye Miller, played by Cara Buono, a consultant hired by Sterling Cooper in the 2010 episode "Christmas Comes but Once a Year.") Weiner described the postwar decades as particularly emblematic in crystallizing this vision of American life as one of aspiration. "It was a very positive culture," he said. "It was capitalism, which was brutal, but it was based in self-improvement." Weiner described it as a gift of American civilization. "We gave that to the world," he said.[6]

That gift has a distinctively materialistic quality. Indeed, more than any other element on *Mad Men*—more even than the writing, acting, or directing—it is conveyed through the series' much celebrated production design. "While the show doesn't gloss over life's harsh realities, it does look gorgeous," noted one observer in a 2009 article in *Adweek*. "The rich cinematography, evocative lighting and fantastic devotion to period furnishings and wardrobe could make a mid-century fetishist out of anyone watching."[7] Indeed, it seems fair to say that no show in the history of television demonstrated a more fanatical devotion to historical detail than *Mad Men* did. This mania for verisimilitude extended to making sure some elements in the show were *not* rooted in the sixties, because, as Weiner noted, people casually incorporate objects and couture from earlier times into the fabric of their everyday lives. The show was also marked by exquisite calibrations of cultural shifts within the decade; in the words of one study, "one can, for example, track the progress of the action through the decade by monitoring the lengthening hair and sideburns of the men, along with the shortening skirts of most of the women."[8] For those old enough to remember the material culture of the sixties, the effect can be startling: that which has long seemed dated, even dowdy, suddenly takes on a shimmering air of modernity. If such artifacts don't necessarily seem beautiful, they somehow seem—almost miraculously—new. Movies do this kind of thing all the time. But the stately pace of *Mad Men*, stretched over seven years and ninety-two episodes, makes the immersion all the more arresting.

The figure at the center of this production, Donald Draper (Jon Hamm), embodies the American Dream of *Mad Men* in all its magnetic attraction—and concealed tawdriness. Tall, handsome, enigmatic, and with a reservoir of insight and empathy that surfaces just often enough to keep you from hating him, Don Draper—his last name indicative of both elegance and concealment; "Don" a verb for something that one wears (in this case an identity)—carries the weight of the show on his shoulders. His interests converge with and diverge from those of other characters, who in many cases have narrative trajectories with intrinsic appeal or weight in their own right. But Draper stands at the center—and much of the time he stands alone.

In many respects, Draper's character is reminiscent of an earlier incarnation of the American Dream: Jay Gatsby.[9] Like Gatsby, Draper is a charismatic man with a secret past. That past includes military service in a dubious war (the First World War for Gatsby; the Korean War for Draper), the details of which are murky. Both lived much of their youth among seedy characters that respectable people tend to avoid, yet both had mentors (Dan Cody, Roger Sterling) whose lessons they learned—and successes they surpassed. Both attain riches scarcely imaginable in their youth, and both engender curiosity on the part of strangers as well as those who know them—or think they do. They elicit admiration and resentment from the elite into whose ranks they have managed to enter, where there is room for them in an economically dynamic society marked by explosive economic growth. Both are workaholics for whom business is constantly intruding into their private lives.

There are differences too. Draper is a family man—his wife, Betty (January Jones) is a Daisy Buchanan figure of the kind Gatsby cannot attain—and he's the father of three children. Don is a scrupulous businessman and a disgraceful adulterer, while Gatsby is a racketeer whose devotion to Daisy is unshakeable. And while, like Gatsby, a fatalistic air hovers over Draper for the length of the series, their secrets always on the cusp of revelation and self-destruction, Draper's fate is neither as decisive or spectacular of that of Gatsby, whose ambivalent admirer, Nick Carraway, finally decides is great. And yet Nick could be speaking for Draper no less than Gatsby when he famously says, "If personality is an unbroken series of successful gestures, then there was something gorgeous about him, some heightened sensitivity to the promises of life."[10]

One key difference is that Gatsby isn't really that bright ("Can't repeat the past? Of course you can!"),[11] which is why he needs an interlocutor who can frame his behavior and endow it with a dignity he could not confer on himself. Don Draper needs no such mediation. We see him vividly, if never quite transparently, through a small screen where he—and the imperial republic for which he stands—looms larger than life.

RICH DICK

The seeds of Mad Men germinated for a long time. They were planted by Weiner, a Baltimore native born in 1965 to a neurologist father (Ronald Reagan's personal doctor) and attorney mother who left the law to raise the couple's four children.[12] The family relocated to Los Angeles when he was a child, giving him early exposure to show business—his family home was used as a location in a Hollywood movie—though his parents strictly rationed his television viewing. Weiner graduated from Wesleyan University, and earned an MFA from the University of Southern California's School of Film and Television.

Initially hoping for a career as an actor, Weiner focused on writing, sustained by a wife who worked as an architect. After a few small gigs, he got his first big break writing for Becker (1998–2004), a sitcom starring sitcom fixture Ted Danson as a maverick doctor. From there he made a big leap into the golden age of cable television by landing a producing job with *The Sopranos* (1999–2007), David Chase's classic drama about a gangster family in New Jersey. Weiner won a pair of Emmy Awards for his work on the series and wrote a dozen episodes. He was widely admired for his talent but also had a reputation for testing his colleagues' goodwill. "There were some days when it'd be nice if he stopped talking," Terence Winter, who would go on to success with *Boardwalk Empire*, once noted.[13]

Weiner had written a script for *Mad Men* on spec as early as 1999, which he carried in his briefcase for years. It was actually the credential that led Chase to hire him. Weiner pitched the project to HBO—a plausible prospect given that he was working for the network's most successful program to date. But no one bothered to call him in rejecting it. Weiner shopped the project around to other networks, where it was finally bought by an unlikely suitor: American Movie Classics (AMC).[14]

Founded in 1984 as a premium cable channel, AMC was nevertheless considered a second-tier operation for much of its history, lagging behind Ted Turner's Turner Classic Movies (TCM). By the turn of the new century, AMC was facing an existential crisis in an increasingly crowded cable landscape squeezed by a raft of alternatives that included home video, pay-per-view, and alternative media like videogames. Network executives decided to take a gamble on producing original programming and doubled down on it by undertaking a relatively expensive and unusual show—not a classic police procedural or family drama, but rather a period piece on an industry that was not widely known (or, for that matter, admired).[15] Weiner, a strong-minded auteur, nevertheless faced spending restraints, which among other things meant working with lower-priced actors, something that did not bother him in that it allowed him to mold the personae of his characters in ways that would have strong and lasting associations. This could be risky for those who were cast: Christina Hendricks, who played the role of the voluptuous, competent Joan Holloway, was let go by her agent for deciding to do *Mad Men* rather than pursue traditional network opportunities.[16] Suffice it to say that she, among others, ended up doing just fine.

But *Mad Men* was no ratings blockbuster. The pilot episode scored relatively good numbers—good for a struggling small cable network, that is. About 1.65 million viewers tuned in for its debut, though subsequent episodes hovered closer to a million. By the time the show ended in 2015, it averaged 3.7 million viewers, a figure that combined live and a week's delayed watching. This was a long way from the glory days of shows like *The Waltons* or *M*A*S*H*, when tens of millions of viewers would watch any given episode.

There were, however, other metrics that mattered. The show's audience was decidedly upscale; 53 percent of *Mad Men* viewers were in the coveted 25 to 54 age demographic, with incomes that exceeded $100,000. This allowed AMC to charge premium advertising rates; ad space for the finale was sold out.[17] Eventually *Mad Men* would win fifteen Emmys and four Golden Globes. By that point, the series had already made an outsized imprint on popular culture far beyond easily measurable dollar figures. It became shorthand for a certain kind of sixties nostalgia that showed up in magazine stories, fashion, and trends in advertising.

That nostalgia had a distinctly vicarious element to it, centered on behaviors that have since become decidedly taboo. One was cigarette smoking, probably the most rampant vice on the show and one embraced by most of the major characters. This portrayal reflected historical realities; a 1967 Department of Agriculture study reported that Americans smoked 551 billion cigarettes annually—about 215 packs for every adult over 18 years old—all this despite the famous Surgeon General's Report of 1964 reporting the dangers of smoking.[18] Cancer rates were accordingly high, and it's unsurprising that the disease would ultimately claim the life of Betty Draper. It's also not surprising that cigarette advertising—soon to be restricted—loomed large in the plots of *Mad Men*. The largest client at Don's agency is Lucky Strike, and the pilot episode of the show climaxes with his coining a specious feature of the company's product—"It's toasted!"—that in fact figured prominently in Lucky Strike marketing.

Another vice was alcohol. Drinking of course has not receded in American society to the extent smoking has, but it's much more contained now than it was back then. Driving while intoxicated was routine—Don gets into a car accident with a comedian's wife with whom he's having an affair. A dry bar was a standard feature of many corporate offices, as indeed it is in *Mad Men*, where mixed drinks were a standard part of the workday. A number of characters have a drinking problem, among them Freddie Rumson (Joel Murray), who loses his job over it, and Don himself, who teeters on the verge of self-destruction (one website calculated that his alcohol consumption averaged nine drinks per day).[19]

And then there's the sex—and sexism. Both run rampant on *Mad Men*, though it's the latter that's really striking. The leering, the put-downs, the casual assumption of female inferiority: you're going to see plenty in any given episode. "What do women want?" Don asks in Freudian bemusement in the show's second episode. "Who cares?" Roger replies. Lines like these can be shocking, and their cumulative effect can be appalling. Yet they can also elicit a perverse fascination, a jarring recognition that cultural mores can change sharply, which might be experienced as a reassuring sense of progress or a troubling recognition that today's commonplace realities may be tomorrow's atrocious offenses. The effect is an implicit statement that social "progress" is merely an illusion, a temporary set of circumstances that will change in unforeseeable ways, leaving one with an unsettled feeling about the arbitrary standards of morality that govern our everyday lives.

As in so many other ways, Don is a complex figure in this regard. A compulsive womanizer, he routinely assesses the women he meets in terms of their suitability for a tryst, an extramarital affair, or as wife material. And yet he also has a capacity to recognize intelligence and talent when he finds it, whether in the relationship of mutual respect he cultivates with Joan or the way he mentors Peggy (Elisabeth Moss), who will evolve into a rare advertising talent. In the pilot, Pete

Campbell (Vincent Kartheiser) arrogantly appraises Peggy, pre-sumptuously calling her "honey" and suggesting that she's a prude by asserting "it wouldn't be a sin for us to see your legs." Don is dis-gusted. "Sorry about Mr. Campbell here," he tells Peggy. "He left his manners back in the fraternity house." Over and over again, Don will have authentic conversations with a variety of women from different walks in life while simultaneously indulging in sexually duplicitous behavior. He seems to have real regard for many of these women—the Greenwich Village bohemian Midge Daniels (Rosemary DeWitt); the Jewish department store executive Rachel Menken (Maggie Siff); the manager-wife of a comedian Bobbie Barrett (Melinda McGraw); his daughter's primary school teacher Suzanne Farrell (Abigail Spen-cer); the consumer research analyst Dr. Faye Miller (Cara Buono); his downstairs housewife neighbor Sylvia Rosen (Linda Cardellini); and the diner waitress Diana Baur (Elizabeth Reaser)—but cannot commit to any of them any more than he can the two wives he ultimately divorces. The only female relationship in his life he can sustain with any fidelity (in a highly imperfect way) is with his daughter Sally (the gifted Kiernan Shipka), to whom he seems to have bequeathed his intelligence and charisma. "I'm often in the role of Sally," series cre-ator Weiner has said of the character, suggesting the depth of his identification with her (and some presumption).[20]

Insofar as Don's behavior is explicable, it's rooted in his childhood, depicted in flashbacks over the course of the series. Born impover-ished in 1926 as Dick Whitman in rural Pennsylvania, his mother died giving birth to him, and his drunken father was killed by a horse who kicked him in a barn in Don's presence. Don's stepmother (Brynn Horrocks) was pregnant with his half-brother Adam (Jay Paulson) at the time. She subsequently took up with a new man, dubbed "Uncle Mack," (Morgan Rusler) and the two boys were raised in a whore-house. Don lost his virginity to a prostitute (Megan Ferguson), in a scene that could fairly be called a rape, and worked as a pickpocket while she was with her johns.[21] He got out as soon as he could, enlist-ing in the army, whereupon he was sent to Korea. His superior officer—Lieutenant Donald Draper (Troy Ruptash)—is incredulous that Whitman actually volunteered to serve in the war. The two are isolated at the front, and when Lt. Draper is killed in an enemy attack, a wounded Whitman grabs his dog tags and assumes Draper's identity, awarded a Purple Heart at the hospital where he recovers. With "Dick Whitman" now dead, the newly minted Don returns to the States and takes a job as a car salesman. There's a tense moment when the dead man's wife, Anna Draper (Melinda Page Hamilton), shows up, but she agrees to go along with his gambit and the two form a deep bond. (They get a friendly divorce so that Don can marry Betty, who is oblivious to this backstory until the third season of the show. Anna dies of cancer in season 4.) Don remains close with Anna's sister and niece Stephanie Horton (Caity Lotz)—she figures prominently in the final episode—but he completely cuts off his half-brother Adam, whose despair over such rejection leads him to hang himself at the end of the first season.

It's not hard to infer from a youth like this why someone would turn out to be dysfunctional in any number of ways—why indeed such a person would likely lead a life of deceit, paranoia, and failure of multiple kinds. Indeed, as *New Yorker* writer Emily Nussbaum plausibly asserted at one point late in the series run, "This is no longer the backstory of a serial adulterer; it's the backstory of a serial killer."[22] But—and this is really the fundamental point on which *Mad Men* rests—the hard kernel of aspiration at the heart of Don's character allows him to overcome this early deprivation and to fully exploit the environmental opportunities that come to him as he arrives to maturity amid the bounty of postwar America. His hardship became the foundation of, and basis for, his achievement of the American Dream, which lies—in both senses of that verb—at the core of our national mythology.

We see a key moment of Don's flowering in flashback during the 2010 episode "Waldorf Stories," when Roger first encounters him working as a furrier. (Roger's buying a gift for Joan, his mistress) Sensing opportunity, Don wears down Roger with a series of pitches, Roger finally offering him a job at the advertising firm that bears his—actually, and crucially, it's his father's—name. The two men will go on to become close, notwithstanding periodic frictions (Roger hitting on Betty; Don pulling disappearing acts, and so on). Roger is a foil for Don, a child of privilege who for all his wit, generosity, and grace lacks the promethean fire of Don's self-made man, however shoddily constructed.

So is Pete, who also lacks Roger's charm. Young and hungry, he initially seeks Don's approval. But Don isn't much impressed, and when Pete steals the spotlight in a pitch to Bethlehem Steel in the 2007 episode "New Amsterdam," Don fires him. But he's overruled by agency founder Bert Cooper (Robert Morse), who explains that Pete is New York royalty: he's descended from the Dutch Dyckmans, who at one point owned most of upper Manhattan, and the firm cannot afford to alienate its Knickerbocker clientele.

At the end of the first season, in "Nixon vs. Kennedy," Don—who for logical reasons prefers the hardscrabble Nixon over the effortless Camelot princeling—once again flares at Pete, who's angling for a promotion. But Pete now has an important piece of leverage: a box of documents from Don's previous life that Pete filches from Don's desk. Don nevertheless refuses to be blackmailed. "Why can't you give me what I want?" Pete asks. "I've earned this job. I deserve it." Don's response is contemptuous. "Why?" he asks rhetorically. "Because your parents are rich? Because you went to prep school and have a $5 haircut? You've been given *everything*. You've never worked for anything in your life." An angry Pete goes to Bert to spill the beans. What he fails to realize is that Bert, an Ayn Rand acolyte, is more inclined to honor than reject Don's will to power. As a result, he's now amenable to Don letting Pete go, but nevertheless advises against it. "Fire him if you want to," he tells Don. "But I'd keep an eye on him. One never knows how loyalty is born." Don takes this advice, which proves prescient. Pete goes on to be one of the most reliable rainmakers at the firm, and while he's hardly anybody's idea of a decent human being, he and Don forge a relationship based on mutual respect. (In one of the counterintuitive grace notes that animate the series, Pete is genuinely shaken by the death of Martin Luther King Jr., a plot point in the 2013 episode "The Flood."[23])

Don's sense of realized self extends to skepticism toward an entirely different constituency: the nascent counterculture. He reacts with skepticism when a couple of junior execs come into his office with a copy of the idealistic Port Huron Statement in the 2008 episode "The Gold Violin." And he's a good deal more than skeptical in the following exchange with Roy Hazlitt (Ian Bohen), a friend of Don's lover Midge, at a beatnik nightclub in the 2007 episode "Babylon":

ROY: So what do you do, Don?
DON (sardonically): I blow up bridges.
MIDGE: Don's in advertising.
ROY (incredulous): No way. Madison Avenue? What a gas!
MIDGE: We all have to serve somebody.
ROY: Perpetrating the lie. How do you sleep at night?
DON: On a bed made of money.
MIDGE: Isn't this an education.
ROY: You hucksters in your tower created the religion of mass consumption.
DON: People want to be told what to do so badly that they'll listen to anyone.
ROY: When you say "people," I have a feeling you're talking about thou.
DON: And I have a feeling you spent more time on your hair this morning than she [Midge] did.

On the whole, the New Left comes off pretty badly in *Mad Men*—self-indulgent, hypocritical, and naïve.[24] In the 2008 episode "For Those Who Think Young," Don says, "Young people don't know anything. Especially that they're young." But he's no hard-hat: he's too secure for that. Although clearly a man of the fifties, Don is willing to partake of the fruits of the sixties, whether in the form of recreational drugs or the Beatles—when his second wife Megan (Jessica Paré) brings home a copy of their 1966 album *Revolver*, he plays the psychedelic "Tomorrow Never Knows." And while he clearly takes pride in his power as a successful businessman and provider for his wife and children—"I pay the bills, the clothes on your back," he tells Betty in an angry moment—Don shows little concern about money. In an effort to prevent his divorce from Megan from descending into irreconcilable bitterness, he slices through their financial disputes while waiting for a lawyer by writing her a check for a million dollars on the spot. The only thing more breathtaking than the formerly poor Dick Whitman being able to afford such a sum is his evident confidence that he'll be able to make it back.

Don isn't the only self-made man on *Mad Men*. He has something of a junior doppelganger in Bob Benson, a gay confidence man who ingratiates himself with the right people in an impressive rise before he moves on to a job at General Motors in the final season. There's also Michael Ginsberg, a working-class Jew with a sharp tongue and brilliant wordcraft who unfortunately descends into mental illness, something that becomes apparent in his paranoid reaction to an IBM computer's appearance in the company offices. Then there's Lane Pryce, an Englishman whose background is distinguished enough but who sees his arrival at the firm as an opportunity to reinvent himself. This too ends in tragedy after financial desperation leads him to commit embezzlement and then suicide in one of the more somber plotlines of the show.

And then there are the self-made women.

WOMEN'S WORK

There's little doubt that Don Draper is the protagonist of *Mad Men*. And as embodied by Jon Hamm, Don dominates any scene he enters. But in many respects, it's the female characters of the show who command the most interest in the evolving complexity of their characters and in their often jagged relationship with the American Dream.

For no one is this more true than Peggy Olson, whose awkward diffidence and fitful assertiveness makes her arguably the most compelling character on the show. An Irish/Norwegian Catholic working-class woman from Bay Ridge, a distinctly outer-borough precinct of

Brooklyn, she comes to Sterling Cooper to work as Don's secretary. Painfully inexperienced, she makes a series of mistakes, among them believing that it's her job to indicate her sexual availability to Don, who makes it clear he's not interested. Given that the two will go on to enjoy a remarkable degree of intimacy, it's striking that their relationship never becomes romantic, perhaps reflecting a mutual regard whose purity depends on professional respect and intellectual parity. "It's not because you aren't attractive," Don tells her in the pivotal 2010 episode in the arc of their relationship, "The Suitcase." "I have to keep rules about work. I have to. You're an attractive girl, Peggy."

"Not as attractive as some of your other secretaries," she observes.

"You don't want to start giving me morality lessons, do you?"

Don refers to a major plot point from the show's first season, when Peggy makes the mistake of allowing herself to be seduced by Pete, who's a married man with no interest in Peggy but sexual pleasure. In what may seem to be dumbfounding (but not inconceivable at the time) ignorance of her own biology, Peggy does not realize she's pregnant until she goes into labor. She gives the child up for adoption, and the only person who visits her in the hospital is Don. "This never happened," he tells her during a flashback in the 2008 episode "The New Girl." Obviously drawing from his own experience, he adds, "It will shock you how much it never happened." Peggy will also say "This never happened" after she literally bails Don out after he has a car accident with Bobbie Barrett that he wants to keep from Betty.

In this urge to erase, Don and Peggy, like Jay Gatsby, are American Dream archetypes in the way that they leave their pasts behind. But Peggy can't do this as easily as these men, for whom the distance from their origins is literal as well as figurative. Peggy is regularly pulled back toward Brooklyn by her disapproving mother and sister (her father died of a heart attack in her presence when she was a child), and endures painfully empathic entreaties from a local priest, Father John Gill (Matthew Hanks), to acknowledge her sins with her child and return to the fold. "For the little one," he says, handing her a painted

egg on Easter Sunday in the 2008 episode, "Three Sundays," a seemingly innocuous but remarkably sharp-edged injunction for her to
come to Jesus as well as her baby. Peggy will be haunted by her choices
for the rest of her life, even as there's little question such doubts are a
price she's willing to pay.

For it soon becomes clear to Peggy that she not only has real talent,
but that's there's a bona fide path to a promising future as an advertising copywriter. (Just as Don gradually accommodates himself to
Pete's abilities, Pete will gradually accommodate himself to Peggy's.)
Peggy benefits from Don's tutelage—and, inevitably, begins to chafe
at it. "I think, 'I want what he has,'" she tells him in the 2009 episode
"The Fog." "You have everything, and so much of it."

"I suppose that's probably true," he replies. "What do you want me
to say?"

"I don't think I can be any clearer," she says. Peggy, courted by a
rival agency, will ultimately make the jump. But before the series has
run its course, she will be professionally reunited with Don, where
they increasingly operate as equals. Ironically, by that point, Don is
floundering and besieged by self-doubt. "What do you have to worry
about?" she asks him in the 2014 episode "The Strategy" as she con-
fesses her own insecurities about turning thirty. His reply: "That
I haven't done anything. And that I don't have anyone." The episode is
one of the final times we see them together, and this office scene ends
on a lovely note with the two of them dancing to Frank Sinatra's "My
Way." In the remaining episodes of the series, Peggy continues to
chart an upward trajectory with a notable clarity of purpose, one that
includes a satisfying romantic relationship with art director Stan
Rizzo (Jay R. Ferguson), a brutally sexist toad who evolves into an
egalitarian prince.

In addition to Don, Peggy has an additional—and even more
highly charged—foil in the form of Joan. The tetchiness of their relationship is established at the outset, as Joan takes note of the men
who are taking note of Peggy. "You're the new girl. And you're not
much. So enjoy it while you can," Joan tells her on her first day at work

in the show's pilot. The contrast between the two—mousy Peggy versus almost impossibly voluptuous Joan—is almost comic. There's a temptation, one both of them indulge, to view the frictions in their relationship in class terms: the upwardly mobile Peggy versus the working-class Joan, a highly competent secretary with little interest in climbing the standard corporate ladder. But the situation is a little more complicated than that, in that both women have modest backgrounds, both are very good at their jobs, and both must battle sexism on and off the clock. Joan's fiancé (and later husband), a not especially competent doctor, actually rapes her at the Sterling Cooper offices. (He will later abandon her, and "their" son—the secret is that he's actually Roger's—to serve as an army surgeon in Vietnam.) Yet the two women's shared oppression does not always result in solidarity. When Peggy fires a young male staffer who puts up an ugly sexual caricature of Joan on an office window in the 2010 episode "Summer Man," Joan isn't impressed. "You wanna be a big shot," she tells Peggy in an elevator at the end of the workday. "Well, no matter how powerful we get around here, they can still just draw a cartoon. So all you've done is prove I'm a meaningless secretary and you're another humorless bitch. Have a nice weekend," she says, exiting, leaving Peggy stunned.

A perhaps better way to understand the Peggy/Joan divide is to think of them in terms of equality feminism versus difference feminism. Both women think in terms of empowerment, but while Peggy considers her sex something that should be irrelevant in terms of her workplace performance, Joan leverages her sexual power as a means of commanding attention and influence. The starkest illustration of this comes in the 2011 episode "The Other Woman," when Joan agrees to sleep with an obnoxious client who names a night with her as the price facilitating a Sterling Cooper contract with Jaguar, a major coup for the firm. In return, Joan extracts a 5 percent share of the company. Don—whose own connections to prostitution are no doubt a factor here—is appalled on Joan's behalf by the prospect of the transaction; she strokes his face to reassure him. Joan performs the task and vaults into the partnership ranks.

Not that her, or Peggy's, travails or conflicts are over. In the 2015 episode "Severance," both now working for a large larger firm, they're subjected to sophomoric innuendo while trying to pitch a client. Once again, they have an elevator fight after Joan expresses her frustration at their treatment:

PEGGY: You can't have it both ways. You can't dress the way you do and—

JOAN: How do I dress?

PEGGY (*trying to deflect Joan's angry look*): Look, they didn't take me seriously either.

JOAN: So what you're saying is, I don't dress the way you do because I don't look like you. And that's very, very true.

PEGGY: You know what? You're filthy rich. You don't have to do anything you don't want to.

Their relative financial status—Joan, as it turns out, is the one with an equity stake—isn't the only irony. Another is that Joan, who started the series anxious to get married (notwithstanding her on-again, off-again affair with Roger), ends up single, while Peggy has found a soul-mate. But at the end of the day, the two women are aligned in their successful quest for upward mobility in their professional lives, however different the means they pursued to achieve it. They form a part-nership of their own—dubbed Harris Olson—for a company that produces industrial films. "I learned a long time ago not to get all my satisfaction from this job," Joan had told Peggy in the 2010 episode "Tomorrowland." Peggy's response: "That's bullshit." And they both laugh merrily.

One other professional woman worth mentioning here is Megan Calvet, who begins as Don's secretary and marries him on the rebound from Betty. Megan, whose abilities stretch in directions that range from empathic babysitting to ad copywriting, has a different aspira-tion: she wants to be an actor. Her own mother, Marie (Julia Ormond), a French Canadian, is deeply skeptical. "Not every little girl gets to do what they want," she tells Megan in the 2011 episode "The Phantom."

"The world won't support that many parties." Marie advises Don, who's disappointed by Megan's desire to spread her wings, not to worry. "That is what happens when you have the artistic temperament but you are not an artist," she tells him. Noting her daughter's dismay at losing out on a role, she says, "Nurse her through this defeat, and you shall have the life you desire." But Marie underestimates Megan. She embarks on a successful television career in Los Angeles, and would have been more than willing to remain married to Don, even on a bicoastal basis. But Don's demons torpedo that prospect. Megan is arguably the most well-adjusted person in the entire *Mad Men* cast. She suggests that the American Dream remains psychologically viable as well as professionally attainable for women no less than men—and illustrates the tremendous cultural power of California as the national capital for the Dream.

One of the more interesting aspects of *Mad Men* is that there's a whole other side of the female equation: the housewives. Living on the far side of a historical divide separated by third-wave feminism where only 2 percent of girls since 1985 have said they want to be homemakers by the time they're thirty,[25] it's hard to remember—or believe—that this was an aspiration for millions of American women in the aftermath of the Great Depression and World War II. To be sure, there were aspects of it that were highly oppressive (as Betty Friedan's 1963 book *The Feminine Mystique* made clear), and women may have liked the idea better than the reality (as Joan's experience suggests). But the fact remains that it was a widespread if not universal experience, and one celebrated by men and women alike as a plausibly attainable American Dream—with all the hopes, frustrations, and ambiguities that go into the pursuit of a professional career.

The housewives of *Mad Men* are a motley crew. At least initially, the most enthusiastic of the lot is Pete's wife, Trudy, played by the formidable Alison Brie. Over the course of the series we watch her chart her family's way through the Campbells' first apartment, the birth of their daughter Tammy, a move to the suburbs, and relocation to a new life in Wichita. Pete is a self-absorbed narcissist for much of this time, and one can't help but wonder what she sees in him—

unless, of course, he's a means to an end of a lifestyle to which she commits with élan. One of the ironies of their marriage is that while Pete prides himself as a provider, it's really Trudy who calls the shots, as he realizes to his chagrin. "Why do they get to decide what gets to happen?" he plaintively asks the head of Sterling Cooper's television department, Harry Crane (Rich Sommer), with regard to both their spouses in the 2011 episode "Lady Lazarus." Harry's reply: "They just do." Pete transgresses his marriage vow by embarking on an affair, and when Trudy finds out, she throws him out. They reunite at the end of the series when Pete begs her to take him back and she relents. Some of this is a matter of Trudy's class status—she comes from a wealthy family, and her father underwrites that apartment and provides Pete with valuable business connections—but her example suggests that patriarchy may be a little less airtight than both many chauvinists and many feminists may think.

The primary wife and mother of *Mad Men* is Betty Draper. Beautiful, elegant, and remote, Betty is like a Grace Kelly of the suburbs (she hails, as did Kelly, from greater Philadelphia, and like Kelly was a model in her youth). She attended Bryn Mawr and received a degree in anthropology as well as learned Italian, which comes in handy when she and Don make a trip to Rome at the behest of hotel magnate Conrad Hilton, a client of Don's. It's clear early on that Betty is a restless soul. She doesn't much like being a mother to her children, Sally and Bobby (a third child, Gene, comes along as a failed last chance to save the Draper marriage).[26] Her domestic duties are relatively light, because she has a black housekeeper, Carla (Deborah Lacey). Betty dabbles; for a while, equine pursuits divert her. She makes a bid to get back into modeling through Don's connections, but when that falls through she doesn't follow up. Her discovery of Don's secret past, coupled with his infidelities, finally leads her to initiate the break with him, but Betty shows little desire to break out of her traditional gender role, moving on to marry the Republican operative Henry Francis (Christopher Stanley). While Henry is largely a man of his time and place—he gets annoyed with Betty for expressing her political opinions—he is exceptionally decent in his handling of Betty and her children and in his dealings with Don.

Henry is also appalled when, in a fit of pique, Betty fires Carla, who stayed with the family after Betty's divorce from Don. "You get rid of [the children's] nanny since they were born?" he asks her, incredulous. "I wanted a fresh start, okay?" she responds irritably. "There *is* no fresh start," Henry says. "Lives carry on." It's hard not to admire his realism here, though Henry is ultimately a tragic figure in that he hitches his wagon to Nelson Rockefeller (who will be shoved aside by Richard Nixon) and seems more shattered than Betty herself is when she's diagnosed with fatal lung cancer.

Betty gives Pete a run for the money as the least likeable character in *Mad Men*, but her character is indicative of the way even the most boring housewives can have fascinating wrinkles in their lives. The most intriguing relationship she has is with her neighbor Helen Bishop's son Glen, played by Matthew Weiner's son Marten. Glen is besotted with Betty, and she shares startling confidences with him. Their interactions have a remarkable intimacy that never quite crosses a sexual line—there's a riveting parking lot scene in the 2007 episode "The Wheel" in which Betty's gloved hand clasps Glen's mittened one—even when Glen, as a young adult, comes to tell Betty that he's enlisted in the army to impress her. With a combination of scruples, fatalism, and distaste, she spurns him, perhaps because the charm of his innocence is now gone.

Interestingly, it's the offspring of *Mad Men* who have the least clear path forward. Glen enjoys a long friendship with Sally Draper, who has no clue of Glen's tie to Betty and is angrily appalled by his decision to go to Vietnam. Sally herself, who heads off to the prestigious Miss Porter's School, will counsel the heartbroken Henry through her mother's death. She's compassionate yet sharp, in multiple senses of that term, but there are no hints to her future as the series ends. Roger's daughter Margaret, played by Elizabeth Rice, is a truly lost soul; Roger unsuccessfully tries to rescue her from a commune to return to her husband and son. Children of affluence, their dreams are shrouded in mist.

Actually, the uncertainty these children feel is indicative of a larger truth about domestic life in *Mad Men*: it's not very happy.[27] No family that we see is fully functional, and the locus of the show's energy is on the workplace, not the home. A family seems at best a means to an end, at worst a grim necessity. "Do you want to be right, or do you want to be married?" Roger counsels Don as his relationship with Betty heads for the rocks in "Six Month Leave." His advice: "I know marriage isn't a natural state, but you do it."

"Why?" Don asks.

"I dunno. Kids. . . ." Roger responds, his voice trailing off.

There are occasional gestures in a familial direction. Duck Phillips, an ad executive who drops out of and reappears in the series over the course of its run, is a drunk who forfeits his family for his career, something we see happen in the 2008 episode "Maidenform." In the 2014 episode "The Better Half," he's a recovering alcoholic and corporate recruiter working with an adrift Pete, who is living apart from his wife and child and struggling to find suitable arrangements for his mother, who has descended into dementia.

> DUCK: Pete, one day I looked in the mirror and I realized I had regrets because I didn't realize the wellspring of my confidence.
> PETE: Gin? [Typical Pete snark.]
> DUCK: My family.
> PETE: My family is a constant distraction.
> DUCK: You better manage that or you're not going to manage anything.

Ironically, the most full-throated affirmation of family life—of a sort—comes in the form of an advertisement. Peggy and Don are charged with coming up with a campaign for Burger Chef, a fast-food chain, and of course search for a way to suggest that takeout is the best way to make everybody happy. "*Are* there people who eat dinner and smile at each other instead of watching TV?" she asks Don during 2014 episode "The Strategy." "Did you ever do that with your family?" Don's answer: "I don't remember." In their back and forth, Peggy hits on a winning pitch: "What if there was a place where you could go where there was no TV? Where you could break bread, and whoever you were sitting with was family?" The episode ends with

Pete, Don, and Peggy enjoying a meal at a Burger Chef, with veteran director Phil Abraham deploying a standard *Mad Men* technique of moving (in this case in a fluid single shot) from close-up to wide angle to situate the characters in a broader historical context.[28] The happiest families, it appears, are the ones you make yourself. That's a dream that gets pursued, and sometimes achieved, with every generation in which two people unite to form a household. But part of what makes a family a family is that you don't always get to choose who the members are. This, you might say, is an American dilemma.

DREAM MARGINS

Not surprisingly, the sharpest commentaries on the limits of the American Dream come from the characters on the margins. *Mad Men* is at heart a show about rich white people in metropolitan New York City (which is partly what makes their parochialism all the more striking). But there are enough characters outside that charmed circle to offer a useful foil for the dominant discourse on the dream—and in some cases to provide pointed critiques of it.[29]

The primary messengers of such messages in the series are African Americans. Their oppression is established in the opening scene of the series, "Smoke Gets in Your Eyes," when we first meet Don at a bar scribbling down notes on a cocktail napkin as he tries to formulate a slogan for Lucky Strike cigarettes. With his usual combination of clarity in his vision and instrumentalism in his motives, Don strikes up a conversation with a black waiter for his take on what he smokes and why. But they're interrupted by the waiter's white boss, who says, "I'm sorry, sir. Is Sam here bothering you? He can be a little chatty." Don responds, "We're just having a conversation." When in response to Don's subsequent queries the waiter says simply, "I like smoking," Don seizes on the simplicity and appeal of such a statement, though he will later settle on "It's toasted," which sounds good even as he readily admits it's meaningless. Don shows a similar clarity—and, perhaps, a similar finitude in his empathy—when Roger notes that a rival firm has hired an African American in the 2008 episode "Six Month Leave." "What do you think of that?" he asks. Don's reply: "I think I'm glad I'm not that kid."

Black characters make their own observations. There's the women's room attendant who notes Betty Draper's parsimony to a colleague with tart dismay: "Those purses get any smaller we're gonna starve." When, in "Six Month Leave," Peggy laments the suicide of Marilyn Monroe by saying, "You don't ever imagine her being alone," the black elevator operator, Hollis, responds by saying, "Some people just hide in plain sight." In the 2005 episode "The Fog," Pete is disappointed that he can't pump a lot of information out of Hollis as part of his market research on for Admiral televisions. When Pete expresses surprise that Hollis doesn't watch TV, he replies, "Why should I? We've got bigger problems to worry about than TV, okay?" Pete presses the point: "The idea is that everyone is going to have a house, a car, a television—the American Dream." Hollis's silent skeptical look in response is more effective than anything he chooses not to say.

The most (intentional) cringe-worthy moments in the series come from the interracial relationship between ad-man Paul Kinsey (Michael Gladis) and Sheila White (Donielle Artese). "It's so good to see you and Paul together," Joan, whose backstory includes a romance with Paul, says in the 2008 episode "Flight." "I have to say, when Paul and I were together the last thing I would have taken him for is open-minded." Sheila's response takes the form of a pained expression. When, after some dickering, Paul later joins a freedom ride with Sheila, he instructs his fellow bus travelers on his professional contribution to civil rights. "Advertising, if anything, helps bring change," he explains in "The Inheritance," also from 2008. "The market—and I'm talking in a purely Marxist sense—dictates that we must include everyone. Consumer has no color." Once again, Sheila's reaction is silent, this time an amused smile. Paul will later become a Hare Krishna who writes a spec script for *Star Trek* that he hopes Harry will help him sell, suggesting the way superficial quests for fulfillment can lead one to spiritual emptiness, among other kinds.

For other characters, disillusionment is swift and brutal. Salvatore Romano, a married closeted gay man who's the art director at

Sterling Cooper, is a fixture for the show's first three seasons. (The look on the face of his wife Kitty, played by Sarah Drew, when he unwittingly reveals he's gay in the 2009 episode "Out of Town" is one of the most crushing images in the series.) Don and Sal go on a business trip to Baltimore in which Sal acts on his long suppressed desires with a hotel bellhop, his secret revealed to Don when he sees the two through a window while descending a fire escape after an alarm goes off. Don takes this in stride. "Limit your exposure," he tells him in a spirit of friendly advice. But later that season, when a gay Lucky Strike client comes on to Sal, calling him "Sally," Sal recoils in fear—and, apparently, distaste for a man who's not his type. The jilted client, whose sexual identity remains secret, then demands that Sal be fired, which he is. "I guess I was supposed to do what he wanted?" Sal asks Don, incredulous. "What if it was some girl?"

Don's merciless response: "That would depend on what kind of girl it was and what I knew about her." He shakes his head in disgust over Sal's lack of recognition of the power rules of the road for anyone who's not a heterosexual white male. "You people," he adds, his prejudices rising to the surface.

"I didn't do anything but turn him down," Sal pleads. "He's a bully."

"Lucky Strike could shut off the lights," Don says. "I think you know this is the way this has to be. You'll do fine."

We don't learn if he does. (Don thought Lane Pryce would be fine and he committed suicide.) In any event, Sal's exile from the snake-filled garden of the Mad Men is complete. We never see him again.

SECULAR GRACE

Intimations of doom hover about Donald Draper. Indeed, they're there even before we actually meet him in the first episode, adumbrated in the iconic animated credit sequence of the show, accompanied by a synth-heavy and percussive theme song, "A Beautiful Mine" (an instrumental version of a song from the rapper Aceyalone's 2006 album *Mag-*

nificent City). The sequence shows a man falling from a skyscraper, the buildings around him plastered with advertisements, which is to say a cascade of questionable claims. *Mad Men* has a high-concept premise that's typical of many TV shows, where their protagonists—from Samantha Stevens of *Bewitched* (1964–1972, mentioned on *Mad Men*) to Mike Ross of *Suits* (2011–2019)—live lives at variance with who they say they are. This friction drives such shows: can they get away with it? All of them, *Mad Men* included, include a series of close calls as well as strategically placed disclosures, often near or at season finales, meant to regulate their pacing. As *Mad Men* proceeded toward its conclusion—its final season strategically stretched out over two seven-episode halves separated by almost a year in 2014–2015—there was widespread speculation among devotees about when and how Don would, like Icarus, fall from his semi-manufactured grace.

Certainly there were plenty of events in the last twenty or so episodes where Don was in trouble. His second marriage is over. His firm has been absorbed by the real-life colossus Batten, Barton, Durstine & Osborn (BBDO), something he finds difficult to accept, even though he's made a fortune and has vast new opportunities. He's estranged from his daughter Sally, who has caught him *in flagrante delicto* with Sylvia Rosen (among other things, a notable betrayal of her husband, a heart surgeon he deeply admires). Claustrophobic during a corporate meeting to figure out how to advertise a newfangled product to be dubbed "light" beer—"low-calorie" deemed too feminine for men—Don leaves, hops in his car, and keeps on driving. He ends up in California, in so many ways the locus of his imagination: his chosen family, his professional prospects, and a site of leisure in ways that range from recreational drugs to casual sex. It's while he's there that he learns in a phone call with Sally that Betty is dying. By this point, Sally is caring for her siblings and explains to Don that his notions of charging back home are unrealistic—a point reinforced by Betty in a subsequent phone call with Don where she insists that the children be cared for by her brother and sister-in-law, because they need a woman in their lives.

Don has washed up at the home of Anna Draper's niece Stephanie, who is herself adrift following the birth of a child out of wedlock whom she has given up (Don had helped out financially during her pregnancy). She's headed to a retreat at an Esalen-styled New Age resort, and she takes Don along. But Stephanie ditches the retreat when a participant questions her choice to give up her child, leaving Don alone. He's at his wit's end. "I broke all my vows. I scandalized my child. I took another man's name and made nothing of it," he tells Peggy from a payphone in the 2015 series finale, "Person to Person," a reference to a way long-distance calls were once placed. Don's connections are tenuous, but Peggy is still there for him.

Don attends a group encounter session in which an unprepossessing figure named Leonard describes his bland life and compares himself to an object in a refrigerator that no one ever takes out. He breaks down in tears. For some reason, these remarks tap a wellspring of empathy in Don, who embraces him fervently and breaks down in tears himself. This appears to be a turning point. The next time we see Don, he's sitting in the lotus position on the gorgeous Pacific coast with other retreat participants, chanting with a beatific smile on his face. The camera cuts to, and the series concludes with, an iconic document: the real-life classic 1971 BBDO ad "I'd Like to Buy the World a Coke"—which, the episode slyly implies, was Don's handiwork. The ad features a notably diverse group of young people singing in harmony in a verse that culminates with the chorus: "It's the real thing." (One can wonder if there's anything more artificial.) This is an ironic and perhaps even a cynical ending, suggesting the way that capitalism relentlessly commodifies our deepest spiritual yearnings. But in an important sense, that's precisely what the American Dream is: a form of secular grace.

Don has been redeemed. Of course he has: he's a white man. The difference between his time and ours is that he could safely ignore that fact. But Matthew Weiner, who wrote and directed the episode, casts his net of benediction widely: "We leave everybody slightly improved," he told *Variety* in 2015.[30] (One wonders how or if this applies to Betty; it appears we're supposed to believe she has made her peace with her fate and her family.) From our perspective in the twenty-first century, we sense the limits of that redemption—the aperture of our society has widened, even as our collective prospects have narrowed in a nation whose lack of confidence in its mythology continues to unravel. Those of us fascinated by the Great Draper watch *Mad Men* as a dream, uneasy yet reluctant to wake from its world of bright shadows.

THE KIDS ARE ALRIGHT

Publicity still from season 2 of *That '70s Show*, 1999. More liberal and less innocent than its predecessor, *Happy Days* (1974–1984), the sitcom injected a fillip of realism to keep its sentimental tendencies in check, but quickly became dated in the more censorious environment of the early twenty-first century. Shown clockwise from left: Ashton Kutcher (Michael Kelso), Danny Masterson (Steven Hyde), Mila Kunis (Jackie Burkhart), Wilmer Valderrama (Fez), Laura Prepon (Donna Pinciotti), and Topher Grace (Eric Forman).

CHAPTER 5

WE'RE ALL ALL RIGHT

That '70s Show as a 1990s Version of the 1970s

Key Cast Members
- Topher Grace as Eric Forman
- Laura Prepon as Donna Pinciotti
- Danny Masterson as Steven Hyde
- Ashton Kutcher as Michael Kelso
- Mila Kunis as Jackie Burkhart
- Wilmer Valderrama as Fez
- Kurtwood Smith as Red Forman
- Debra Jo Rupp as Kitty Forman

Key Episodes
- "Battle of the Sexists" (1998)
- "Hyde Moves In" (1999)
- "The Velvet Rope" (1999)
- "Kitty's Birthday (Is That Today?!)" (2001)
- "Canadian Road Trip" (2001)
- "Street Fighting Man" (2005)

*A*LL POPULAR CULTURE gets dated, but *That '70s Show* (1998–2006) got dated especially quickly. A genial series about a group of teenagers and adults in the fictive small town of Point Place, Wisconsin, in the years between 1976 and 1979, the show was reminiscent of one it frequently referenced: *Happy Days* (1974–1984), which was also a show about teenagers who happened to be living in Wisconsin, albeit in the 1950s. In both cases, there were plenty of adolescent hijinks, high school romances, and occasional teachable moments, awash in nostalgia. The difference was the history that occurred between those generations—specifically the loosened cultural mores in which pre-marital sex and casual drug use had become accepted facts of everyday American life. In this regard, *That '70s Show* could plausibly be called more liberal and less innocent than *Happy Days*, injecting a fillip of necessary realism to keep its sentimental tendencies in check.

But that's not how it looks now. Instead, the sitcom rapidly acquired a retrograde air. In the decade after its final episode was first broad-cast in 2006, you could type the words "*That '70s Show* politically incorrect" into a Google search and get hits with titles like "20 Story-lines from *That '70s Show* That Wouldn't Fly Today" and the sitcom's presence in stories like "The 50 Most Racist TV Shows of All Time" and "15 Iconic TV Shows That Are Totally Inappropriate Today."[1] Of course, such pieces are themselves products of a fleeting cultural moment (listicles, that characteristic fad of the 2010s, dominate the results, many of which are likely to be gone by the time a reader of this book tried to track down the citations for them). Actually, the tone of such stories may end up saying more about the censorious tenor of the Trump era than they do the 1970s setting of the show or the 1990s context of its origins.

Which is not to say that the show was ever really respectable. Indeed, its cheekiness was something its creators embraced. During its eight-year run, the sitcom was a mainstay of the Fox network, and while its TV shows were not as uniformly right-wing as its news pro-gramming, challenging pieties of all kinds—whether from the left with *The Simpsons* (1989–ongoing) or the right with *Married . . . With Children* (1987–1997)—has always been Fox's stock in trade. The Los Angeles–based Parents Television Council (PTC), an advocacy organ-ization founded by conservative activist L. Brent Bozell, named *That '70s Show* one of the ten worst shows of the 2001–2002 television season.[2]

The offensiveness of *That '70s Show* generally seems more casual than edgy, which in a way makes it all the more striking. The adolescent male characters casually make references to "jugs," "boobs," and "racks" as indeed teenaged boys often did in in the seventies—but not to the accompaniment of the raucous laughter of a studio audience of a generation later that might have been expected to know better. A reporter for the *Los Angeles Times* noted in 1999 that the sitcom "possesses one of the loudest studio audiences, which the series must have inherited from Fox's late raunchy comedy, *Married . . . With Children*. Every comic and sexual situation is met with not only laughs, but catcalls, wolf whistles and 'wooooooooos.'"[3] Perhaps even more striking is the equanimity with which female characters condone or even savor such transgressions. When Donna Pinciotti (Laura Prepon) congratulates her friend Michael Kelso (Ashton Kutcher) in the 2001 episode "The Relapse" for having "finally gotten past the stage where you have to look at every woman's chest," he responds, "Not exactly. I'm looking at yours right now." Donna's riposte: "You're such a perv. And thank you." And when, in "I Can See for Miles" (2004), Kelso— who in a later age might be regarded as a sexual predator—makes the mistake of grabbing the derriere of a woman who turns out to be his buddy's mother, Kitty Forman (Debra Jo Rapp), she delivers a requisite lecture scolding that ends with "Thank you for the compliment. It made my day." Such issues took on a more serious, real-life turn in 2017 when series star Danny Masterson, who played the key character of Steven Hyde, was named in multiple accusations of sexual assault in the wake of the #MeToo movement.[4] Masterson, who contested the charges, was written out of his role in the Netflix series *The Ranch* (2016–2019), which included many *That '70s Show* alumni, among them Kutcher, Masterson, Valderrama, and director David Trainer.

If *That '70s Show* sex jokes are crude, the gender politics aren't much better. The show's pivotal character, Eric Forman (Topher Grace) is dogged by questions about his masculinity, very often by his father, Red (Kurtwood Smith). Terms like "nancyboy" and "pantywaist," which would likely be regarded as offensive were they still in general circulation, get thrown around. Despite the fact that the show was reportedly the first in North America to depict a gay male kiss, Eric's panicked response and hostile reactions from viewers led to the shelving of the character.[5] A recurrent character named Fenton, played by Jim Rash, is never explicitly identified as gay but his mincing manner in dress, voice, and gestures are meant to be understood in a negative way. Eric's older sister, Laurie, is routinely— one could say mercilessly—taunted for her sexual appetite. Critics of her treatment on the left would today call what she's subjected to slut-shaming; those on the right would wonder about self-esteem issues driving a promiscuity that's no laughing matter. Tragically, the woman who played Laurie, Lisa Robin Kelly, was an alcoholic who died in a rehab facility in 2013.

That '70s Show is also racist. The most egregious example is a running joke involving the identity of Fez (Wilmer Valderrama), whose nickname is a bowdlerized acronym for "foreign exchange student." Fez's friends can't pronounce his real name; in the 2006 episode "Killer Queen" he explains that "the first five Ks are silent." The double problem here is that while he's deracinated as an immigrant, he's consistently depicted as a comic other whose foibles are routinely attributed to his foreigner status. Red never even refers to him as Fez, invoking a series of monikers that include "Anwar," "Tonto" and "Tutankhamen" when he's not simply "that foreign kid." Jackie Burkhart (Mila Kunis) regularly makes heartlessly offhand remarks that aren't intended as jokes, as when she dismissively tells Fez, who has just acquired a green card in the 2003 episode "I'm Free," that "This is America. And you still look foreign. So don't expect to be treated equally." Though Fez's name is vaguely Middle Eastern, his features are Latino; sleuthing by fans centers on former Dutch colonies in the Caribbean.[6] Ironically, Valderrama is a native-born American, while Kunis is a Ukrainian immigrant. Also ironically, the two characters would end up as a romantic pair.

Still, however vulgar or offensive it may seem now, *That '70s Show* was much beloved in its day and continues to retain the residual affection of the millennials who form the core of its audience. In fact, in late 2018, it was among the top ten shows streaming on Netflix as a percentage of all views on the platform.[7] Even those outside its core demographic recognized its appeal; no less august a figure than Edward Albee—best known for his searing 1962 play *Who's Afraid of Virginia Woolf?*—noted in an email to a *New York Times* writer that "The characters are outrageous stereotypes and yet sweet and believable at the same time."[8] In short, *That '70s Show* was, and is, widely viewed as a guilty pleasure, whether that guilt is measured in terms of questionable cultural politics or hackneyed aesthetics. But what are the sources of that pleasure?

HAPPY DAZE

That '70s Show originated with seasoned television veterans. It was created by the Carsey-Werner Company run by Marcy Carsey and Tom Werner, responsible for such hits as *Roseanne* (1988–1997) and *The Cosby Show* (1984–1992). By the mid-nineties, the firm, affiliated with the U.K.-based producer Caryn Mandabach, was the last independent sitcom shop in a Hollywood now dominated by network-owned shows as a result of the 1993 expiration of government rules preventing them from doing so. Werner and Carsey noticed a seventies boom that cropped up in the nineties, one that included now-classic films such as Ang Lee's 1997 *The Ice Storm* (the movie featured a "key party" sequence involving wife swapping that would be comically reproduced in *That '70s Show*), Paul Thomas Anderson's *Boogie Nights* (1997), and Richard Linklater's *Dazed and Confused* (1993). The latter film seems a particularly apt parallel for *That '70s Show*, given its high school setting, its stoner ethic, and its role as a springboard in launching careers for young actors (Ben Affleck and Matthew McConaughey, among others, for *Dazed and Confused*; Ashton Kutcher and Mila Kunis, among others, for *That '70s Show*). Werner and Carsey asked the husband-and-wife writing team of Terry and Bonnie Turner, who had written screenplays for *Wayne's World* (1992) and *The Brady Bunch Movie* (1995), if they had any ideas for a seventies-based show. They in turn brought in their colleague Mark Brazill, with whom they worked on their hit series *3rd Rock from the Sun* (1996–2001). Brazill tapped his memories of an adolescent growing up in upstate New York; "Eric is basically me," he explained of the show's protagonist. The sitcom was purchased by Fox Entertainment president Peter Roth. It enjoyed unusual continuity in that every episode except the pilot, which was directed by Terry Hughes, was helmed by Trainer. While never a huge hit, it performed steadily with its core demographic, garnering an audience that hovered in the neighborhood of 10 million viewers weekly for most of its eight-season run.[9]

The sitcom's creators hoped to title it *Teenage Wasteland* or *The Kids Are Alright*, both the names of songs by the British rock band the Who. But songwriter Pete Townshend refused to sell the rights, and so they considered *Feelin' All Right,* the title of a song by Traffic that was recorded by Joe Cocker. But according to Bonnie Turner it didn't go over well with advertisers. Both she and Valderrama reported that the project was routinely referred to as "that 70s show" in the development process and so the producers decided to go with that.[10]

Which begs a question: *which* seventies? The seventies of Watergate and the energy crisis? The seventies of disco, feminism, and gay liberation? All these would in fact be referenced over the course of the show's run. But *That '70s Show* depicted a very specific rendition of the decade—a small-town Midwestern one that resonated widely—whose components merit unpacking.

Before doing so, it's worth discussing the element of the show that distills the sitcom's ethos most completely: its theme song, "In the Street," named in a *Rolling Stone* poll as one of the ten best in television history.[11] "In the Street" wasn't commissioned for *That '70s Show*; it was written by veteran rock artists Alex Chilton and Chris Bell of the band Big Star, and included on its 1972 album *#1 Record*. (Chilton was reportedly paid a $70 royalty per airing of an episode.)[12] A fresh version of the song was recorded for the sitcom's first season by musician Todd Griffin; the lyrics were joyfully sung by teen members of the cast, who were shown in a rapid-fire opening sequence of shots while riding in Eric Forman's antiquated, boat-sized Oldsmobile Vista Cruiser passed down to him by his dad, which figured in many a plot.

The words of "In the Street" deftly capture the pleasures and boredom of a middle-class adolescence to the accompaniment of heavy-metal guitars:

> Hangin' out, down the street
> The same old thing we did last week
> Not a thing to do but talk to you . . .

A couple of crucial revisions were made in this song/sequence after the first season. The first is that the cast of participants was widened to include parents of the characters (and, notably, to put Eric's on-again, off-again girlfriend Donna in the driver's seat for part of the ride). The other is that the song was rerecorded yet again, this time by the famed seventies rock band Cheap Trick. This was a clever move on a number of levels: Cheap Trick was an Illinois-based act that would have been near and dear to the hearts of the characters—their hit "I Want You to Want Me" plays in the background of the 1999 episode "Red's Last Day," and Eric has a poster of Cheap Trick guitarist Rick Nielsen in his bedroom—and their version of "In the Street" is exceptionally catchy (hence its citation in that reader's poll). But the real kicker is a new tag line that was repeated at the end of theme song: "We're all all right!" This is actually an allusion to the signature line in one of Cheap Trick's biggest hits, "Surrender," a sly commentary on the generation gap in which the protagonist gradually realizes that his parents actually had a life before he was born and comes upon them dancing, leading to a furtive mutual recognition of—and awkward surrender to—youthful exuberance by all.

It's this essentially benign spirit which, notwithstanding the transgressions noted above, finally governs *That '70s Show*. There's plenty of friction and misunderstanding among the parents and the kids, foregrounded by the tendency of the latter to indulge in sex and drugs

(limited here to alcohol and marijuana; in an effort to avoid censorship and controversy, the makers of the show resorted to a ritual
known as "the circle," in which a rotating camera showed obviously
high characters making foolishly sober pronouncements amid a
cloud of smoke).[13] But at the end of the day, the problems and issues
the characters grappled with were not all that far from earlier teen-
based sitcoms like *The Adventures of Ozzie and Harriet* (1952–1966),
The Brady Bunch (1969–1974), or *The Fresh Prince of Bel-Air* (1990–
1996). Happy Days, indeed.

Those problems and issues were, nevertheless, grounded in their
time and place. This was most obviously apparent in devices like having the character of Steven Hyde shout "Hello, Wisconsin!" like a rock
star on tour at the end of the theme song, and in the final image of
every episode, a Wisconsin license plate with an expiration year that
corresponded to the episode in question. There were also details like
Debra Jo Rapp's Midwestern accent in her portrayal of Kitty Forman
(Kurtwood Smith, who played her husband Red, is actually a native of
Wisconsin). Other episodes involve trips to the Wisconsin Dells, a
popular local tourist destination, and road trips the characters take to
Chicago or Canada. There are also the recurring local settings like the
Hub, a fast-food joint, and Point Place Hospital, where Kitty works
and where the characters go after miscellaneous injuries.

But placement of the sitcom's historical milieu was more subtle
than that. In his review of the series for *Entertainment Weekly* at the
time of its debut in 1998, the prominent culture critic Ken Tucker
complained that the show was meant to depict "the last gasp of pop-
culture innocence, a prelude to the deluge of slick, debilitating irony
that would grease our way into the '80s." But, he said, "this is a willed
misunderstanding of the period," citing evidence like the breakout
album of the Sex Pistols to argue that the seventies was much edgier
than the sitcom would suggest.[14] In some important sense Tucker is
right, though it's worth remembering that the show is set in a heart-
land town, somewhat insulated from such coastal and transatlantic
currents. The self-styled rebel of the cast, Hyde, does indeed know
about the Sex Pistols; when Kitty comes into the record store where

he works looking for a Bette Midler album, he passes it on to her as a joke (she gets an unpleasant jolt when she plays it while taking a bath). But Hyde's musical tastes, as indicated by the concert T-shirts he wears, suggest more conventional white-boy fare: Led Zeppelin, Black Sabbath, Jethro Tull, the Allman Brothers, and so on. The episode titles for the final four seasons are all song titles from such acts: season five is Zeppelin, season six is the Who, season seven is the Rolling Stones, and season eight is Queen. One episode involves Eric's desire to land tickets to see Styx; he's roundly mocked for his affection for the critically maligned Chicago-based band, but it is revealed that a number of the characters are secretly fans. In an allusion to an actual event that took place in 1979, Hyde leads a disco record–burning party in the woods near Point Place.

Hyde's T-shirt collection is indicative of the main way *That '70s Show*—like most specimens of visual media with historical themes—conveys its setting: through material culture. The sitcom is lovingly curated in terms of costumes (we get requisite jokes about the leisure suit Donna's father Bob Pinciotti, played by Don Stark, wears), hairstyles, furniture, automobiles, and actual period magazines that the characters thumb through occasionally.[15] Viewers who may know nothing of historical events of the decade can nevertheless take such cues as indicative of a temporal gap between their own lives and those of the characters they're watching, which is the main way most of us experience history.

Another form of historical referencing more specific to *That '70s Show* is a penchant for metatextual jokes, many of which are conveyed through fantasy sequences in which characters imagine alternative realities to the ones in which they find themselves. So it is that we get a steady stream of parodies that include seventies touchstones like the *Star Wars* movies, *Rocky*, *Charlie's Angels* (1976–1981), and the like. (There's a wink here in that the actor who plays Donna's mother Midge, Tanya Roberts, actually *was* one of *Charlie's Angels* back when that series aired.) Such sequences are particularly amusing when they involve actual pop culture icons from the period, like Jamie Farr of *M*A*S*H* (1972–1983), Shirley Jones and Danny Bonaduce of *The*

Partridge Family (1970–1974), and Mary Tyler Moore of *The Mary Tyler Moore Show* (1970–1977). Moore had a recurring role in which she played against type as an abrasive broadcaster for a local Wisconsin station. In one especially clever intertextual allusion, Dwayne Johnson—a.k.a. The Rock—portrays his father, Rocky Johnson, who was a professional wrestler in the 1970s. (Thirteen years later, after *That '70s Show* went off the air, Kutcher, starring in *The Ranch* as former football player Colt Bennett, answers a query as to how he managed to get into the office of a business rival with another such inside joke: "Let's just say your assistant is a fan of Michael Kelso, who she thinks I look like.")

There are also a couple of unintentional ironies worth noting here that couldn't have been known at the time. At one point in the final season when Donna is pulling a prank, she gleefully says, "I could go to a girl prison!" In fact, Laura Prepon, who played her, would go on to a major role in the Netflix series about incarceration, *Orange Is the New Black* (2013–2019). And in the 2004 episode "Let's Spend the Night Together," Donna and Eric attend a Take Back the Night rally, where an amorous moment between them is mistaken as sexual assault, leading Eric to be confronted by a feminist mob. "Run, Eric! Run like Bruce Jenner!" she tells him. A decade later, Bruce became Caitlyn, which puts the gender politics of that moment retrospectively in a different light.

Generally speaking, *That '70s Show* goes light when it comes to portraying specific historical events of the period, most of which occur early in the series. (It can be slipshod in its chronology—there are five Christmas episodes, for example, in the show's three-year sequence.) We get a reference to the energy crisis early in the pilot episode, when Red, a World War II and Korean War veteran, acknowledges that he bought a Toyota. "Yeah, it's mine," he admits at a party. "I tell ya, the last time I was that close to a Japanese machine it was shooting at me." "Well, honey, it's the gas crisis," Kitty commiserates. "What can you do?" Kitty herself feels some bemusement about the ironies of history—and a rising tide of immigration that's increas-

ingly perceptible even in middle America by the 1970s, thanks to the
Immigration and Naturalization Act signed by President Lyndon
Johnson in 1965. "It's thanks to the work of brave men like you that
our enemies are working here for minimum wage," she jokes mor-
dantly at a Japanese restaurant with Red, Bob, and Midge in the 2004
episode "Substitute." In the third episode of the series, "Streaking"—
referring to the seventies fad of people running naked in public—
President Gerald Ford comes to town. At a town-hall styled meeting,
Red asks, "How the hell could you pardon Nixon?" He gets hearty
applause onscreen and off. This points to one of the show's inconsis-
tencies, however; Eric later recites Red's view that Nixon was framed
and jokingly advises a friend that if he's looking for a good conversation starter, "just say we were wrong to go into Vietnam." But Red's
anticommunism has its limits: in a conversation about the arrival of
cable television he tells Hyde that he'd "rather kiss Ho Chi Minh than
pay for TV."

Red is an important figure in the series because he provides an
implicit and explicit point of contrast with the youthful characters.
His biographical background—notably his military experience,
which he clearly regards as the source of the patriarchal authority
that he continues to wield even when he struggles to support his
family—anchors him in the Greatest Generation, leading him to look
with skepticism on the self-indulgent kids of the Me Decade. A
running gag involves countless linguistic variations on kicking them
in the ass. (There's a final variation in the theme song in the show's
final season, which involves the main characters lip-synching the
song a line at a time; a visibly irritated Red refuses do to so.) When
his emotionally adrift son says he needs time to think about his future
in the 2004 episode "You Can't Always Get What You Want," Red
replies, "You know what I got for my eighteenth birthday? A draft
notice and a malaria vaccine. I never had time to think." But by the
conventions of sitcomland with which most viewers are well versed,
we know Red's bark is worse than his bite. He may say in the 2003
episode "Whole Lotta Love" that "Yelling is the only part of being a

father that I enjoy," but he's nevertheless a devoted father, a loving husband, and a mentor to Eric's friends, especially Hyde.

In part, this is because the generations are bridged by shared social conditions. These too are rooted in time and geography. Point Place, Wisconsin, is middle America in more ways than one—it accurately captures a white working class in slow decline. We learn that in the time before the setting of the show, Red was the manager of a now-closed auto plant (hence his lament about his Toyota). He endures patches of unemployment, taking odd jobs along the way, among them at his neighbor Bob's appliance store, which is forced to go out of business when Price Mart, a big retail chain clearly modeled on Wal-Mart, comes to town, and where both Red and Eric will get jobs. When Red gets his first paycheck from Price Mart in 2000 episode "Afterglow," he suggests to Kitty that they should do something nice. "I know!" she replies. "Turn on the heat!" At different points, the Forman family is shored up financially by Kitty, who works as a notably competent nurse at a local hospital, and Eric, who decides not to go to college— the University of Wisconsin, as private schools are out of the question—after Red has a heart attack. Hyde, who is abandoned by his parents and finds himself living on crackers and ketchup late in the first season, comes to live with the Formans and pays rent. At the end of the series we learn Red has put the money aside in a savings account for him (Hyde turns around and uses the funds to buy Red a set of season tickets for his beloved Green Bay Packers). The only clearly rich major character is Jackie, but her father goes to jail for bribery about halfway through the series, casting doubt on her own prospects—at least in the viewer's mind. Jackie herself has little doubt she will marry a man who will keep her in the style to which she is accustomed.

The economic picture isn't entirely grim. Indeed, it rarely becomes a distraction for the more petty matters that dominate given episodes, and a series of windfalls do come to various characters along the way. Red will ultimately buy a muffler shop whose fortunes are uneven until he sells out to a big chain at the end of the series. Hyde is reunited with a biological father he didn't know, who turns out to be a wealthy record-company executive who ultimately deeds him a record store. Bob Pinciotti and his daughter Donna, who remain in Point Place after his wife Midge leaves him, are in rough financial straits when his appliance store closes. But his invention of a device that dispenses tissues from a car visor puts him back in clover. Such happy endings seem less indicative of structural improvements in the economy—which will not arguably arrive until Ronald Reagan comes into office in the next decade—than the good fortune the writers confer on characters whom viewers would like to see rewarded. Similar wishful thinking, if not downright evasion, characterizes the Forman home, which, while hardly luxurious, seems appointed at a level that would appear unlikely for a family given the parameters we're given. That also goes for the vintage car that Red buys, even if he ultimately sells it when it briefly appears that he's about to be the grandfather to Eric and Donna's child (it turns out she's not pregnant; an abortion is in any case beyond mention).

This skewing of the Forman standard of living is hardly unique to *That '70s Show*. As noted in chapter 1, the Walton family also appears to live in a home above its means, something perhaps attributable to a desire for fantasy that often accompanies even TV shows that are presumably meant to be realistic. Though fantasy can sometimes also be oppressive: "You know who had a real family?" a discouraged Kitty asks in the 2002 episode "Ramble On." Her answer: "The Waltons."

Whatever the reality of their circumstances, many of the characters have aspirations of upward mobility. Principal among them are the dreams that parents have for their children. When Donna is embarrassed by her father's circus gimmicks, which include a live monkey, at his appliance store in the 1999 episode "Career Day," he replies by stating, "You see clowns. I see your tuition at Harvard. You see your dad as a ringmaster. I see you going to graduate school. . . . The point is, Donna, you're capable of great things. And if this is what I have to do so you can achieve them, this is what I'll do."

"Geez, Dad, I feel really bad," Donna responds.

Dad characteristically cheers her up: "Hey, nobody feels bad around Bargain Bob—unless you get bit by a monkey."

A similar sense of intergenerational cultural cohesion, not all of it positive, concerns race. *That '70s Show* is very white in terms of its cast, the issues discussed (or not), and, in all likelihood, who watched the show at the time and ever since. These decisions of course reflect the demographic realities of the upper Midwest at the time, which has become significantly more diverse since the 1970s. But a decision to focus on white people, whether as a creator or viewer of the show, can be seen as one more form of fantasy for those nostalgic for a simpler (read: racially homogeneous) time.

Racial diversity is not entirely lacking on *That '70s Show*. A small but steady stream of black characters wander across a series of episodes, notably Gloria Gaynor, the famed disco queen who plays a music teacher attending the junior prom in the first season of the series and belts out a spirited version of her signature hit "I Will Survive." We also get to see Billy Dee Williams play an enthusiastic youth minister who counsels Donna and Eric, and with whom Eric bonds over a shared love of *Star Wars*—which is amusing because Williams played the role of Lando Calrissian, a smuggler turned revolutionary, in that saga.

Then there is Fez, who, as noted, is painfully deracinated but who nevertheless remains a highly visible reminder of the diversity in the world beyond Wisconsin. A further point of contrast is provided by the character of Leo Chingkwake, the aging hippie who owns a Foto Hut kiosk for a stretch of the series, and who's something of a second surrogate father—sometimes it seems like a son—to the less addled Hyde. Leo is played by Tommy Chong, one half of the iconic comedy duo of (Richard) Cheech and Chong that enjoyed a long run of success in the seventies and eighties. (Chong was absent from the show for a while because he was sentenced a nine-month prison term on a drug possession charge in 2003.)[16] At one point in the 2000 episode "Moon over Point Place," Fez tells Leo he should "go home and cry to your big white mama," prompting him to reply with a riposte of typical uncertainty: "First of all, man, I think I'm Chinese." The writers further play with stereotypes late in the series when we learn Leo is a Purple Heart–decorated World War II veteran who drove a supply truck into a German tank formation and rescued a platoon. "I don't know whether to like him a little more or like myself a little less," says the begrudgingly impressed Red. We see a newly discharged young Leo in a brief flashback, who is invited to join a group of jazz musicians in a car dense with the smoke of weed. His future is baked into the plot.

A turning point of sorts occurs early in the seventh season of the show—any series that lasts this long will often need a plot twist of some kind or another. In the second episode, "Let's Spend the Night Together," we learn, along with Hyde himself, that his biological father is black. Hyde himself is exultant; when Eric says he doesn't see a resemblance, Hyde replies, "What are you talking about? My 'fro? [Hyde has curly hair.] My coolness? My suspicion of the Man? This explains so much!" Other characters, with the notable exception of Donna, respond with well-intentioned but embarrassing tone deafness. Eric mentions his affection for the classic seventies sitcom *The Jeffersons* (1975–1985), incorrectly citing the signature catchword "Dy-no-mite!" that's actually associated with a different show, *Good Times* (1974–1980). When Jackie points this out, he says, "I watch them all. I don't discriminate." Kitty, for her part, mentions her affection for Art Garfunkel, not realizing he's white. When she asks her husband, "Red, who's that black person I like?" he ventures, "Martin Luther King?" To which she gleefully says, "Yes!" This is all offered in a comic spirit—certainly audience response suggests as much—but in some quarters the parochialism of the kind Kitty shows is no longer considered a laughing matter.

Hyde's dad, William Barnett, who would appear in nine episodes of the series, is played by Tim Reid, who portrayed the savvy disc jockey Venus Flytrap in the well-regarded sitcom *WKRP in Cincinnati*, which ran from 1978 to 1982. (His colleague Johnny Fever, played by Howard Hesseman, also shows up in three episodes as a station manager in a local radio station where Donna has an internship.)[17] Barnett's reaction to his awkward greeting by these characters is dry: "You know, I'm beginning to feel like we haven't had a lot of black people in this house." Though Barnett is initially suspicious that Hyde is only interested in him for his money, the two go on to enjoy a warm relationship, while Hyde embarks on a sibling rivalry with his (clearly black) half-sister Angie (Megalyn Echikunwoke), who also indulges in a brief romance with Michael Kelso before moving up her dad's corporate ladder. The net effect of these developments is the recalibration of the series on a more diverse integrationist basis, as suggested by Jackie's eventual union with the nonwhite Fez.

Ultimately, however, the most sustained and interesting arena for social history in *That '70s Show*—as is the case with so many television shows in our time—is in the realm of gender roles. As noted, the show now seems dated not simply in the way it depicts them but also in the way its creators and audience seem willing to overlook what in a later age would seem to be appalling behavior by men in particular. There are nevertheless crosscurrents at work in the show—crosscurrents that reflected the complex state of the union in the late nineties.

The nineties were a time, like all times, marked by contradictions, albeit of a distinctive kind. Second-wave feminism, which emerged as a discrete social movement in the 1970s, was still alive and well twenty years later. Women continued getting undergraduate educations (55 percent of bachelor's degrees were going to women by 1996),[18] entering the workforce, and achieving high-profile positions—notably Hillary Clinton, a feminist role model who took on the gargantuan task of trying to overhaul the nation's health care system as First Lady of the United States. To be sure, challenges to equity remained, but those challenges were receiving a new level of attention. A good example was that of sexual harassment, highlighted by Anita Hill, who came forward in 1991 to describe abusive behavior by Supreme Court nominee Clarence Thomas. The seriousness with which Hill's accusations were taken during Thomas's Senate confirmation hearings, combined with the fact that Thomas was ultimately confirmed, suggests both progress and limits in the fight for gender equality.[19]

But not all such battles were fought with the same degree of ideological clarity. When *That '70s Show* debuted in 1998, the nation was gripped by the Clinton-Lewinsky scandal that broke that year and would continue into 1999. Bill Clinton had been elected president in 1992 amid—and despite—abundant evidence that his sex life was at best tawdry and at worst abusive to the point of rape.[20] Enough voters were willing to overlook the tendrils of smoke surrounding his reputation to give him the presidency by a plurality his first election, and to give him a reelection majority four years later. But early in his second term it was revealed that he conducted a sexual relationship with White House intern Monica Lewinsky, and the investigation that followed would lead to Clinton's impeachment by the House of Representatives for lying to investigators, though he would be acquitted by the Senate. Many men and women were appalled by Clinton's behavior, though many of these people were also Democrats who supported Clinton's feminist policies, bona fides that came to him in part by way of his wife. This created an uncomfortable situation for some feminists, notably Gloria Steinem, who found themselves bending their principles in the name of their politics.[21] All of which is to say that when it came to gender relations, hypocrisy, contradiction, and ambiguity were deeply familiar to the viewers of *That '70 Show*, which may explain the air of genial cynicism that characterized much of its humor.

Much of this has already been indicated. And there are plenty more examples to choose from, like Jackie's characteristic observation in the 2005 episode "It's All Over Now" that "women should be valued for their looks, men should be valued for their cars, and foreigners should be valued for their ability to sweep." Actually, in her utter disdain for liberal pieties and her evident embrace of materialism, Jackie sometimes seems like a character who wandered in from the 1980s. (Some of the producers of *That '70s Show* did in fact launch an unsuccessful spinoff, *That '80s Show*, which ran on Fox from January to May of 2002.) To some degree, Jackie really did wander into her social circle—a year younger than the other characters, she's repeatedly told she isn't especially liked, criticism that rolls off her and becomes a weird kind of stoicism that leads the other characters to be similarly stoic in dealing with her, as when Donna, who has little in common with Jackie, ends up sharing her bedroom with her when

Jackie's father goes to jail and her mother declines to come home from abroad. Her mother will resurface, portrayed by Brooke Shields, another seventies icon in a metatextual role, playing the part of a vain sex goddess to the hilt. The left has no monopoly on female gender politics.

Other forms of gender conservatism were rooted in values that were less libertarian than traditional. "There are only a few times in life when it's acceptable for a man to use that phrase," Red tells Eric regarding the words "I love you." "When he's drunk, when he's dying, or when he's in big trouble and it's the only way out. Which usually means he's drunk." Somewhat surprisingly given their sometimes-contentious relationship, Eric can seem as conservative as Red when it comes to his own conception of gender roles. In the 2003 episode "The Kids Are Alright," he tells Donna he assumes she'll be a stay-at-home mom, and his rigidity in such matters will play a major role in their breakup in their junior year of high school. When father and son grapple with Kitty's menopause in the 2002 episode "Heartbreaker," they sit down together to consult the *World Book* encyclopedia because they have little idea about what it means.

One of the saddest—apparently unintentionally so—moments of *That '70s Show* occurs in the 2001 episode "The Ice Shack," when Kitty orders Red to remonstrate with their daughter Laurie, who has flunked out at Madison and is adrift. "I'm not really worried," he tells Laurie as he sits beside her on the living room couch still wearing his Price Mart sports coat from work. "Because I know you're going to find a nice guy and get married."

"Exactly," Laurie says.

"Right. Someone who can take care of you, who's rich, who's not Kelso [with whom Laurie has been hooking up]. And I think this is a plan that just might work out for you."

"Okay. But Daddy, I mean, if I wanted to have a career of my own, I could, right?"

"Well, sure," Red says, an insincere smile pasted to his face. "I just don't want you to set yourself up for like what happened at the college. If you set the bar too high the fall might be [pause] you see [pause]

THAT '70S SHOW 141

you're just so pretty [pause]—here's $5." He walks away with a per-
plexed Laurie still sitting on the couch. The irony here is that it's Kitty,
not Red, who's provided most of the economic security the family has
enjoyed in the late seventies.

And yet for all this, there's one notable, if not always consistent,
bright spot in *That '70s Show*: the character of Donna. Quick-witted,
confident, and more than a match for Eric, she's the most likeable
figure on the show, a fully integrated heterosexual woman able and
willing to challenge gender norms—in a mild but unmistakable ges-
ture of production design, her bedroom is painted blue—as well as to
embrace her femininity. She's also willing to embrace her sexuality.
When Red yells at Eric in the 2000 episode "Parents Find Out" for
having intercourse for the first time, she quietly intercedes: "Mr. Forman, it was my idea, too. So please stop yelling at Eric."

Part of her challenge is that others are less comfortable with her
than she is with herself. This includes Eric, who struggles to keep up
with her—an early episode in the show, "Battle of the Sexes," involves
his embarrassment that she keeps beating him in basketball and other
games. It also includes her parents, who can be dismissive of her aspirations. "If women don't stand up for themselves men will always
control the world," she tells Midge in frustration. "That's what the
Equal Rights Amendment is for."[22]

"That's good," Midge replies. "You stick to your principles. And
forty years from now you can tell all your cats how you won a basketball game."

Even Bob, who had so eloquently made his case for her aspirations,
could still dismiss them. Angry at Eric, whose deferral of his undergraduate matriculation had prompted Donna to do the same, Bob
tells him in the 2005 episode "Gimme Shelter," "My daughter stayed
home from college for you. She could have had a bright future. Sure,
she wouldn't be president of a company or anything, because she's a
gal. But she would have made one *hell* of a secretary."

In the face of such thoughtlessness, Donna soldiers on. In season 3
of *That '70s Show*, she lands an internship at a local radio station, where
her energy, enthusiasm, competence—and looks—result in getting

disc jockey airtime as "Hot Donna." Understandably, she downplays her sex appeal, though others are not inclined to let her. "You got that job because you're hot," Kelso tells her in the final season of the show.

"No. I got my job because I know music," she responds.

"Yeah. That's why your nickname is Music-Knowing Donna."

Part of Donna's problem is that she lacks a clear path forward. She has no mentors at the radio station, or anywhere else, though her penchant for wearing vests of the kind Diane Keaton wore in *Annie Hall* (1977) suggests she's looking for feminist role models. She offers sisterhood of a sort for Jackie, who's too clueless to fully understand it as such, though Donna does enjoy a warm relationship with Kitty. Donna's own mother abandons her at a key stage of her adolescence (Tanya Roberts was written out of the show to deal with her terminally ill husband), while her father embarks on the pleasures of sexual liberation. One paramour, Joanne (Mo Gaffney), seems like she might be good stepmother material—she stands up to Red in amusing ways—but, in an inversion of parent-child concerns, Donna has trouble accepting her father's gleeful embrace of extramarital sex. Meanwhile, Eric, though devoted to her, has a more limited imagination than she does. In the finale episode of season 3, "The Promise Ring," Eric gives her a piece of jewelry meant to signal a premarital commitment. But she's not sure. "How do you see the next twenty years?" she asks him.

"I don't know," he replies. "I guess I always figured we'd go to college together and come home—"

"But you know, Eric, that's not what I want. I've told you that. And who knows, I might want to go to school back east or in Paris."

"Okay, well, you know what, Donna? Whatever. Okay. The important thing is that when you see yourself in Paris I'm there, right?" He repeats, "Right?"

"I dunno. Not always. It's not like there's anyone else. But sometimes I'm by myself. All I mean is that I dunno. Neither of us does. And this ring is just a stupid high school promise. If we're meant to be together, we'll be together." In the short run, they won't.

One finds oneself rooting for Donna as *That '70s Show* proceeds; she's fun to watch—in part because Laura Prepon does such a good job of silently reacting to what the other characters are saying. To some degree, Donna is disappointing: did she really need to defer college along with Eric? (She attends a local junior college, a desultory experience as depicted—when depicted.) Her relationship with Randy Pearson (Josh Meyers) in the final season of the show, when Eric is in Africa—Topher Grace wanted out of the show—seems pleasant but not especially fulfilling for character or viewer. Only at the end of the series does she finally seem to mobilize, resolving to set off for the University of Wisconsin, even as Eric returns in the finale and it appears they do have a future together in which she can be her own person. As a matter of the odds—odds of class as well as odds of gender—Donna's future is likely to be one of unrealized aspirations. But we can nevertheless have hope for her and believe that her inner light will remain—and that a torch will eventually be passed.

Donna isn't the only character on *That '70s Show* who evinces gender complexity. Even the cartoonish Kelso plays with the edges of his Lothario persona. Actually, it's possible to think of him as the "dumb brunette" character transposed into a man. He's the one who delivers stupid lines and lands in physically awkward situations, which may lead one to underestimate the craft of Ashton Kutcher's physicality and timing as an actor, much in the way some underestimated earlier stars such as Marilyn Monroe. One of the more tawdry moments in the series occurs in the Thanksgiving-themed 2002 episode, "Thank You," where Kelso brings his math teacher as his date, hoping to improve his transcript along with his sex life. "I make $11,000 a year," she explains lamely of her foray into exploitation. "I deserve a little something." Kelso, for his part, understands his chief asset. "See what happens when you skate through life using your brain?" he tells Donna in a 2005 episode after she explains to her friends that she lost a position at the radio station to a woman who leveraged her sexuality for professional gain. "For the millionth time, people: it's all about the looks."

Again, much of what Kelso says would be patently offensive (or, at any rate, more offensive) if uttered by another actor. But as portrayed by Kutcher, Kelso's utter buoyancy—and stupidity—overwhelms any malice. It also makes him relatively fearless when it comes to bounding across the frontiers of gender performativity. Kelso frequently remarks on his own beauty and doesn't mind when others suggests its feminine overtones—as long as they get it right. When a minor character mocks him for having "Farrah [Fawcett, iconic sex symbol of the seventies] hair," Kelso's response is indignant: "*Farrah* hair? If I look like any of Charlie's Angels, it's Jaclyn Smith!" ("Wow, that's true," Donna quietly realizes.) In the 1999 episode "The Velvet Rope," Jackie, who is Kelso's paramour at the time, embarks on a gender-bending foray with him, applying makeup so as to make him look like androgynous rock stars such as David Bowie. He balks at donning a dress until she points out that Bowie wears dresses and New York Jets quarterback Joe Namath once wore pantyhose. The fun ends when Jackie's father bounds into the room and begins assaulting him before the camera cuts away. The scene is played for laughs; we don't doubt Kelso will spring back on his feet—this, after all, is a guy who fell off the Point Place water tower every year from middle school through high school. (We periodically see him do so.) We also believe, amid stumbling his way through the local police academy, unwed fatherhood, and an eventual job as a bouncer at a Playboy club, that he will land on his feet in other ways too.

One of the more subtle characters when it comes to gender is Steven Hyde. There's no doubt about his male identity, evident everywhere from his walk, his voice, and the macho role models who adorn his T-shirts. He also evinces a form of conspiratorial libertarianism that reflects a typically male obsession with power and autonomy. The first and last episodes of the series depict Hyde speculating on the existence of a water-powered car, which as he explains in the pilot, is being kept from the marketplace by oil companies. In the 2005 episode "Don't Lie to Me," Kelso's prank call to the White House leaves him, Eric, and Hyde panicked about a pending FBI raid on the Forman home. A stoned Hyde says the 1969 moon landing was a hoax: "Spielberg shot the whole thing on a movie set. That's how he got the job for *Jaws*!" Such conspiratorial, loner instincts may be why he and

Red gradually bond over the course of the show. One of the more unlikely pairings in the series is the romance Hyde has with Jackie in the fifth season. Insofar as it makes sense, it's because the two are the most polarized in their gender identities among the teen characters, allowing Hyde to play a strong, silent type to Jackie's feminine extrovert.

And yet it's Hyde who consistently exhibits a unique degree of emotional sensitivity among all the characters. Sometimes his intuitions are comic, as in the split-screen scene in the 2001 episode "Who Wants It More?" where Jackie tells Donna that "sex is how we control men. If they ever find out we want it too, we'll never get jewelry again." Hyde, meanwhile, is telling Eric, "Secretly, I think they want it as much as we do." Eric's reply: "You and your crazy conspiracy theories."

But there's also a string of moments where Hyde demonstrates an understanding of women that's genuinely empathic. In the "Kitty's Birthday" episode later in the same season, he's the only one who notes the date, and he leaves money to help the Forman family, where he's a long-term boarder, when it's in tight financial straits. He's also the first person to congratulate Kitty on what appears to be a late-in-life pregnancy. It's a false hope, but Hyde, unlike Red and Eric, recognizes that it *is* a hope for her rather than a burden to be dreaded. Early in the series, Hyde tries to move in on Donna, but once he recognizes the strength of her tie to Eric settles in as a true friend. In the 2000 episode "Baby Fever," he advises her during a rough patch with Eric: "As the voice of a new generation of smart, independent women, you need to make this dillhole [a censor-friendly euphemism for asshole] realize that a mind and spirit like yours has more options than your mother had." The fact that they're both stoned, and Donna is fixated on the Hostess cupcake she's about to eat, doesn't change the truth of what he's saying. In the 2006 episode "Good Company," Hyde procures what appears to be a lame birthday gift for Donna bearing the words "My parents went to Lake Michigan . . . and all I got was this lousy T-shirt." But it turns out she's been collecting such shirts for the other Great Lakes and this was the only one she lacked.

It would be a mistake to make too much of any of these examples or suggest *That '70s Show* is a progressive portrayal of gender relations or anything else, whether the point of reference is the 1970s, the 1990s, or the 2020s. (Though who knows—decades from now an interested observer may find that the show was ahead of its time in ways scarcely any of us are thinking about now.) It seems fair to say that engagement—whether actually liking or simply choosing to watch—with a television show or any cultural document will implicitly ask a viewer to put aside any number of objections one may have to it. This will be easier or harder for a given viewer to do based on that person's constellation of values and prejudices, which are likely to be widely, but never universally, shared. A lot will depend on who—and when—you are.

CHOOSING THE PAST

Given all its shortcomings, what, then, is the appeal of *That '70s Show*? At bottom, it's an exercise in nostalgia—certainly for any Baby Boomers who may choose to watch it, but also for millennials who may have first looked to it for the origins of their milieu (most of us, for example, show some interest in pop music from before our time) and whose subsequent viewings may serve to remind them of where they were at the time the show was first seen. Though nostalgia—defined by Merriam-Webster as "a wistful or sentimental yearning to return to some past period or irrecoverable condition"[23]—is often considered in hazy emotional terms, it also has an inevitable ideological character: one woman's nostalgia is another man's myth (in the false, as opposed to unverifiable, sense of the term). Operating somewhere inside both, but not quite captured by either, is history: what actually happened. This is never entirely knowable, not only because there was always more going on than we can document but also because we typically have to choose *which* facts that we *do* have are going to be the basis of the stories we tell and hear. And because any such stories are inevitably going to involve human fallibility, we're going to have to choose which shortcomings we're willing to condone or overlook—assuming they're not simply ignored. This is a political decision, even if many of us make it unconsciously.

Which is why there are so many shows out there—and new ones emerge to reach newly formed constituencies. We're not *all* all right, and no one is all *all* right. But sometimes we have to act like we are to get through the day (or the decade) as a matter of practicality or sanity. A little goodwill, a little tolerance, and a sense of humor go a long way in Point Place. And other places, too.

LEFT IN THE KITCHEN

Kerri Russell and Matthew Rhys as Elizabeth and Philip Jennings in a 2017 episode of *The Americans*, set in 1984. The show evinced sympathy for its doomed Soviet idealists even as it affirmed a New Right interpretation of the Cold War.

CHAPTER 6

DOMESTIC FRONT

The Americans as a 2010s Version of the 1980s

Key Cast Members

- Keri Russell as Elizabeth Jennings
- Matthew Rhys as Philip Jennings
- Holly Taylor as Paige Jennings
- Keidrich Sellati as Henry Jennings
- Noah Emmerich as Stan Beeman
- Costa Ronin as Oleg Burov
- Lev Gorn as Arkady Zotov
- Alison Wright as Martha Hanson
- Richard Thomas as Frank Gaad

Key Episodes

- "Pilot" (2013)
- "The Deal" (2014)
- "Echo" (2014)
- "March 8, 1983" (2015)
- "The Magic of David Copperfield V: The Statue of Liberty Disappears" (2016)
- "Persona Non Grata" (2016)
- "Amber Waves" (2017)
- "Dead Hand" (2018)
- "START" (2018)

*F*OR THOSE AMERICANS who were alive during the last couple of decades of the Cold War—the first couple of decades were a different story—it's possible to look back on the tense state of relations between the United States and the Soviet Union with a kind of nostalgia. Yes, the prospect of nuclear war was ever present, and yes, the militarization of American society meant that resources that might have gone into social welfare programs were instead diverted into weapons systems and proxy wars. But compared to the early postwar years, when volatile conflicts in Korea and the Cuban Missile Crisis pushed the world to the brink of apocalypse, such threats and diversions were relatively minor. Moreover, it was the Soviets, not the Americans, who were bogged down in Afghanistan in the 1980s, a conflict that sapped that society even more than the Vietnam War did the United States in the 1960s—or indeed more than Afghanistan would bedevil the United States after the Cold War. By the 1970s, the two superpowers had settled into the diplomatic state known as détente like a bickering old married couple who would never do anything really rash. More importantly, many Americans in the late twentieth century felt comfortable, even smug, about being on the right side of history. The capitalist system on which its economy rested could seem like common sense: flawed for sure, but demonstrably better than the obvious alternative of communism, which seemed worse as both an unattractive theory and a failed reality.

Or so it could seem. In fact, the economic stagnation of the United States in the 1970s and early 1980s was deeply unsettling to Americans who had grown up with expectations of recurring generational upward mobility. And when the economy did begin to pick up in the eighties, it was under the leadership of a president—Ronald Reagan— who engendered worldwide concern over saber-rattling that marked a return to the Cold War's chilliest days. (One good example: Operation Able Archer, a nuclear war simulation that the Soviets briefly believed was the real thing.)[1] Antiwar protesters mobilized in huge numbers at home and abroad over the new militarism that Reagan fostered, most notably in his Strategic Defense Initiative (a.k.a. "Star Wars") that dominated the end of the Cold War. Reagan was widely

derided as an idiot who would be contemptible if he wasn't so dangerous (perhaps that sounds a little familiar).

The Americans, which ran on the FX network from 2013 to 2018,
sought to capture both these realities. The show depicts an affluent
suburban Washington, D.C., family from 1981 to 1987—son, daughter,
parents running a travel agency—in lovingly recreated period detail.
The twist is that those parents, presumably Elizabeth and Philip
Jennings, played by Keri Russell and Matthew Rhys, are actually
undercover KGB agents actively working to sabotage American
political and military operations from within the United States. The
further twist is that by sheer coincidence, they live across the street
from the family of an ambitious FBI agent, Stan Beeman (Noah
Emmerich) who works in counterespionage operations. Over the
course of seventy-five episodes, we witness the everyday lives of Elizabeth and Philip with an intimacy that invites implicit sympathy. As
such, the show is part of a long tradition in American popular culture,
stretching from Gone with the Wind to The Man in the High Castle,
that depicts events from the point of view of losers in a repellent
cause. Like those other examples, The Americans is finally a vindica-
tion of what used to be called the American way of life, a sensibility
that views itself as above ideology—a matter of "the humane trump-
ing the political," in the words of Emmerich.[2] Whether or not this is
actually true, and for all the ambiguities and tragedies that surround
it, The Americans is finally a patriotic love song: the Cold War as a
good war in which right values and necessary actions prevailed.

SPYING POSSIBILITIES

The immediate roots of The Americans lie in a real-life espionage
case. In 2010, the Federal Bureau of Investigation arrested ten illegal
Russian agents in the United States, including Cynthia and Richard
Murphy, a.k.a. Lidiya and Vladimir Guryev, who lived in Montclair,
New Jersey, with their two daughters. Cynthia held degrees from
NYU and Columbia and held down an accounting job that earned
her $135,000 a year. Another couple, Donald Heathfield and Tracey

Lee Ann Foley, were based in Boston, though their two sons were born in Canada. One son successfully pleaded to retain his citizenship in a 2019 case, while the other was denied because he was suspected to have been recruited as an agent by his parents (as indeed the Jennings daughter, Paige, played by Holly Taylor, would be in *The Americans*). Yet another agent, Mikhail Semenko, worked for a travel agency; the Jenningses of *The Americans* would own one.[3]

"That was absolutely the inspiration for the series," Joe Weisberg, who developed it with his partner Joel Fields, told *Time* magazine in 2010. Weisberg read John le Carré's classic 1963 novel *The Spy Who Came In from the Cold* as a child and went on to Yale, where he took classes in a history department that was anchored by Richard Pipes, a prominent—and strongly anticommunist—historian of the Soviet Union. Weisberg, the son of a civil rights lawyer, whose brother Jacob edited the pioneering online magazine *Slate*, went on to serve a stint in the Central Intelligence Agency between 1990 and 1994 before moving on to writing fiction, supporting himself by teaching. He was intrigued by the 2010 arrests, but he also believed he needed to adapt the stories he was hearing. "A modern day [setting] didn't seem like a good idea," he explained. "People were both shocked and simultaneously shrugged at the scandal because it didn't seem like we were really enemies with Russia anymore. An obvious way to remedy that for television was to set the scenario back in the Cold War. At first, the '70s appealed to me just because I loved the hair and the music. But can you think of a better time than the '80s with Ronald Reagan yelling about the evil empire?"[4] Indeed, the title of season 3 finale of the show, "March 8, 1983" (2015) takes its title from the date of the speech when Reagan used that phrase—he's seen making it on television—and other episodes of *The Americans* explicitly name Able Archer, the ARPANET (the military forerunner of the Internet), and arms control negotiations as part of their plots.

Weisberg came to the attention of Canadian television producer Graham Yost, whose credits include the riveting FX series *Justified* (2010–2015), based on the crime fiction of the great Elmore Leonard. Yost liked Weisberg's 2007 novel *An Ordinary Spy* and went on to be executive producer of the show, brokering a connection between

Weisberg and network executives, who in turn introduced Weisberg to veteran writer and producer Joel Fields. The two—known as "J&J," or "the Js"—secured backing from FX and Steven Spielberg's company, Amblin Entertainment.[5]

The showrunners adopted a strategy of casting against type for the two leads. The first major actor to be recruited for the show was Keri Russell—previously known for appearing in *The All-New Mickey Mouse Club* (1989–1995) and as the star of the now-classic *Felicity* (1998–2002), which focused on the adventures of a college student in Manhattan. A lustrous-haired beauty, Russell absorbed what seems like a punishing regimen of close-ups without vanity and was oddly believable in her role, since in fact so much of her character involved pretending to be somebody else (the show was notable for its almost comic, but always compelling, hair, makeup, and costume changes). Russell was followed by the Welsh Matthew Rhys (who sounds remarkably different in real life than the character he plays but maintains a similarly affable off-screen persona). Rhys would later form a romantic attachment with Russell, with whom she would have a son. One noteworthy addition to the cast was Richard Thomas of *The Waltons* fame as Stan Beeman's boss, Frank Gaad. Forty-one years separate the debuts of the two shows.[6]

The Americans made an unprepossessing entrance onto the cultural landscape when it premiered on January 30, 2013. It did so as a standard cable TV show two days before Netflix inaugurated a new era in television viewing with its simultaneous release of thirteen episodes of *House of Cards*, creating the possibility of binge-watching new shows. Besides the sheer novelty of *House of Cards*, which was an instant hit, *The Americans* was also competing with cable giants such as *Mad Men* (2007–2015), *Breaking Bad* (2008–2013), and *Game of Thrones* (2011–2019).[7] By prevailing and earlier standards, the show was not a major hit, averaging a little over a million viewers over the course of its six seasons.[8] But it also arrived at a time when such figures were increasingly less relevant, since time-shifting and streaming increasingly meant a television show was becoming something like a back-listed book: a piece of content whose audience could grow over time, and an asset that could become part of a larger cultural stable for the media company that acquired it. Like good literary fiction, *The Americans* developed a coterie of positive critical opinion and was soon a fixture of cultural commentary for the length of its run.

One reason for the show's appeal is that it's more than an action-thriller of the James Bond variety (even if there was plenty of suspense, along with sex and violence). *The Americans*, as Weisberg and Fields have repeatedly testified, is a show about unholy matrimony—"the most profound show about marriage on television," in the words of one headline at the time. "*The Americans* is a show of heartbreaking marriage moments," Fields said after its run was over. Weisberg agreed. "It all goes back to the marriage," he said in 2018. "It started out as a show about a marriage and it stayed that all along. It's about a couple in a very odd and unusual situation. Despite that, everything they experience and felt and went through, we always thought could be relatable to everyone."[9] In a shrewd observation, *New Yorker* writer Amy Davidson agreed: "It's often said, admiringly, that *The Americans* is a show about marriage that is dressed up as a spy drama. One of its premises is that marriage itself is a matter of dressing up and performing, and that those enactments, particularly when children are watching, can be its most genuine part."[10]

That said, it's equally evident that Elizabeth and Philip—Nadezhda and Mikhail, or "Mischa," as they are known to almost no one else—are not a typical married couple. Elizabeth was born in 1940 in Smolensk, in western Russia, living through World War II in extreme privation. Her father was a deserter in the Soviet army; she lived with her mother in an apartment with three other families and cared for her when she was afflicted with diphtheria. Philip was born in the Asian Russian city of Tobolsk in 1942, also raised by his mother (Philip believed his father, who died when he was six, was a logger; we later learn he was a prison guard at a logging camp). Both Elizabeth and Philip were recruited into the KGB in late adolescence, where their training included the arts of self-defense—and offense—as well as techniques of sexual seduction and control. They are paired for the purposes of espionage and given cover as a married couple who actually do produce two children. As the series opens, there's some ambiguity about the actual degree of their attachment to each other—Philip seems to love Elizabeth more than she loves him—but while they have their ups and downs, which includes a trial separation, their marital bond deepens over time, sealed by a religious ceremony with a Russian Orthodox priest in the finale of the show's fifth season.

Besides the shared experience of often harrowing joint operations, Elizabeth and Philip do have important things in common. One is the occasionally dizzying experience of American affluence after childhoods of Soviet deprivation, reinforced by the show's set design.[11] "We didn't have anything; now we have everything. It's so strange sometimes," he muses to her one night in bed during the 2017 episode "Crossbreed." "I know," she replies. The two are also linked by their evident devotion to their children: elder daughter Paige and younger son Henry (Keidrich Sellati). In the early years of the show, Elizabeth and Philip are able to hide their activities from the kids, though this becomes increasingly difficult. It also becomes increasingly difficult to suspend one's disbelief that genuine love and devotion can coexist alongside an espionage career. As *New Yorker* TV critic Emily Nussbaum tartly noted, "*The Americans* would be a romantic story if they weren't such murderous psychopaths."[12] As such, the show is of a moment with others, among them *Breaking Bad* and *Mad Men*, that invite viewers to empathize with people who do truly terrible things—and lead us to ask ourselves why we do so.

Elizabeth and Philip are not the only ones who must weigh the state of their souls against those of the state and sheer self-preservation. Stan Beeman, whose backstory includes infiltration of the Ku Klux Klan, battles estrangement from his wife, whom he eventually divorces, and their teenage son. Stan confides his troubles to (as he believes) his good friend Philip, who appears to sincerely like Stan, notwithstanding the fact that he's his professional enemy.

The Americans also features a whole set of plot lines set in the Soviet rezidentura in Washington, where staff of the Russian embassy live and which acts as a hub of activity, legal and otherwise, for the staff there. These include Arkady Zotov (Lev Gorn), who manages the operation, along with agents Oleg Burov (Costa Ronin) and Nina Krilova (Annet Mahendru), who gets involved in a complex romantic triangle involving Stan and Oleg. This side of the operation is rounded out by a couple of different handlers, notably Gabriel (Frank Langella) and Claudia (the magnificently versatile Margo Martindale) who mediate between the rezidentura and the Jenningses. Over the course of the series all of these people must weigh competing imperatives and make dangerous, often excruciating choices—none more than Nina, who is eventually jailed and killed for her choices, which include sacrifice for a Soviet scientist who defected to the West and was repatriated by force thanks to Philp. Though they are all presumably villains in the eyes of American audiences, we come to recognize these Soviets as honorable, if fallible, people. Actually, notwithstanding the marriage discourse, it's such dilemmas of competing loyalties more than anything else that comes to define *The Americans*: the question of what, finally, is worth living—and dying—for.

NOTHING PERSONAL

For Elizabeth, there's little question about what she's living and willing to die for: the Motherland. For all the twists and turns in the show's plot, it's the lodestar that guides all her actions. This includes her treatment of her husband and children, though she's never inclined to see an irrevocable conflict between them. "I am a KGB officer. Don't you understand that?" she tells Philip in the show's pilot episode when they disagree about how to handle a KGB agent who has defected to the West (Philip thinks the situation is too hot to handle and wants to make a deal with the Americans). "After all these years, I would *die*, I would lose *everything* before I would betray my country," she tells him. Elizabeth also has personal motivations here: this agent raped her when she was in training, and she will ultimately kill him. But the episode shows how tightly bound the personal and the political are for her.

The Americans can also show how disposable the personal can be in the service of the political. When, in the 2015 episode "Do Mail Robots Dream of Electric Sheep?" (an allusion to the 1968 Philip K. Dick story "Do Androids Dream of Electric Sheep?" which was the basis of the 1982 film *Blade Runner*, contemporaneous with the setting of this episode), Elizabeth comes upon the mother of the person whose work the couple is in the process of sabotaging. It's clear that Elizabeth intends to kill this unwelcome complication of her mission, but they have a revealing conversation before this happens:

BETTY: Do you have children?
ELIZABETH: Yes.
BETTY: And this is what you do?
ELIZABETH: Sometimes.
BETTY: By yourself?
ELIZABETH: Sometimes with my husband.
BETTY: Why?
ELIZABETH: To make the world a better place.
BETTY: You think doing this to me will make the world a better place?
ELIZABETH: I'm sorry, but I do.
BETTY: That's what evil people tell themselves when they do evil things.

Betty is forced by Elizabeth to take an overdose of her prescription medicine, then dies in what will be regarded as an accidental death. Elizabeth is shaken—we do see necessary moments of humanity in a character whose sense of competence and commitment are as impressive as they are appalling—but she never fundamentally changes course.

We get a glimpse of why in one of the periodic flashbacks that pepper *The Americans*. "Do you know why you were chosen for America?" her mentor, General Viktor Zhukov, asks her in a 1976 flashback. "Because of my commitment," she answers. "Yes," Zhukov says. "Loyalty. Intelligence. Skills. But most of all you were chosen for your fear."

"My fear?" a surprised Elizabeth responds.

"Of surrender. Surrender for you would be an act of suicide." But, he warns her, "not everyone is your enemy." Elizabeth shows unfeigned grief when she learns Zhukov has been murdered in Moscow.

Philip is also a Soviet patriot. We seem him capable of all manner of violence, and he commits a truly awful betrayal by presenting himself as Clark Westerfeld, a suitor for the credulous Martha Hanson (Alison

Wright), an FBI secretary whom he marries in a civil ceremony—passing off Elizabeth as his sister and Claudia as his mother. This sustained ruse will ultimately result in Martha's unceremonious exfiltration to Russia, where she will have to begin her life all over again, alone. Despite such ruthlessness, Philip is less of an ideologue than Elizabeth, a stance that at times shades into explicit doubt. "What's *so* bad about it?" he asks her about the United States in the pilot, suggesting that maybe they should defect to the West for the sake of the family. "The electricity works all the time, the food's pretty great, closet space—" But she's incredulous, slapping him in the face, and he backs off. The following season, in "New Car," in which Philip buys a new Chevy Camaro, he tries again:

PHILIP: Don't you enjoy any of this? Sometimes? This house, the clothes, all those beautiful shoes? It doesn't make you bad at what you do. It just makes you a human being. Don't you ever like it?
ELIZABETH: That's not why I'm here.
PHILIP: Don't you ever like it?
ELIZABETH: We *have* to live this way. For our job, for our cover. Five miles from here there are people—
PHILIP: Do you like it?
ELIZABETH: You know how I grew up. It's nicer here, yes. It's not better.

And in some ways, she's right. *The Americans* does give us glimpses into the darker side of American life. Having sex with other people is just part of the job for Elizabeth and Philip, but she has genuine feelings for Gregory Thomas, an African American civil rights activist she recruited into the KGB many years earlier. While we may not accept Gregory's belief that the Soviets represent a viable alternative, it's clear that he has legitimate grievances with American life, which are indicated by the gritty milieu in which we find him. While Philip's stance is more muted—in part because he rightly considers Gregory a rival for Elizabeth's affections—he professes a similar idealism. "I still believe in those things," he tells his daughter Paige, who has learned, in the partial way she always does about her parents, that they were activists in their youth. "You just get older, and other things become more important," he says, tousling Henry's hair. "And you realize there are a lot of ways to make a difference."

The most ominous stretch of episodes of *The Americans*, which center on season 4 (2016), involve biological warfare research. This is something both sides in the Cold War have pledged not to do, but both seem to take for granted that neither will honor their promises, and it's yet another front in which the Americans have a clear advantage. In these episodes, Elizabeth and Philip team up with William Crandall (Dylan Baker, an actor who brings a creepy yet sympathetic overlay to his characters) who plays a Soviet secret agent who has been working in an American biological warfare plant. They're able to acquire a pathogen they consider necessary to maintain a balance of power—and we will later learn the Soviets deploy it in their war in Afghanistan. There are limits to how much access they can gain, however, for reasons that go to the heart of Soviet-American conflict. "There's a military facility we can't get into," another agent observes at one point in the 2016 episode "Munchkins." "But they can't stop being Americans," she notes dryly. "They subcontract it out to a private lab." William will ultimately die an agonizing death when he purposely infects himself rather than become a captured asset for the Americans, but his semi-delirious meditations on his loneliness and admiration for Elizabeth and Philip, whom he describes as living the American Dream, will become a valuable clue for Stan when he finally begins to realize who his neighbors really are.

The harshness and even terror of the Cold War also surfaces in more quotidian ways. There's the 2016 episode "The Day After," for example, which refers to the two-part movie broadcast by ABC in 1983 that realistically portrays the outbreak of a nuclear war. "That's why your mother and I do what we do," Philip tells a shaken Paige, who has been watching the show and is learning more about her parents' work. "To keep things like that from happening."

"Do you really think it makes a difference?" she asks.

"I don't know."

Philip's uncertainty on this question becomes the source of the key conflict in the Jennings marriage: how and whether to tell their children about their identities. The couple is deeply unsettled by an event that absorbs much of the show's second season in 2014: the brutal murder of another KGB couple and their daughter in a hotel room near an amusement park both families had visited. This is perplexing to both the FBI and the KGB; we learn in the season finale, "Echo," that it was the family's teenaged son who committed the act because his parents were opposed to his recruitment as a Soviet spy, which had taken place through another agent with whom he had fallen in love. Dying himself after aiding Elizabeth and Philip in killing a navy special operative who was out to get the Jenningses over their disruption of his operation in Nicaragua, the boy describes the killings of his as "what we do; it's for something greater than ourselves." What's even more chilling is that Claudia informs Elizabeth and Philip that the KGB has similar designs on their eldest child, who is now an adolescent: "Paige is your daughter. But she's not just yours. She belongs to the cause and the world. You haven't forgotten that, have you?" Philip flatly rejects this premise, and tells Arkady (whom he's not supposed to meet) that if the KGB approaches Paige, he'll quit. But Elizabeth is not so sure. "She's looking for something," she tells Philip. His response: "It would destroy her." One way to read the ensuing four seasons of *The Americans* is as a struggle for Paige's soul.

The problem, as anyone who has raised a child knows, is that Paige has a mind of her own. While still ignorant of what it is her parents actually do for a living, she rebels in a manner that's both amusing and characteristic of her moment in the early eighties: she becomes an evangelical Christian, joining the congregation of Pastor Tim (Kelly AuCoin), a charismatic preacher who is eager to mentor her. Paige's parents are appalled. Elizabeth reacts like a mother who's learned that her daughter has just befriended a drug dealer. "You protect them from the big things out there, the big life and death dangers, and then something finds its way into your *house*," she tells Philip disgustedly in the 2014 episode "A Little Night Music." Elizabeth then connects that disgust to a broader ideological critique: "We're failing to help them stand up to the distractions, the consumerism." she tells Philip of their children. "I mean, look at this country. Church, synagogue—that's what's holding this all up. The opiate of the masses."

It's not exactly clear how consumerism connects to evangelicalism, since they're presumably antithetical impulses, but there's no question the two grew in tandem in the eighties.

Philip isn't any happier about Paige's discovery of Christ than Elizabeth is, but he handles it in a characteristically more personal way, going to the pastor's church and physically threatening him. But Tim doesn't back down; one of the more interesting aspects of the show is its refusal to turn him into an evangelical caricature. "There is grace and forgiveness for everyone," he tells Philip during that confrontation in the 2014 episode "Martial Eagle."

"You really believe that?" Philip retorts.

"I do," Tim responds, and Philip backs off. For the next few years, the Jenningses are stuck with Pastor Tim, who becomes even more of a millstone around their necks after Paige learns about her parents' activities and confides in him. They are eventually able to secretly orchestrate an appealing missionary position for him and his family in Buenos Aires, but his take on the Jenningses, which they learn from a pilfered diary in the 2017 episode "Darkroom," is brutal in its clarity. "Are they monsters?" he asks. "I don't know. But what they did to their daughter I'd have to call monstrous. I've seen sexual abuse, I've seen affairs, but nothing I've seen compares to what P. J. [Paige Jennings] has been through." Another passage that's photographed and hanging in the Jenningses' improvised darkroom: "There's a psychic injury. Faith may help but I fear the damage is done. How can she trust anyone ever again?"

This, as it turns out, is a key question. Paige is increasingly suspicious of her parents' whereabouts—they seem awfully solicitous of their travel agency clients—and they're eventually compelled to let her in on their secret. But this proceeds in stages. When, for example, Paige asks them in the 2016 episode "Experimental Prototype Community of Tomorrow" (EPCOT) whether "people get hurt because of things you're involved with," they answer "No" and "Of course not" simultaneously. "Paige, you know us better than that," Elizabeth tells her.

Elizabeth takes primary responsibility for Paige's education, which ranges from martial arts classes in the garage to indoctrination marked by more than a whiff of disinguousness. When, in the 2016 episode "Glanders" (which refers to a form of biological warfare)

Paige asks her to explain what a source is and whether cultivating them is dangerous, she replies, "It's more about getting people to trust you. To help them understand that you want the same thing they want, which is to make the world a safer place for everyone. Not everyone sees it that way, so it has to be done in secret." Elizabeth recites Marxist doctrine without an air of irony: "Revolution is necessary to create and achieve a worker's state so that no one is exploited," she tells Paige in the 2017 episode "Crossbreed." "I mean, my whole country came out of those ideas." Late into the final season, Elizabeth continues to tell Paige outright lies, as when she denies she has ever used her sexual power as a means of getting information. In the service of her mission, she ends up secretly seducing a young man in whom Paige had a personal interest.

Over the course of the series, Paige increasingly falls under her mother's sway, eventually discarding the cross necklace she wears. (Ironically, Elizabeth orders her to put it back on: Pastor Tim must continue to be managed, and Paige's work with the church now becomes a tedious piece of espionage management.) Philip is not happy about his daughter's steady ensnarement, but he's powerless to stop it. His scruples about the Jenningses' activities eventually reach the point by the end of season 5 that he opts out entirely. In the final season of *The Americans*, he's working at the travel agency full-time for real—and slouching toward bankruptcy—taking primary responsibility for Henry while Elizabeth continues espionage activities as well as her tutelage of Paige, who by this point is down with the program and actively mentored by Claudia. But as many a mobster has learned in the history of popular culture, a life of crime has a way of catching up with you, even when you're determined to put it behind you. (Oleg Burov, who returns to Moscow after the death of his brother in the Afghan war, also finds that his double-dealings in Washington cast long shadows.) But in an important sense, it's the series that's written itself into a corner. How long can Stan Beeman, who among other things is a surrogate father to Henry, stay clueless? When will the looming end of the Cold War, which was ordained from the outset, finally breach the walls of Elizabeth's certitude? And how much longer can we the viewers take seriously the proposition that a couple can be dedicated spies and good parents at the same time? These questions loom increasingly large by the fifth season, which is marked by something of a course correction.

THE RIGHT STUFF

The Americans is a show that seeks to convey a sense of clear-eyed realism. One way it does so is through graphic depictions of sex and violence that can be discomfiting in their detachment, as when we get grim or distracted facial shots of Elizabeth or Philip, for whom seduction of people they barely know or viscerally dislike is all in a night's work. The show also makes some effort to depict the cynicism that marks both Soviet and American life in giving us unlikeable figures on both sides and characters who make knowing asides. When, in the 2014 episode "The Deal," Arkady notes that "we are better at vodka; they are better at tobacco," he's making a statement about more than Soviet and American vices—he's also ironically conveying a credible assertion of moral equivalence between the superpowers.

In the last two seasons of *The Americans*, however, there's a perceptible shift in the tenor of its depiction of the Cold War in which the Americans are not only winning but are also *right* to be winning. In the season 5 premiere, "Amber Waves," we are introduced to a family of Russian immigrants, the Morozovs, whom the Jenningses are in process of infiltrating with what will be disastrous results for the family. The father, Alexei (Alexander Sokovikov), is working as a consultant with the U.S. Department of Agriculture, which is why the Jenningses are stalking him. With their own kids in a more independent adolescence, Philip and Elizabeth are now running a second fictive household as Brad and Dee Eckert, which includes an adopted Vietnamese son, Tuan (Ivan Mok), also an operative, who is manipulating the Morozovs' son so that he and his mother will want to leave the country. Over a cordial dinner with their new neighbors, Alexei complains about the Motherland. Alexei's wife Evgheniya (Irina Dvorovenko) remonstrates about his kvetching with their American guests, but Alexei persists. "It's the truth. You want food, you stand in line," he says of the Soviet Union. "Do you see any lines for food here? No, go to store, they have so much of everything, it's a beautiful sight. You choose. You would not believe what you see in Soviet Union."

"That bad?" Philip asks in his most ingenuous voice.

"We share apartment with three families," Alexei says of his former life. "We share toilets, bathroom. You want a phone, you pay a bribe. Phone breaks, you bribe."

"What did you do there?" Philip follows up in a spirit of polite inquiry.

"Complain," Evgheniya interjects. "Same like here."

"You hear me complain about America?" he asks her in Russian, oblivious that Elizabeth and Philip understand every word.

The argument here is plain: prosperity trumps ideology, though it may be more accurate to say that prosperity becomes its own form of ideology. This notion actually animates a big part of the season, which turns on a Soviet fear that the Americans are developing pests to decimate the Soviet grain crop, a plot they believe Alexei is furthering. The truth, however, is far different: the U.S. government is working to develop hardier strains of wheat in ways that will help capitalism while ensuring a more secure global food supply, something Elizabeth learns when the Kansan biologist she's developing turns out to be actually kind of a good guy. It doesn't take the KGB long to decide it doesn't matter: they still need to steal the technology. In the case of biological weapons, which both sides were using in violation of treaties with each other, it was easier to argue for moral equivalence. But here the KGB's conspiratorial mindset continues in the face of positive intentions, because whatever's good for one side is going to be bad for the other.

This is something that Stan, for all his cluelessness, understands very well. He gives what amounts to a brief speech in another dinner table scene, this one a Thanksgiving toast in the 2018 episode "Rafifi":

> "You know, not everybody around the world wants us to live in peace and freedom. But aren't those the things that Pilgrims came here for in the first place? You ask me, we should all be willing to fight to hang

on to them. Because there are people out there who don't like our way of life. They're afraid of it. Of us. And we have an administration right now, President Reagan and his people, they know the only way to get to peace is to stand firm against those who wish us harm—and believe me, they wish to do us harm. Make no mistake about that. Happy Thanksgiving."

Elizabeth is missing this meal because she's frantically trying to stop the exposure of her identity by an operative in Chicago; Philip and Paige look on grim-faced. Stan's partner Dennis Aderholt (Brandon J. Dirden), who is African American, nods approvingly. (One of the key plot points in season 1 was the death of Stan's previous partner, Chris Amador, played by Maximiliano Hernández. He was killed by Philip in his guise as Martha's paramour.) As Dennis says to Stan at one point in the episode, "They want to look peaceful, but they're really just trying to screw us."[13] The fact that there are people of color on the team—and that Gregory Thomas dies a tragic death protesting American racism by siding with an ally of questionable legitimacy— is indicative of the tilt of the show.

In a 2018 podcast noting the fidelity of his character to a country where "the American Dream has failed people who look like me," Dirden notes Aderholt's "extreme faith in the United States of America and the promises that it will offer." Dirden observes that a number of characters, American and Soviet, nevertheless pledge their allegiance to question-able institutions.[14] But while Dirden's own implicit skepticism is clear, the overall thrust of the show suggests that Aderholt's faith is not ultimately misplaced—just as President Reagan's hard line on the Soviet Union, after a long period of détente between the Soviets and the United States, showed that the Cold War could be won without mutu-ally assured destruction. This appears to be the implicit logic of the series.

Meanwhile, the dubiousness of the Soviet model comes into stark focus—first for Philip, eventually for Elizabeth—in perhaps the only way it can: a fractious debate from within. In 1985, Mikhail Gorbachev succeeded to the premiership of the Soviet Union after a generation of sclerotic leadership and began to vigorously advocate reform of its government. Not surprisingly, the entrenched bureaucracy—and the military—found such moves threatening and maneuvered to stop it, a campaign that dominates the final season of *The Americans*. Oleg Burov decides to risk his family and his career in an effort to aid the reform efforts, enlisting a reluctant Philip back into the spy game, which he secretly rejoins without telling Elizabeth. That's because she sides with the old guard: "All this talk of perestroika [restructuring] and glasnost [openness]," she irritably says to Philip in the 2018 episode "Urban Transport Planning," using the buzz terms of the Gorbachev moment. "The Americans eat it up. They want us to be just like them. I don't want to be just like them! And neither do the people back home." Given how long she's been in the States, Philip wonders how she'd know. She bounces the same point back to him.

These episodes take place against the backdrop of the so-called Washington Summit of December 1987 between the United States and the Soviets. That event, in turn, took place against another summit in Reykjavik, Iceland, the previous year in which Reagan stunned Gorbachev—and his own advisers—by boldly pressing a "zero option" to remove intermediate range nuclear weapons from Europe entirely. Gorbachev was not prepared to accept the idea then but would ultimately do so in Washington, an outcome that Elizabeth's faction is frantically trying to prevent with a body count that gets high even by *Americans* standards. Elizabeth's growing unease about what she's being told to do leads her to change her mind—and to part company with Claudia, with whom she and Paige, now a full-fledged agent, have grown close. In some sense, this is all moot, because the walls are finally closing in on the Jenningses as Stan begins to put the pieces together. The showdown moment of the series is a ten-minute scene between him and a fleeing Elizabeth, Philip, and Paige in an underground garage at George Washington University, where Paige is a student. (Henry, off in boarding school in New Hampshire, remains innocent.) Stan is understandably furious at what he sees as a personal betrayal. He regards Philip as his best friend and has come to think of Henry as a surrogate son. But in the words of Noah Emmerich, who plays him, "Stan is bigger than his anger," and he lets them go.[15] This, in the foundational logic of the show, is what makes the Americans American: a sense of limits. A value that Philip—and, yes, even Elizabeth—finally assimilates.

There is a rough justice in the outcome of Elizabeth and Philip Jennings. They end up back in Moscow—a place that, after so many years away, cannot but be experienced as a kind of exile, especially since they return without their children. Henry was agonizingly relinquished without a word of explanation (we are meant to understand that Stan will stand by him); Paige makes a breathtaking decision to leave her parents behind at the Canadian border. In the end, Philip and Elizabeth's—Nadezhda and Mischa's—real legacy is what they've generated together and what they leave behind. Wars are for the world. But home is where your heart is.

THE NEXT FUTURE

One of the more curious aspects of The Americans is that it invites us to commiserate with Elizabeth and Philip Jennings—the enemy. We watch them knowing, as they do not, that the Soviet system to which they've pledged their allegiance is doomed, and there's a certain pathos to this: all their efforts, strenuous as they are, will ultimately be for naught. Some of us may also feel a twinge of identification in that we also know that the American way of life—something we're so squarely in the middle of it that its contours can be hard to grasp, which is precisely why shows like this one are appealing—is also mortal.

Nowadays, it's the other great Communist power on the bloc, China, that now seems far more challenging. What's striking about this is not so much China's military might, which is considerable and growing. It's that Chinese society seems to have a dynamism, an optimism about the future, that used to be the hallmark of American identity, even if China has more than its fair share of problems and the United States was never as pristine as its fondest champions imagine. Still, such mythologies are potent, which is one major reason why The Americans has such a nostalgic feel to it: once upon a time, we were the future.

COMPUTER GAMES

Donna Clark (Kerry Bishé) and Cameron Howe (Mackenzie Davis) play office politics in a 2016 episode of *Halt and Catch Fire*. The show depicted the rise of the Internet from a series of unusual perspectives: Texas rather than Silicon Valley; women rather than men; losers rather than winners.

CHAPTER 7

PROGRAMMING HOPE

Halt and Catch Fire as a 2010s Version of the 1990s

Key Cast Members

- Lee Pace as Joe MacMillan
- Scoot McNairy as Gordon Clark
- Kerry Bishé as Donna Clark
- Mackenzie Davis as Cameron Howe
- Toby Huss as John Bosworth

Key Episodes

- "I/O" (pilot, 2014)
- "Giant" (2014)
- "SETI" (2015)
- "Limbo" (2015)
- "neXt" (2016)
- "You Are Not Safe" (2016)
- "Ten of Swords" (2017)

OVER THE COURSE of the last half-century, computers have gone from large, highly complex, expensive, and remote pieces of machinery to pervasive, ordinary facts of everyday life. The pace of change in this transformation was particularly notable in the decades on either side of the year 2000, which witnessed the rise of personal laptop computers and the transformation of the Internet from a government-run military and research utility to the engine of the

American economy. This was a big deal—and experienced as such by those of us who lived through it.

That said, while we moderns tend to think that which has happened most recently represents the most momentous of changes, the computer revolution is not all that big in the larger scheme of things. The advent of the railroad, for example, transformed the nation's landscape more dramatically, literally and figuratively, than the Internet has (and required a lot more people to do it). Electric lighting, telephones, motor vehicles—these too were transformative. Most transformative of all are less dramatic but decisive innovations in saving, extending, and improving lives: modern sewage systems and clean water. A person who witnessed the changes in the United States between 1850 and 1900 experienced more change in the fabric of daily life than anyone in the century or so since.[1]

Computers don't even represent the most important communications revolution in American history. That honor belongs to the invention of telegraphy by Samuel F. B. Morse in 1844, which represented something new under the sun: the conquest of time and space. For the first time in history, it was possible to transmit a message instantly without anyone having to deliver it in person, merely by stringing a copper wire over which electrical signals could be sent in the form of Morse code. In the years that followed, the world became dramatically smaller; cables were laid across the ocean, reducing message travel times from weeks to seconds. The spread of the telegraph also sparked the drive the next technological quest, to eliminate the need for the wire and achieve wireless communication—what came to be known as radio.

That this process took the remainder of the nineteenth century and another generation before it assumed a modern form as broadcasting is a reminder that the measure of technological revolutions is decades, even lifetimes. The first movies were available to viewers on kinetoscopes—machines for individual viewing that were set up in parlors in major cities—but it wasn't until the 1920s that film projection, studio production, and a star system created the culture of Hollywood as we know it. Television, which grew out of radio, was technically possible in the 1920s, but it wasn't until the 1950s that it became a household fixture (in large measure because the Great Depression and World War II impeded the refinement of the necessary technology, which was diverted into radar, and delayed the economic conditions necessary for mass production, distribution, and purchase). For long periods of time, it wasn't clear where any of these new media were headed or how long they would take to arrive—and, perhaps most importantly, who would control them. There were false starts, wrong turns, and unforeseen developments that eluded even the most farsighted people.

Such considerations are worth keeping in mind when considering the trajectory of computers in American life, because doing so reminds us that for all its uniqueness, this technological revolution was not unprecedented in some important respects. It also reminds us that any attempt to tell the story of such a revolution will inevitably have selective contours in terms of when it starts, ends, and is situated relative to other pivotal moments in U.S. history. It's in this light that *Halt and Catch Fire*, a television drama covering the period between 1983 and 1994 that ran between 2014 and 2017, emerges as a surprising and revealing interpretation of national experience, a quirky rendering of a story whose sharper edges have sanded down by familiarity.

Considered in the context of television history as a whole—or, for that matter, considered in the context of the other shows in this book—*Halt and Catch Fire* is a curio, even a blip on the screen. While titanically successful shows like *The Waltons* or *M*A*S*H* routinely drew tens of millions of viewers weekly, *Halt and Catch Fire* barely crept over the million mark in its debut episode (when it had a lead-in from *Mad Men*, a show with which it was often compared) and pretty much went steadily downhill from there, bottoming out at roughly 270,000 viewers at one point in its fourth and final season.[2] That it lasted as long as it did was itself something of an accident of history, as the show debuted right in the heart of the era of Peak TV, when cable networks were willing to take chances on shows that could find audiences through streaming later.[3] Of course, an audience of a quarter of a million would be huge in some media (like publishing), and it's likely that many more people have seen the show, a critical darling, in the years since.[4] But it's safe to say that in a television context *Halt and Catch Fire* is, and may always be, relatively obscure. It is nevertheless worth noting and remembering, not only in terms of its intrinsic merit as a piece of storytelling but for the important statement it makes—a statement about how the blend of technology, capitalism, and personality fuels the engine of history.

TEXAS TECH

It was not only unlikely that *Halt and Catch Fire* would last as long as it did; it's also surprising that it ever got made in the first place. The show's creators, Christopher Cantwell and Christopher Rogers, were new to television, and the concept was initially developed as a practice run, a version of something they never expected to get made but as training for something that eventually would.

Cantwell was born in Chicago circa 1982 and moved to Dallas as a child, where his father, a salesman, made his way into the computer business. Cantwell attended the University of Southern California, where he learned the craft of television writing. He eventually landed a job at Disney as the creative director for social media online marketing, where he hired Rogers to organize and manage content on Facebook. Rogers, for his part, also trained to be a television writer at the University of California at Los Angeles, and graduated from the Writer's Guild of America's prestigious Showrunner Training Program. The two began collaborating and an early result was "The Knoll"—a screenplay about the Kennedy assassination that made it onto the famed "Black List" of unmade projects that nevertheless raises the profiles of those on it. Their agents told them to develop something new as a way of refining their fledgling craft. The result was a script on speculation for *Halt and Catch Fire*, which they completed in 2011. Their agents sent the project to HBO and Showtime, where they got the requisite encouraging rejection (no thanks, but send us what you do next). After extensive deliberations, AMC decided to take the plunge, signing the project in 2012 and beginning production the following year, bringing in veteran producers Melissa Bernstein and Mark Johnson of *Breaking Bad* fame to help steer the ship.[5]

A big part of the appeal of *Halt and Catch Fire* derived from the unusual angle from which Cantwell and Rogers approached their material. The story of the early computer business is usually one that ends up sooner or later in Silicon Valley (as indeed theirs would, too). But Cantwell mined his Texas childhood, augmented by Rogers's penchant for research, and set the origins of their tale in the so-called Silicon Prairie surrounding Dallas, home of Radio Shack, Texas Instruments, Tandy, and Dell. "I loved the idea that it took place in Dallas and that I didn't hear Steve Jobs' or Bill Gates' name," recalled Ben Davis, one of the AMC executives who greenlighted the project. "It approached it from the backdoor instead of straight ahead."[6]

That backdoor wasn't only a matter of geography; it was also one of timing. As with any technology story, there's always a question of when to begin. In the case of computers, there are any number of entry points. One could, for example, go back to the invention of the abacus in ancient Mesopotamia, or the seventeenth-century work of John Napier, whose development of Napier rods (or Napier's bones) simplified complex calculations.[7] But these would not likely make for gripping television. More promising, perhaps, would be a story based on the work of nineteenth-century mathematician Charles Babbage, who developed what he called an analytic engine, a machine which involved wooden cards and rods that could perform calculations faster and more accurately than if done manually. Babbage's work was taken significantly further by his friend Ada Lovelace, daughter of the famous British poet Lord Byron. Lovelace had a crucial insight: that the work of a machine of the kind Babbage was designing need not be about mathematical calculations alone. She was pursuing what she called "a poetical science," pointing the way to the first computer program—an algorithm to be executed by machine.[8] So it is that one of the major characters in *Halt and Catch Fire* names the basic input/output system (BIOS) that she invents after Lovelace, to the snickering of sexist men who regard it as an excessively feminine term rather than an act of homage to a digital pioneer. There is of course a lot to be done with World War II, when Grace Hopper, who worked on the pivotal development of the Electronic Numerical Integrator and Computer (ENIAC), also led the way in the development of the common business-oriented language (COBOL) that remains in use to this day. (Note the pivotal role of women here, whose history has been somewhat lost—something *Halt and Catch Fire* would redress with its prominent pair of female characters.) And there's the saga of the Internet, which began in the crucible of the Cold War but became a fixture of civilian life.[9] In modern times, computer mythology has tended to focus on the promethean genius of hackers in garages, most vividly embodied by the so-called two Steves, Wozniak and Jobs, who invented the Apple computer.

Halt and Catch Fire pushes all this history aside. By the time its story begins in 1983, the frontier phase of computing has long since ended—not only have computers become routine features of business and academic life, but they have shrunk in size and price, becoming consumer electronics one would buy in a big-box store. The closing frontier seemed sealed by IBM—the corporate colossus of the industry, positioned to dominate the nascent personal computer market with the introduction of its PC in 1981. As anyone familiar with the story knows, however, there was a loophole. In its haste to develop the PC, IBM subcontracted the development of its operating system to Bill Gates's Microsoft Corporation, which retained the right to sell it to other computer manufacturers. This opened the door for competitors, notably the Compaq Computer Corporation, whose "clone" of the PC gobbled up a huge share of the market in the 1980s and 1990s. The initial storyline of *Halt and Catch Fire* is clearly modeled on that of Compaq—and springboards from there into the dawn of the Internet era.[10]

CREATIVE DESTRUCTION

The phrase "halt and catch fire," or HCF, is a term of art in computer engineering explained on a desktop screen in the establishing shot of the series: "An early computer command that sent the machine into race condition, forcing all instructions to compete for superiority at once. Control of the computer could not be regained." The "catching fire" part is a techie joke meant to capture the idea of system overload.

The phrase is actually a pretty good description of what happens over the course of the first season of the show. The first character we meet is Joe MacMillan (Lee Pace), a dashing young man in hurry— he runs over an armadillo in his sports car—on his way to deliver a guest lecture in a computer class as one of the leading figures in the development of IBM's personal computer. But Joe is not what he seems. For one thing, he's a renegade who quit IBM, where his father is a senior executive, under murky circumstances. For another, he's on something of a fishing expedition, seeking to recruit a hot-shot programmer, whom he finds in an alienated, punk rock and video game addicted young woman named Cameron Howe, who will have energetic sex with him in the arcade where he hunts her down. (Their fraught relationship will drive the series.) Joe next makes his way to Cardiff Electric, a stodgy but profitable midsized mainframe computer company, and talks one of the executives there, John Bosworth (Toby Huss) into hiring him as a salesman. But Joe has no interest in that job. Actually, he's on another recruiting mission, this time with a known target: Gordon Clark (Scoot McNairy); his character's name seems to be an amalgam of semiconductor pioneer Gordon Moore and graphics trailblazer Jim Clark. It turns out the fictive Clark wrote an article for *BYTE* magazine on open architecture that MacMillan believes could be the foundation for a machine that would compete with the IBM PC. But Clark is resistant to joining MacMillan's project, not only because he rightly suspects Joe is a little too slick but also because he's gun shy in the aftermath of the failure of Symphonic, a personal computer he developed with his wife Donna (Kerry Bishé), who works at an unfulfilling job at Texas Instruments and bears most of the weight of raising their two young daughters. But the allure of Joe's entrepreneurialism is too strong for Gordon to resist.

Over the course of the first season, we learn just how creatively destructive Joe MacMillan can be. The quest for a new machine begins with Gordon reverse-engineering the IBM PC, an act of questionable legality that secretly crosses the line. The twist is that Joe (partially) discloses what he and Gordon are doing to intentionally precipitate litigation against Cardiff Electric in a fashion that leaves the company little practical choice but to actually develop the machine, forcing the furious John Bosworth to reluctantly put Joe in charge of the project. Meanwhile, Joe puts Cameron to work in developing an operating system for the Cardiff PC—and then secretly destroys her data on the eve of a visit from a journalist at a major computer magazine sniffing for a juicy story. Joe's gamble that Cameron will rise to the occasion is vindicated—"You're the modern Ada Lovelace," he tells her—and he gets an unexpected assist from Donna, who, like Gordon, has a degree in computer engineering from Berkeley. She pitches in at the moment of crisis. (She also made an earlier crucial suggestion involving putting hardware on both sides of a board in the quest to limit space and maximize speed in creating a laptop that will weigh a "mere" fifteen pounds.) Joe will further anger Cameron, who gets intrigued by the possibility of personalizing the PC with interactive features, by dropping these features at the last minute in the rush to get the machine to market. At great literal and figurative cost, Cardiff's machine, dubbed the Giant, does indeed become a success. But as the season ends, we see the writing on the wall in the form of the Apple Macintosh—which, considering the omnipresence of Apple in our lives, we in the audience know will inevitably vanquish the Giant.

Which points to a major theme of *Halt and Catch Fire* as a whole: failure can be as dramatic and interesting as success, which is as much a matter of timing and luck as it is the intrinsic merits and talents of the people involved.[11] Such a message takes on particular resonance when one considers that the show was made in the decade after the dot.com bust in 2001, a speculative boom that rested on a great number of Internet dreams of varying solidity turning to ashes. This, in turn, points to another theme: the quality of the people involved *as* people—the role of personality and temperament in any story of technology and/or business. Though he will fade in importance over the course of the series, Joe MacMillan is the catalytic force of *Halt and Catch Fire*—often to the exasperation of the other characters (and, perhaps, viewers of the show who might wish the profit motive was less decisive in the history of computing than it has proven to be). "It must be nice to have a job where you get to say words without having to do anything," says an irritated Gordon, who races to implement the ideas that Joe airily imagines, in the fifth episode, "Adventure." Three episodes later, a bitter Cameron tells Joe, "You only destroy things. You never created anything."

"I created the both of you," he responds to her (and Gordon, who's in the room). She slugs him.

But he's not entirely wrong, as John Bosworth, who has at least as much reason to be mad at Joe as Cameron or Gordon, realizes. "In five years, every one of us could have one of these damn things in the house," he notes, grasping the reality of an incipient consumer revolution. Desperate to save a company collapsing amid layoffs and rising debt, he colludes with Cameron to digitally embezzle money from company founder Nathan Cardiff, for which he will serve a short prison term and emerge as "Bos," a transformed man who casts his lot with the brilliant young programmer, for whom he becomes a surrogate father. He also reinforces *Halt and Catch Fire*'s argument about the importance of good business sense in the computer revolution, because while he has a decidedly different style than Joe MacMillan, Bos repeatedly demonstrates commercial acumen and good sense that sustains the other characters over the course of the story. Nor is this cheer for capitalism sustained only by men, as suggested by a tense exchange between Donna and Cameron late in the series. As an audience member at a conference presentation, Donna queries Cameron on "the relationship between a creator like yourself and the business side of gaming. You seemed to indicate there was some difficulty there and I was wondering if you felt any culpability in that."

"Well, it's an inherently fraught relationship, right?" Cameron asks.

"Huh," Donna responds. "How so?"

"Well, in that we have the ability to create something out of nothing and that can be threatening to the business side, because they can't." When Donna replies by stating "that relationship should be symbiotic," Cameron says, "I would say it's parasitic." She has the last word for the moment, though she will later apologize for saying it. But the debate—and *Halt and Catch Fire*'s consistent affirmation of the profit motive, however ugly, as a generative force—is one of the consistent themes of the series.

In the second and subsequent seasons of *Halt and Catch Fire*, the locus of the series shifts more decisively to the women—who, by the way, receive crucial funding from venture capitalist Diane Gould (Annabeth Gish), who forms a romantic attachment to Bos. A restless Joe leaves Cardiff Electric—and Cameron—to try a new life with a new woman in Austin (her wealthy father, an oilman, gives Joe a job that he quickly turns into a scheme to sell time on the company's huge mainframe). Gordon stays on at Cardiff, but when the company is sold he cashes out and tries to find himself, a task complicated by a diagnosis of brain damage caused by too much exposure to lead in his geek days.

But in an important sense, Gordon's and Joe's problem is that the two are focused on hardware when the future really belongs to software. This is a characteristic pitfall of communications technology pioneers, who focus on the machines (projectors, radios, televisions) rather than the content, where the real money ultimately lies.[12] It falls to Cameron, a gamer at heart, to exploit the untapped insights she's gained about interactivity to found a new company, Mutiny, that attracts Donna, who's similarly drawn to the human dimension of computing. Indeed, she's even more attuned to its incipient social media implications than Cameron, and her efforts to build chat rooms become even more important to Mutiny's bottom line than gaming does, pointing the way toward a future of social media.

The relationship between Donna and Cameron—conventional working mother versus mercurial punk individualist—now occupies center stage in *Halt and Catch Fire*. The two come to like, respect, and depend on each other even as their differences (Cameron's sometimes uncompromising vision; Donna's increasingly ruthless pragmatism) drive them apart. One particular source of tension is a decision to deal with Mutiny's ever-growing need for processing power by becoming a customer of Joe's company. Joe is up to his usual scheming, though the women are wrong in believing he's conspiring against them (he in fact is the one being outmaneuvered by his prospective father-in-law). When Gordon develops a program that accidently devours Mutiny software, Cameron in turn uses the malware on Joe's company. But Joe recognizes that Gordon's solution to that crisis is a brilliant piece of antivirus software. He sees a golden commercial opportunity that he exploits—and fights with Gordon about—in subsequent episodes.

The third season of Halt and Catch Fire finds the principal characters in Silicon Valley, where Donna notes a potent trend among Mutiny users: a desire to swap goods with each other in what is clearly a nod toward what will become eBay. There are growing tensions between Donna and Cameron, rooted in Donna's quest for venture capital so that she can further commodify Mutiny by accepting credit card payments, something Cameron considers anathema to her coding ethic. Information may want to be free, goes the saying widely attributed to computer guru Stewart Brand, but it appears plastic is greater than silicon.

Joe, for his part, has ended his short-lived marriage and is now a computer security baron—but one who's as restless as ever in his quest to find the Next Big Thing. With the help of a disaffected coder from Mutiny, a South Asian named Ryan Ray (Manish Dayal), he thinks he's found it: the pending commercialization of the Internet, which until this point has been a network controlled by the government.[13] This is yet another tricky proposition that will require various kinds of subterfuge that will culminate in the suicide of his protégé. The third season ends with Donna in effect trying to get the band back together to take advantage of the emergent Internet. She finds an eager collaborator in the figure she's been consistently skeptical about—Joe, who we learn has met Tim Berners-Lee at a conference, where he acquired the conceptual building blocks for what will become the World Wide Web. But the baggage the characters have accumulated with each other have become too great to allow such a merger.

By now it is 1994. The fourth and final season of Halt and Catch Fire begins with the main characters groping toward an opportunity on the horizon—the invention of a search engine—and compete to develop it, a contest all the more awkward because Joe's inspiration is none other than the younger of Gordon and Donna's daughters, Haley (Susanna Skaggs), with whom he is increasingly close in a paternal way. The rivalry becomes more complex still when Gordon's condition, which he has largely managed for the past two seasons, results in his sudden death. The series reaches a climax with a sudden death of another kind: with their collective effort focusing their efforts on attracting Netscape, the net browser developed by famed coder Marc Andreessen, another firm—Yahoo, which Donna has difficulty even pronouncing properly—has beaten them to the punch. Cameron and Donna will live to fight another day, as well as find a way to put aside their fights with each other. For Joe, this crushing defeat effectively ends his tech career, especially after Cameron leaves him. (He wants children; she doesn't.) Our final view of him, in effect, is back where he started: in a classroom, where his power to inspire remains intact—as a historical artifact.

GROWING PAINS

Like a lot of its television peers—such as the CBS series *The Good Wife* (2009–2016) with the legal profession, or *Mad Men* and the advertising business—the creators of *Halt and Catch Fire* made a strong effort to portray their industry settings with a high degree of verisimilitude, not only in terms of their sets but also in the level of technical detail in their dialogue, which was authentic but worn lightly. But they also made some effort to document the social history of their time. Actually, sometimes it was a lack of emphasis—a casual, matter-of-fact manner of portrayal—that made a statement in its own right.

Take sexuality. *Halt and Catch Fire* coincided with a major cultural turning point in American cultural history, when homosexuality— increasingly widened to include a series of categories that now fall under the general rubric of queer—were incorporated into the fabric of everyday life, a reality ratified by the 2015 Supreme Court decision *Obergefell v. Hodges*, which secured the right to marry as federally protected by the Fourteenth Amendment to the U.S. Constitution. But a few years before that—and even afterward—many LGBTQ people nevertheless had to tread carefully in their public and private lives. This was less true of the American intelligentsia, and it's reflected as such in *Halt and Catch Fire*. We learn early on in the series that Joe MacMillan is bisexual, an orientation that he is willing to deploy in the service of office politics when he plays a game of one-upmanship with a haughty investor by seducing her boyfriend. One of the more striking plotlines of the 2014 episode "Giant" involves Joe hiring an old paramour (D. B. Woodside), an African American industrial designer, to burnish the looks of Cardiff's PC. Cameron, who may not be as tough as she seems, is consumed with jealousy. But the fact that her rival for Joe's affection is both black and gay seems entirely irrelevant to her—she never refers to either. What we do see is the primal emotion of jealousy that appears to transcend race or sexuality. This is not necessarily anachronistic, especially among the technocratic elites of the 1980s and 1990s. But it is nevertheless a world of don't ask, don't tell, where the public display of affection we see between the two men pushes a social envelope. Then again, this is what Joe is all about. Which means, among other things, he has to worry about AIDS—his erstwhile lover tells Joe he's dying without specifying why; Joe later has a test that proves negative, to his enormous relief.

As befits the world it portrays, *Halt and Catch Fire* is an overwhelmingly white show. This is not only a matter of casting but of culture, as suggested by the songs selected for the series by music supervisor Thomas Golubić, which tend to run toward early eighties punk and new wave artists such as the Talking Heads (two episodes, "Heaven Is a Place" and "And She Was" allude to the band's songs) and the Clash ("Working for the Clampdown" is another song that's the title of an episode). There are occasional recurring characters of color, notably Ryan Ray, and Donna's African American assistant Tanya Reese (Sasha Morfaw), whom she promotes to an executive position. But the milieu here is decidedly that of the highly educated, upwardly mobile white elite.

Actually, the racial diversity we see is more substantial than portrayals of working-class life, which are almost entirely absent. We do get a glimpse of one such character, John Bosworth's secretary at Cardiff, Debbie (Bianca Malinowski), but she disappears once the company does. Despite the fact that we get regular exposure to the private lives of the main characters, there are no nannies, housekeepers, or other kinds of people who have always allowed places like Silicon Valley to function.

Gender is another story. Perhaps this isn't surprising given the prominence of women behind the camera in *Halt and Catch Fire*: eight of its twenty-one directors were female, as were six of eleven credited writers (not including showrunners Cantwell and Rogers). When it comes to the portrayal of marriage, the early episodes of the series begin with conventional, even stereotypical, depictions of gender roles. The first time we see the Clarks, Donna has bailed Gordon out after a bender, picking him up at a police station in the middle of the night with the girls asleep in the back of the family station wagon. He's the distracted husband and father seething with repressed ambitions; she's the increasingly resentful mom burdened with excess emotional labor. But as we've seen, *Halt and Catch Fire* will play with this script as Donna becomes an increasingly powerful figure inside and outside their home. In its unfussy way, the writers also show Gordon—described in the uncharitable words of Cameron as "the guy who hung two kids on [Donna] and now she's trapped"—growing into an effective parent in ways that range from basic housekeeping to attending to the emotional state of his children.

Those children are also interesting characters. The oldest, Joanie (Morgan Hinkleman) grows up to become an adolescent hellion, mercilessly mocking her parents in front of their post-divorce paramours. And yet her quiet statement in the aftermath of a disastrous dinner party that the woman Gordon is dating is beneath him, whether true or not, speaks to her regard for her father. It's also interesting that Joanie harbors no animus at all toward her sister Haley, who emerges as the most interesting character in the series in its final episodes. Her skills as an online curator attract Joe's curiosity and respect. One heartbreaking moment occurs when Haley, who is apparently gay, fails to connect with a girl in whom she's interested. One nevertheless finishes the series hopeful that these young women of the nineties are coming of age equipped with skills to take on the world.

And it's this underlying optimism that's ultimately the key to appreciating *Halt and Catch Fire*. As has been discussed, it's a show that repeatedly dramatizes failure—both in terms of the history of technology and in the lives of the characters who dedicate their lives to it. And yet it's not the whole, or even dominant, chord on which the story ends. This is not only because a number of these people are granted what can plausibly be considered happy endings—Bos finds true love in retirement; Cameron and Donna patch up their differences; a chastened Joe finds a calling. It's also that the show affirms the role of computers as a positive force in our lives. They're a source of hope.

This point is captured in an incidental but powerful fashion in the 2015 episode "Limbo," when an unabashed fan of Cameron's named Gretchen (Cait Pool) shows up at a party for Mutiny subscribers. "I just want to say thank you," she tells Cameron. "My family is kinda screwed up—well, really screwed up. I didn't have anyone to talk to until I found Mutiny. There are a bunch of people dealing with the same sort of stuff and they helped me—they helped me realize that I could walk away. That there wasn't anything wrong with me. And I couldn't have done it without you." Cameron is awkwardly stunned by this revelation and the hug that follows. But the value of the moment sinks in and she's able to fully embrace the grateful Gretchen.

Actually, it was Donna who first made Gretchen's point to Cameron four episodes earlier in the aptly named "Play with Friends." Donna tries to address Cameron's skepticism over Mutiny's chat rooms by appealing to Cameron's own longings: "You know that feeling when you're sending private messages with [her boyfriend] Tom, that feeling where you had a place to go where you could say things you wouldn't say in person? That—*that*—is the value of community." Given where the culture was headed, a world of social networking where people routinely meet and develop their most intimate relationships, this statement resonates.

By the time *Halt and Catch Fire* was made in the mid-2010s, however, such an affirmation could not be credibly made in an entirely uncritical way: we'd come to know too much about the dark side of technology. This point is underlined by the voiceover suicide note of Ryan at the end of the 2016 episode "You Are Not Safe." Set in December of 1986 (just before the series takes a leap forward into the nineties), his words are prescient: "There's something on the horizon. A massive connectivity. The barriers between us will disappear. And we're not ready. We'll hurt each other in new ways. We'll sell and be sold. We'll expose our most tender selves only to be mocked and destroyed. We'll be so vulnerable and we'll pay the price. We won't be able to pretend that we can protect ourselves anymore. It's a huge danger. A gigantic risk." Nevertheless, he concludes, it's worth it— albeit with a caveat: "If only we can learn to take care of each other."

That's a big if, of course. "All we have to do is build a door," a breathless Joe says as he imagines the Internet in the finale of season 3, "neXt," an allusion to a high-end computer sold at the time. Five deceptively simple words: *all we have to do.* As Joe would learn, building that door was much more difficult, and dangerous, than he imagined. But people like him built it, and the rest of us have sailed through it. So we beat on, bits with the current, forced forward ceaselessly into the ether.

CONCLUSION

Visualizing the Future of the Past

*F*OR MOST OF human civilization, recorded history was typically a matter of writing, the primary way to transmit accounts of past events across time and space. (Painting as well as theater were also forms of historical storytelling, but both usually rested on printed sources for inspiration.) And then, in the middle of the nineteenth century, two powerful new media emerged: photography and sound recording. Both were useful as a means of creating documentary artifacts, but neither was especially good for crafting seamless narratives. The advent of moving pictures at the turn of the twentieth century was an important step in that direction—D. W. Griffith's 1915 film *The Birth of a Nation* offered viewers a grandiose (and racially grotesque) history of the Civil War. But not until the advent of sound on film in the 1920s was it possible to create audiovisual experiences that could rival print in terms of offering interpretive accounts of the past. Television literally brought this audiovisual capacity home in midcentury, and by the turn of this century you could carry it around in your pocket. At this point, it's safe to say, most people watch and listen, rather than read, historical accounts.

Print hasn't disappeared. Indeed, the creation of the codex—a set of pages bound on one side, an improvement on the scroll—two thousand years ago has proven remarkably versatile, especially since it doesn't require batteries, electricity, or wireless connections. Nor has it grown obsolete as so many information delivery formats have already. (It might, but so far e-books have supplemented rather than replaced them.) Since the next big war will almost certainly involve electronic disruptions of any number of kinds, it seems safe to say books will be around for a while longer and will continue to be an important source of material for other media, even if they are ultimately relegated to museum pieces.

Meanwhile, we continue to watch "TV," a term that by this point refers to a form of segmented narrative more than it does a means of transmission. Most television shows, historical and otherwise, are interpretations of events in one form or another. But over time, those interpretations will themselves become artifacts—time-bound explanations of the world. (They considered *this* entertaining? They really believed *that*?) Those artifacts, however varied and even opposing in their interpretations, will become dated, obsolete, or even false in what they assert, explicitly or implicitly. But they will be no less valuable for that, because they will help people in the future to understand themselves by measuring themselves against us—the way we measured ourselves against those who came before us.

This book has been an effort to accomplish something along these lines: to look at how interpretations of the past look now. But the book is no less an artifact than that which it chronicles. It's a product of the second decade of the twenty-first century, a time when television, which was a quintessentially American invention, was losing its centrality in national life, just as the nation itself was losing centrality in the world at large. American television took its American audience for granted, but America itself—the very notion that the geographic space it signifies can be considered synonymous with "United States"—can no longer be. A nation is itself a form of storytelling, a collection of myths its members tell each other to explain and justify their laws, rituals, and common sense. But all stories become dated, their relevance, such as it survives, increasingly metaphorical than factual. And so new stories, new myths, get told in new ways.

In the meantime, we'll keep looking for the truth behind the screen in the faith that we will find some that will work for now—and maybe, just maybe, later too.

ACKNOWLEDGMENTS

*T*o BEGIN WITH a few words of thanks: I've benefited from discussing and showing parts of this book to friends and colleagues, notably Nancy Banks, William Norman, and Andy Meyers. I'd also like to thank my agent, Roger Williams of the Roger Williams Agency, for helping me pitch the book and steer it through contractual waters once I crossed into the publishing domain.

I'm grateful for the opportunity work again with the talented staff of Rutgers University Press. This includes my editor, Lisa Banning, sales and marketing director Jeremy Grainger, and publicity director Courtney Brach. Thanks also to copyeditor Lunaea Weatherstone and designer Pamela Rude for their work on my behalf.

This book, like a number of previous ones, was substantially written at the Starbucks coffee shop in Dobbs Ferry, New York. I was gladdened by the proficiency and goodwill of the staff there and the camaraderie of that community. The project was completed in the shadow of COVID-19, a somber reminder of the limits of human endeavor, but also a useful one in appreciating the views from windows on the world that remained available through small screens.

My family continues to be a source of sustenance. My sons Jay, Grayson, and Ryland Cullen have begun amassing interests and talents of their own, as has my daughter Nancy, who is beginning her undergraduate adventure as I write these words. My wife, Lyde, remains by my side. My final words of thanks are to her.

Jim Cullen
Hastings-on-Hudson, New York
October 2020

NOTES

INTRODUCTION

1. See the HBO featurette *"Boardwalk Empire* Sets: Designing an Empire," at the History vs. Hollywood website, http://www.historyvshollywood.com/video /boardwalk-empire-sets-designing-an-empire/ (accessed September 4, 2020).

2. Jim Cullen, *The Art of Democracy: A Concise History of Popular Culture in the United States*, 2nd ed. (New York: Monthly Review Press, 2002), 213.

3. Brett Martin, *Difficult Men: Behind the Scenes of a Creative Revolution: From* The Sopranos *and* The Wire *to* Mad Men *and* Breaking Bad (New York: Penguin, 2013), 285.

4. The basic outline of the narrative offered here draws on Peter Novick's classic study, *That Noble Dream: The "Objectivity Question" and the American Historical Profession* (Cambridge: Cambridge University Press, 1988).

5. For a brief analysis of Civil War historiography and its connection to twentieth-century popular culture, see Jim Cullen, *The Civil War in Popular Culture: A Reusable Past* (Washington, DC: Smithsonian Institution Press, 1995).

CHAPTER 1: LEFT TO THE RIGHT

1. "Statistics: The Impact of the Depression," History Resources, Gilder Lehrman Institute of American History, https://www.gilderlehrman.org/content /statistics-impact-depression (accessed August 31, 2020).

2. The culture of the 1930s has been richly documented. Important studies include Richard Pells, *Radical Visions and American Dreams: Culture and Thought in the Depression Years* (1973; Urbana/Chicago: University of Illinois Press, 2004)

and Morris Dickstein, *Dancing in the Dark: A Cultural History of the Great Depression* (New York: Norton, 2009).

3. See Jim Cullen, *The American Dream: A Short History of an Idea that Shaped a Nation* (New York: Oxford University Press, 2003), 3–5.

4. Josh Ozersky, *Archie Bunker's America: TV in an Era of Change, 1968–1978* (Carbondale: University of Southern Illinois Press, 2003), 2–5.

5. James E. Person Jr., *Earl Hamner: From Walton's Mountain to Tomorrow* (Nashville: Cumberland House, 2005), 20. *Spencer's Mountain* and its 1970 sequel, *The Homecoming*, were reissued in a dual e-book edition by Rosetta Books in 2017.

6. Hamner befriended Serling when both were writing for a radio station in Cincinnati in the late forties). See Person, *Earl Hamner*, 15.

7. Earl Hamner and Ralph Giffin, *Goodnight John-Boy: A Celebration of an American Family and the Values that Have Sustained Us through Good Times and Bad* (Nashville: Cumberland House, 2002), 44–45; Person, *Earl Hamner*, 72. Richard Thomas says flatly that it was Paley who made the series happen. See his remarks in his Archive of American Television interview (Part II), curated by the Television Academy Foundation, November 16, 2016, https://interviews.television academy.com/interviews/richard-thomas.

8. Person, *Earl Hamner*, 68; Hamner and Giffin, *Goodnight John-Boy*, 49.

9. "This is homespun material, and I love this kind of thing, but this show belongs to the boy and I'm too old to play second fiddle to a fifteen-year-old kid," Fonda told Hamner. See Hamner and Giffin, *Goodnight, John-Boy*, 57.

10. Person, *Earl Hamner*, 75; Hamner and Giffin, *Goodnight, John-Boy*, 59.

11. John J. O'Connor, "TV: Varying Norms for 'Family Entertainment,'" *New York Times*, September 14, 1972.

12. Cyclops [John Leonard], "Wholesome Sentiment in the Blue Ridge," *Life*, October 13, 1972, 20.

13. Anne Roiphe, "Ma and Pa and John-Boy in Mythic America," *New York Times*, November 18, 1973.

14. Thomas makes this point about word-of-mouth success in his American Academy of Television interview; Hamner and Giffin, *Goodnight, John-Boy*, 64; Person, *Earl Hamner*, 91.

15. Person, *Earl Hamner*, 10.

16. Quoted in Person, 59.

17. Large chunks of Hamner's memo are included in Person, 72.

18. Thomas notes this from his firsthand recollections in his American Academy of Television interview. He also skillfully renders an amusing anecdote of a good-natured offer of sexual initiation from an old artist to a young one that might well be regarded as harassment today but which Thomas accepted with mirth and gratitude (without any obvious indication that he accepted it).

19. See Michael Learned's interview in her 2014 Archive of American Television interview, curated by the Television Academy Foundation, November 11, 2014, https://interviews.televisionacademy.com/interviews/michael-learned?clip =chapter1. She revealed her emotional involvement with Waite in an interview with the UK newspaper the *Daily Mail* on February 12, 2019, https://www.dailymail .co.uk/news/article-6695381/The-Waltons-husband-wife-love-screen-worried -things-messy.html.

20. This information is included as part of the trivia accompanying the Amazon streaming service for *The Waltons*.

21. These figures derived by analyzing data provided on *The Waltons* by the International Movie Database, https://www.imdb.com/title/tt0068149/ (accessed August 31, 2020).

22. For an excellent review and context of this family history, see Robert Moore, "Confederates, Southern Unionists, and . . . The Waltons?" *Cenantua's Blog*, October 23, 2011, https://cenantua.wordpress.com/2011/10/23/confederates -southern-unionists-and-the-waltons/.

23. Hamner and Giffin, *Goodnight, John-Boy*, 82–83.

24. The writers of the show make this point in a lighthearted way in the 1976 episode "The Rebellion," when a restless Olivia defies John's wishes and gets a new (curly) hairstyle, which she instantly regrets and has trouble trying to undo. At one point she visits Verdie, assuming she will know how to straighten hair, presumably as all black people do. But Verdie informs her she doesn't know; it's not something her family ever taught her.

25. Hamner and Giffin, *Goodnight, John-Boy*, 138–139.

26. David Sheff, "The Waltons Come Down Off the Mountain as Jon (Jason) Walmsley Marries His Lady of Three Years," *People*, July 16, 1979, https://people .com/archive/the-waltons-come-down-off-the-mountain-as-jon-jason-walmsley -marries-his-lady-of-three-years-vol-12-no-3/.

27. Thomas, American Academy of Television interview.

28. Learned, American Academy of Television interview.

29. Thomas agreed that the movies just didn't work (even if he enjoyed them as literal and figurative family reunions). "The show's tone and character was based on the sort of filter of memory, you know, and there's an element of childhood being remembered," he explained. That's what was missing in the films. See his American Academy of Television interview.

30. For a notably incisive analysis of this development, see Mark Crispin Miller's essay "Deride and Conquer" in *Watching Television*, ed. Todd Gitlin (New York: Pantheon, 1986).

31. Roiphe, "Ma and Pa and John-Boy in Mythic America."

32. Thomas, American Academy of Television interview.

33. Andrew Rosenthal, "In a Speech, President Returns to Religious Themes," *New York Times*, January 28, 1992.

34. *The Simpsons*, "Stark Raving Dad," with new opening scene, January 30, 1992.

35. Steven Malaga, "Hallmark Channel's Competitive Advantage? Red State Appeal," *Los Angeles Times*, January 9, 2018, https://www.latimes.com/opinion /op-ed/la-oe-malanga-hallmark-success-20180109-story.html; Samantha Rose Hill, "Why the Hallmark Channel Is Completely Dominating in 2017," Thrillist, December 22, 2017, https://www.thrillist.com/entertainment/nation/hallmark -channel-movies-success-2017.

36. See, for example, All About the Waltons, http://www.allaboutthewaltons .com, and Fandom's Walton's Wiki, https://thewaltons.fandom.com/wiki/The _Waltons_Wiki, both of which were invaluable in writing this chapter. The Walton's Mountain Museum's website is http://walton-mountain.org/. As for reunions, see the footage from the 2017 gathering at https://www.youtube.com/watch?v =umINVexySqs. (All sites accessed August 31, 2020.)

CHAPTER 2: CAMP HISTORY

1. Jack Gould, "TV and Radio: New Programs Reviewed," *New York Times*, September 18, 1965, https://timesmachine.nytimes.com/timesmachine/1965/09 /18/290271472.html?pageNumber=35; Martin Oppenheimer, "Did the Nazis Win the War?" (letter), *New York Times*, October 25, 1970, https://timesmachine.nytimes .com/timesmachine/1970/10/25/129395522.html?pageNumber=167; Renee Hamilton, "*Hogan's Heroes* Deservedly on Hold," *Boston Globe*, October 25, 1998. There were a flurry of stories about a possible *Hogan's Heroes* movie again in 2013; see "'Hogan's Heroes' Rights Won Back by Creators Al Ruddy and Bernard Fein; They're Plotting New Movie," *Deadline*, March 13, 2013, https://deadline.com /2013/03/hogans-heroes-rights-won-back-by-creators-al-ruddy-and-bernard-fein -theyre-plotting-new-movie-454636/.

2. Brenda Scott Royce, *Hogan's Heroes: Behind the Scenes at Stalag 13* (New York: Bedford Books, 1998), Kindle 2013, location 86. A transcript of the interview, "Bob Crane Talks with Stan Freberg about Hogan's Heroes," is available on You Tube, https://www.youtube.com/watch?v=dd8obtKO904 (accessed September 1, 2020).

3. On the intricacies of syndication, see Royce, *Hogan's Heroes*, locations 57, 869. See also Robert R. Shandley, *Hogan's Heroes* (Detroit: Wayne State University Press, 2011), 52, 100. Perry Lafferty discusses the laugh track issue in Allan Neuwirth, *They'll Never Get That on the Air: An Oral History of Taboo-Breaking Comedy* (New York: Allworth, 2006), 172.

4. Jack Gould, "No Time for Situation Comedy," *New York Times*, December 17, 1967, https://timesmachine.nytimes.com/timesmachine/1967/12/17/93228182.html ?pageNumber=119.

5. Shandley, *Hogan's Heroes*, 57.

6. "A Military Invasion of Television," *Chicago Tribune*, March 27, 1966. As the story noted, not all these shows were about World War II (*F Troop*, for instance, was set just after the Civil War). But most were.

7. Shandley skillfully limns this trajectory. See *Hogan's Heroes*, 68–74.

8. Richard Powell, who cowrote the pilot, said he based his creation of Schultz on a character in the 1942 Ernst Lubitsch movie *To Be or Not to Be*, noting that Schultz is a very common German name. See Royce, *Hogan's Heroes*, location 253.

9. Royce, *Hogan's Heroes*, location 253.

10. The authoritative account of the show's creation comes from Royce, who spoke with many of the principals; see locations 158–240. Richard Dawson mentions the crucial role of Philip Morris and General Foods in his interview with the American Academy of Television, December 1, 2010, https://www.youtube.com /watch?v=lytPqkXbC6I, as does Werner Klemperer in a 1992 interview, https:// www.youtube.com/watch?v=2Gl_smVVkEI.

11. Royce, *Hogan's Heroes*, location 1576.

12. Information on these actors drawn from the brief chapters on each included in Royce, *Hogan's Heroes*, as well as Shandley, *Hogan's Heroes*, 52–56. See also "*Hogan's Heroes* Cast Included an Actual Holocaust Survivor, WWII Heroes," Groovy History, July 25, 2018, https://groovyhistory.com/hogans-heroes-the-lighter-side-of -wwii.

13. Royce, *Hogan's Heroes*, locations 429, 99.

14. On Clary, see Royce's chapter on him; Shandley notes the blackface history on p. 54. Banner quoted in Shandley, *Hogan's Heroes*, *Hogan's Heroes*, 55–56; Klemperer in Royce, location 1366. On O'Connor's portrayal of Archie Bunker, see Jim Cullen, *Those Were the Days: Why* All in the Family *Still Matters* (New Brunswick, NJ: Rutgers University Press, 2020), chapters 6, 8.

15. Thomas Saylor, *Long Hard Road: American POWs During World War II*, Kindle edition (St. Paul: Minnesota Historical Society Press, 2007). On the Geneva conventions, see preface; on POW figures, see p. 5. Saylor devotes a chapter to hell ships and slave labor (see ch. 7).

16. Shandley, *Hogan's Heroes*, 64, 49.

17. John J. O'Connor, "TV Weekend," *New York Times*, April 14, 1978, https:// www.nytimes.com/1978/04/14/archives/tv-weekend.html. The piece was excerpted two days later. See also Shandley, 51, for a good treatment of the issues.

18. For a vigorous argument on the depth and breadth of anti-Semitism in Germany before and during the Third Reich, see Daniel Jonah Goldhagen, *Hitler's*

Willing Executioners: Ordinary Germans and the Holocaust (reprint, New York: Vintage, 2007).

19. Stuart Elliot, "Enron's Many Strands: Congressional Sidelight; TV Catch-phrase from the 1960's Is Evoked in a Hearing over Enron," *New York Times*, February 9, 2002, https://www.nytimes.com/2002/02/09/business/enron-s-many -strands-congressional-sidelight-tv-catch-phrase-1960-s-evoked.html. *Hogan's Heroes* reruns were part of Nickelodeon's "Nick at Nite" programming at the time.

20. This backstory is sketched on the Sgt. Schultz page of Fandom's *Hogan's Heroes* site, https://hogansheroes.fandom.com/wiki/Hans_Schultz (accessed September 4, 2020).

21. Royce, *Hogan's Heroes*, locations 1731, 1542, 1556.

22. Shandley, *Hogan's Heroes*, 58.

23. Shandley, 67; Peter Gumbel, "Does the World Need the Idea of 'Bad' Germans?" *Wilson Quarterly*, January 1, 2015. Gumbel notes, as have others, that *Hogan's Heroes* was popular in Germany (it began airing there in 1992; see Royce, *Hogan's Heroes*, location 922).

24. Josh Ozersky, *Archie Bunker's America: TV in an Era of Change, 1968–1978* (Carbondale: Southern Illinois University Press, 2003), 2. Ozersky's table is based on Nielsen ratings.

25. Shandley, *Hogan's Heroes*, 25.

26. Royce, *Hogan's Heroes*, location 1930.

27. See "Robert Butler Discusses Directing the *Hogan's Heroes* Pilot," January 14, 2004, Archive of American Television, https://www.youtube.com/watch ?v=iEdB1vBUHJM.

28. Shandley, *Hogan's Heroes*, 95–97.

29. Paul Buhle and David Wagner, *Hide in Plain Sight: The Hollywood Blacklist-ees and Television* (New York: Palgrave Macmillan, 2002), 62; Shandley, 75. Clary discusses the political affiliations of the cast in his AAT interview.

30. See Royce's chapter "Auf Wiedersehen, Hogan: The Cancellation," in *Hogan's Heroes*; on the rise of *All in the Family*, see Cullen, *Those Were the Days*, ch. 3.

31. Shandley, *Hogan's Heroes*, 15, 103.

CHAPTER 3: A FUNNY WAR

1. A little context here. "Goddamn war" is uttered by Staff Sergeant Gorman, a minor character, followed rapidly by "That is all," which comes over the loud-speaker that serves as a source of announcements—and sly subtext—in the film as well as the later TV series. Houlihan's line comes from the episode titled "As Time Goes By," which was shot last but aired as the penultimate episode of the series.

2. As will be discussed, MASH is an acronym for "mobile army surgical hospital," and as such was the title of a 1968 novel. When that book was made into a film, the studio that released it, 20th Century Fox, was concerned that viewers would take it literally and added asterisks—*M*A*S*H*—to avoid confusion. That convention was carried over into the TV show. See Dale Sherman, *MASH FAQ: Everything Left to Know about the Best Care Anywhere* (Montclair, NJ: Applause Books, 2016), xii–xiii.

3. The telegrams are reproduced in Arlene Alda and Alan Alda's keepsake book *The Last Days of MASH* (Verona, NJ: Unicorn, 1983).

4. Travis M. Andrews, "106 million people watched 'M.A.S.H.' finale 35 years ago. No scripted show since has come close," *Washington Post*, February 28, 2018, https://www.washingtonpost.com/news/morning-mix/wp/2018/02/28/106-million-people-watched-mash-finale-35-years-ago-no-scripted-show-has-come-close-since/. As explained in the analysis of the episode at the fan website MASH4077TV.com, the official Nielsen rating figure of 106 million was based on who was watching at any given minute; something on the order of 125 million (a figure widely cited in media reports of the time) saw at least some part of it. Such figures shattered the previous record held by the famous "Who Shot J.R.?" episode of *Dallas* from November 1980. See "Goodbye, Farewell and Amen Ratings Analysis," https://www.mash4077tv.com/articles/gfa-ratings/, accessed September 4, 2020.

5. "*M*A*S*H* Ratings and Rankings," MASH4077TV.com, https://www.mash4077tv.com/episodes/ratings/, accessed September 4, 2020. On the cultural power of *All in the Family* and its ratings, see Jim Cullen, *Those Were the Days: Why* All in the Family *Still Matters* (New Brunswick, NJ: Rutgers University Press, 2020), 45–46.

6. Sherman, *MASH FAQ*, 25–30.

7. Richard Hooker, *MASH* (New York: Pocket Books, 1978), 5. In the 1974 episode "A Rich Full Day," we learn that Hawkeye got his nickname because *Last of the Mohicans* was his father's favorite novel.

8. Hornberger quoted in Sherman, *MASH FAQ*, 46.

9. Suzy Kalter, *The Complete Book of M*A*S*H* (New York: Abradale, 1988), 26–27.

10. Sherman, *MASH FAQ*, 209–210; Allan Neuwirth, *They'll Never Put That on the Air: An Oral History of Taboo-Breaking TV* (New York: Allworth Press, 2006), 159–160. Larry Gelbart also talks about the role of Self in launching the show in his memoir *Laughing Matters: On Writing* Tootsie, M*A*S*H, Oh, God! *and a Few Other Funny Things* (New York: Random House, 1998), 30.

11. Gelbart discusses the circumstances of his life in England before undertaking *MASH* in *Laughing Matters*, 27–31.

12. Neuwirth, *They'll Never Put That on the Air*, 161. On Gelbart's decision and involvement in the show, see his May 26, 1998, interview with the Archive of American Television https://interviews.televisionacademy.com/interviews/larry -gelbart#interview-clips, especially chapters 3 and 4.

13. See the August 26, 2000, Gene Reynolds interview at the Archive of American Television, https://interviews.televisionacademy.com/interviews/gene-reynolds #interview-clips. These remarks come at the end of chapter 6.

14. Kalter, *The Complete Book of M*A*S*H*, 27. Alda talks about his decision to join the show in his November 17, 2000, interview with the Archive of American Television, especially chapters 2 and 3, https://interviews.televisionacademy.com /interviews/alan-alda#interview-clips. His remark about high jinks appears in his memoir *Never Have Your Dog Stuffed and Other Things I've Learned* (New York: Random House, 2006), 149.

15. See Gelbart's essay on the show's first season in Kalter, *The Complete Book of M*A*S*H*, 37.

16. For a list of Korean characters on *MASH*, see Fandom's page on the subject with links to the actors: https://mash.fandom.com/wiki/Category:Korean _characters, accessed September 4, 2020.

17. Gelbart, *Laughing Matters*, 33.

18. See Alda, AAT interview. On the censorship fights, see Neuwirth, *They'll Never Put That on the Air*, 165–67. "They did not have any problem with the politics," Gelbart remembered (Gelbart, *Laughing Matters*, 167). In his research, which included conversations with the principals, David Marc found them reticent on the subject of *MASH* as Vietnam allegory, as obvious as it was to anyone watching at the time. See Marc, *Comic Visions: Television Comedy and American Culture* (Boston: Unwin/Hyman, 1989), 197, 192.

19. Linville makes this remark in the 1981 PBS documentary *Making M*A*S*H*, https://www.youtube.com/watch?v=jiFqjhSYomA, accessed September 30, 2019. The documentary is narrated by fellow CBS sitcom star Mary Tyler Moore.

20. David Reiss, *M*A*S*H: The Exclusive, Inside Story of TV's Most Popular Show* (Indianapolis: Bobbs-Merrill, 1983), 67.

21. Gelbart, *Laughing Matters*, 57.

22. Sherman, *MASH FAQ*, 315. See also Gelbart's AAT interview.

23. "Lenny Bruce's Gay Naval Ruse," The Smoking Gun, August 31, 2010, http:// www.thesmokinggun.com/documents/celebrity/lenny-bruces-gay-naval-ruse. Alda also cites the Lenny Bruce story in *Never Have Your Dog Stuffed*, 153.

24. Elizabeth Kolbert, "Alan Alda; Hawkeye Turns Mean, Sensitively," *New York Times*, May 18, 1994, https://www.nytimes.com/1994/05/18/garden/at-lunch -with-alan-alda-hawkeye-turns-mean-sensitively.html. A quick ProQuest search of "Alan Alda feminism" between the years of 1970–1984 yields a trove of results.

25. Howard Fishman, "What M*A*S*H Taught Us," *New Yorker*, July 24, 2018, https://www.newyorker.com/culture/culture-desk/what-mash-taught-us.

26. See Swit's August 13, 2004, interview with the Archive of American Television, chapters 2 and 3, https://interviews.televisionacademy.com/interviews/loretta-swit#interview-clips.

27. Marc, *Comic Visions*, 197.

28. Tom Wolfe, "The 'Me' Decade and the Third Great Awakening," *New York*, August 23, 1976, republished April 8, 2008, http://nymag.com/news/features/45938/.

29. Daniel E. Slotnick, "Alan Arbus, M*A*S*H Psychiatrist, Dies at 95," *New York Times*, April 23, 2019, https://www.nytimes.com/2013/04/24/arts/television/allan-arbus-mash-actor-dies-at-95.html. Alda makes this remark in his AAT interview, cited above.

30. Metcalf explains in an essay included in Kalter, *The Complete Book of M*A*S*H*, 217.

31. Alan and Arlene Alda's *The Last Days of MASH* is a keepsake volume with a clutch of photographs and documents marking the end of the series.

32. Gail Milgram's *WSJ* piece, "M*A*S*H a S*M*A*S*H as a Museum Show," is reproduced in *The Last Days of MASH*.

33. President William Jefferson Clinton, State of the Union Address, 1996, https://clintonwhitehouse4.archives.gov/WH/New/other/sotu.html.

34. Marc, *Comic Visions*, 194.

CHAPTER 4: DREAM ADVERTISEMENT

For a useful compendium of *Mad Men*—including an excellent timeline that situates individual episodes of the show amid actual events of the 1960s—see Matt Zoller Seitz, *Mad Men Carousel: The Complete Critical Companion* (New York: Abrams, 2017).

1. Matthew Weiner, Television Academy interview, June 8, 2015, https://interviews.televisionacademy.com/interviews/matthew-weiner. See chapter 10 of the video. Earlier installations of the interview date back to 2010.

2. For more on this, see Andrew Cracknell, *The Real Mad Men: The Remarkable True Story of Madison Avenue's Golden Age* (New York: Running Press, 2012).

3. For one such example, see Weiner, Television Academy interview, chapter 5.

4. The firm's name undergoes a series of permutations over the course of the show's run—its unwieldiness a topic of discussion among the characters—but for the sake of simplicity it will simply be referred to here as Sterling Cooper, reflecting its founding by the (now dead) father of Roger Sterling, who remains a principal, and Bert Cooper, played by Robert Morse. Morse is a veteran actor cast with

a wink of intertextuality, as his first major role was in the 1961 stage version of *How to Succeed in Business without Really Trying*. He also appeared in the 1967 film.

5. The phrase "fable of abundance" was coined by T. J. Jackson Lears. See *Fables of Abundance: A Cultural History of Advertising in America* (New York: Basic Books, 1995).

6. Weiner interview, chapters 8, 9.

7. Barbara Lippert, "It's a Mad, Mad World," *Adweek*, August 16, 2009, https://www.adweek.com/brand-marketing/its-mad-mad-world-100110/.

8. Weiner, Television Academy interview, chapter 5; M. Keith Booker and Bob Batchelor, *Mad Men: A Cultural History* (Lanham, MD: Rowan & Littlefield, 2016), xv. For a good precis of the show's production design, see Martin Filler, "Designing Mad Men," *New York Review of Books*, July 29, 2010, https://www.nybooks.com/daily/2010/07/29/designing-mad-men/.

9. The Draper-Gatsby comparison has been widely made. For one succinct set of juxtapositions, see *Daily Beast*, July 11, 2017, https://www.thedailybeast.com/don-draper-and-jay-gatsby-two-men-with-a-parallel-and-lurid-past. Baz Luhrmann's 2013 film version of *The Great Gatsby* was released during *Mad Men*'s run.

10. F. Scott Fitzgerald, *The Great Gatsby* (1925; New York, Scribner, 2004), 2.

11. Fitzgerald, 110.

12. Much of the biographical sketch that follows draws from Brett Martin, *Difficult Men Difficult Men: Behind the Scenes of a Creative Revolution, from The Sopranos to The Wire to Mad Men and Breaking Bad* (New York: Penguin, 2013).

13. Martin, 244.

14. Alex Witchel, "'Mad Men' Has Its Moment," *New York Times Magazine*, June 22, 2008, https://www.nytimes.com/2008/06/22/magazine/22madmen-t.html.

15. Martin, *Difficult Men*, 260.

16. "*Mad Men's* Final Season, Matthew Weiner Tells All," 92nd St. Y interview, April 30, 2015, https://www.youtube.com/watch?v=Ln3dvXzjetM.

17. Anne Becker, "Not a Hot Cable Summer for All," *Broadcasting and Cable*, August 10, 2007, https://www.broadcastingcable.com/news/not-hot-cable-summer-all-83511; Frank Pallotta, "Mad Men Brings, Prestige, If Not Powerful Ratings, to AMC," CNN Business, April 4, 2015, https://money.cnn.com/2015/04/03/media/mad-men-ratings/.

18. Booker and Batchelor, *Mad Men*, 45.

19. Erin Mosbaugh, "How Much Does Don Draper Drink in One Day?" *First We Feast*, March 15, 2015, https://firstwefeast.com/eat/2015/03/don-draper-is-an-alcoholic-infographic.

20. Martin, *Difficult Men*, 262.

21. Weiner makes this point in his Television Academy interview, chapter 8. For further discussion of the issue, see Abigail Rine, "Don Draper Was Raped,"

Atlantic, June 8, 2013, https://www.theatlantic.com/sexes/archive/2013/06/don
-draper-was-raped/276937/.

22. Emily Nussbaum, "Faking It: Mad Men's Don Draper Problem," *New Yorker,* May 13, 2013, https://www.newyorker.com/magazine/2013/05/20/faking
-it-emily-nussbaum.

23. For an analysis of the show's deft depiction of King's death, see Juli Weiner, "Why *Mad Men* Got the Martin Luther King Jr. Assassination So Very Right (and Why *The Newsroom* Would Have Failed)," *Vanity Fair,* April 29, 2013, https://www
.vanityfair.com/news/2013/04/why-mad-men-got-the-martin-luther-king-jr
-assassination-so-very-right-and-why-the-newsroom-would-have-failed.

24. "I can't wait until next year when all of you are in Vietnam, agency executive Jim Cutler (Harry Hamlin) tells the young liberal men in the office in the 2010 episode "Summer Man," set in 1966. "You will be *pining* for the day when someone was trying to make your life easier. When you're over there, when you're in the jungle, and they're shooting you, remember you're not dying for me because I never liked you." Cutler also observes at one point that it's hard to take the pieties of these guys too seriously given that they're collecting paychecks that derive from Dow Chemical (maker of napalm, an incendiary product it sold to the military).

25. Claire Cain Miller, "The Costs of Motherhood Are Rising, and Catching Women Off Guard," *New York Times,* August 18, 2017, https://www.nytimes.com
/2018/08/17/upshot/motherhood-rising-costs-surprise.html.

26. For a feminist analysis of Betty's difficulties, see Stephanie Newman, *Mad Men on the Couch: Analyzing the Minds of the Men and Women of the Hit TV Show* (New York: Dunne, 2012), 87–99.

27. One of the people who noticed this most incisively is *New York Times* columnist Ross Douthat. See his blog post "The Three Dramas of *Mad Men,*" May 22, 2015, https://douthat.blogs.nytimes.com/2015/05/22/the-three-dramas-of-mad-men/.

28. This point is made in a discussion of the 2010 episode "The Chrysanthemum and the Sword," in Seitz, 205.

29. For an overview of the role of black characters in the series, see Rod Carveth, "We've Got Bigger Problems to Worry About: *Mad Men* and Race," in *Mad Men and Philosophy: Nothing Is as It Seems,* ed. Carveth and James B. South (Hoboken: Wiley, 2010), 217–227. In *Mad Men Carousel,* Seitz observes that the general absence of black characters of the show believably reflects the reality of its setting. But he complains that such a setting "doesn't seem a convincing excuse for treating civil rights as a historical background that occasionally affects action occurring in the dramatic foreground" (219). Such objections are characteristic of a moment when race is the primary consideration in contemporary cultural discourse.

30. Debra Birnbaum, "*Mad Men* Finale Explained by Matthew Weiner," *Variety*, May 21, 2015, https://variety.com/2015/tv/news/matt-weiner-mad-men-finale-12015 02982/.

CHAPTER 5: WE'RE ALL ALL RIGHT

1. Robin Zabiegalski, "20 Storylines from *That '70s Show* that Would Not Fly Today," *The Talko*, January 1, 2019, https://www.thetalko.com/21-storylines-from -that-70s-show-that-wouldnt-fly-today/; "The 50 Most Racist TV Shows of All Time," *Complex*, June 3, 2013, https://www.complex.com/pop-culture/2013/06 /most-racist-tv-shows/; Jessica P., "15 Iconic TV Shows that Are Totally Inappropriate Today," *TheTHINGS.com*, May 17, 2017, https://www.thethings.com/15 -iconic-tv-shows-that-are-totally-inappropriate-today/.

2. Parents Television Council, https://www.parentstv.org/.

3. Susan King, "The Right Time for Nostalgia," *Los Angeles Times*, June 13, 1999, https://www.latimes.com/archives/la-xpm-1999-jun-13-tv-45920-story.html.

4. Niraj Choksi, "Netflix Fires Danny Masterson amid Rape Allegations," *New York Times*, December 5, 2017, https://www.nytimes.com/2017/12/05/business /media/danny-masterson-fired-netflix.html. Masterson was formally charged in Los Angeles in 2020.

5. Nicki Swift, "Dark Secrets the Cast of *That '70s Show* Tried to Hide," April 7, 2017, https://www.youtube.com/watch?v=mpNIuNkoCFA.

6. See Fez's page in Fandom's *That '70s Show* Wiki, https://the-70s.fandom .com/wiki/Fez, accessed September 4, 2020; see also the "Where Is Fez From?" Reddit feed, circa 2017, https://www.reddit.com/r/That70sshow/comments/56gnw3 /where_is_fez_from/.

7. David Hochman, "Even Those 70's Kids Should Have Seen It Coming," *New York Times*, February 12, 2006, https://www.nytimes.com/2006/02/12/arts /television/even-those-70s-kids-should-have-seen-it-coming.html. Hochman notes that the show did exceptionally well with the 18 to 34 demographic, and that it continued to do so once it went into syndication. A 1999 profile of the show noted that while it rated fifty-fourth overall among prime-time shows, it was sixth among teenagers and twelfth among adults 18 to 34. See Andy Meisler, "Clothes and Hairstyles Do Not a Decade Make," *New York Times*, October 10, 1999, https://www .nytimes.com/1999/10/10/arts/television-radio-clothes-and-hairstyles-do-not-a -decade-make.html. The statistic on Netflix viewership comes from the table included in Rani Molla, "Here Are Some of the Most Popular Shows on Netflix— Which May Be Leaving Netflix Soon," *Vox*, December 21, 2018, https://www.vox.com /2018/12/21/18139817/netflix-most-popular-shows-friends-office-greys-anatomy -parks-recreation-streaming-tv.

8. Hochman, "Even Those 70's Kids Should Have Seen It Coming."

9. Meisler, "Clothes and Hairstyles Do Not a Decade Make"; Erik Adams, "*That '70s Show* Took TV Adolescence Down into the Basement (Where It Belongs)," *AV Club*, July 30, 2014, https://tv.avclub.com/that-70s-show-took-tv-adolescence-down-into-the-baseme-1798270795. A table with viewership of the show, complete with citations, is included in the *That '70s Show* entry in Wikipedia.

10. Michaela Morgan, "How *That '70s Show* Got Its Name," *10 Daily*, October 28, 2018, https://10daily.com.au/entertainment/tv/a181028kow/the-real-story-of-how-that-70s-show-got-its-name-20181028; Lacey Rose and Marisa Guthrie, "From *Lost* to *Friends*, The Strange Art of Picking a TV Title," *Hollywood Reporter*, March 6, 2012, https://www.hollywoodreporter.com/news/picking-tv-titles-friends-lost-examples-297288.

11. Andy Greene, "Reader's Poll: The Best Television Songs," *Rolling Stone*, September 21, 2011, https://www.rollingstone.com/music/music-lists/readers-poll-the-best-television-theme-songs-23185/7-that-70s-show-in-the-street-32090/.

12. John D. Leursson, "Alex Chilton Set to Go," *Rolling Stone*, February 28, 2000, https://www.rollingstone.com/music/music-news/alex-chilton-set-to-go-243920/.

13. Jill Webb, "15 Things You Didn't Know about 'That '70s Show,'" *TheTHINGS.com*, April 5, 2017, https://www.thethings.com/15-things-you-didnt-know-about-that-70s-show/.

14. Ken Tucker, "*That '70s Show*," *Entertainment Weekly*, September 18, 1998, https://ew.com/article/1998/09/18/70s-show-2/.

15. For visual diagrams and explanations of the *That '70s Show* set, see Judith Rumelt, "Home Sweet Home: Hard Work and Dedication Make the Set for *That '70s Show* as Garish as the Real Thing," *Hollywood Reporter*, April 29, 2002. See also an accompanying article, "Fashion Flare," on costumes, along with a sidebar on music. The pieces were published to coincide with the broadcast of the sitcom's one-hundredth episode.

16. Torsten Ove, "Actor Tommy Chong Gets Nine Months for Selling Pot Pipes," *Pittsburgh Post-Gazette*, September 12, 2003, http://old.post-gazette.com/localnews/20030912chong0912p5.asp. Chong was charged and sentenced in Pittsburgh.

17. Reid and Hesseman's performances are listed on their respective entries in the Internet Movie Database, https://www.imdb.com/.

18. See "All Bachelor's Degrees Earned by Women" at the "Women and Computer Science" website, https://cs.stanford.edu/people/eroberts/cs201/projects/2000-01/women-in-cs/statistics.html#nsfdata, accessed September 4, 2020. Data was obtained by the National Science Foundation, the Computer Research Association, and the Stanford Science Department.

19. The most comprehensive treatment of the Hill-Thomas hearings is Jane Mayer and Jill Abrahamson's *Strange Fruit: The Selling of Clarence Thomas* (New York: Houghton Mifflin Harcourt, 1994).

20. Accusations leveled (but largely dismissed at the time) by two women—Kathleen Wiley and Juanita Broaddrick—got new attention in the 2016 presidential campaign amid suggestions that Hillary Clinton had resorted to subtle intimidation to keep Broaddrick quiet. For two overview treatments of the accusations, see those in *Vox* by Dylan Matthews, "The Accusations Against Bill Clinton, Explained," October 9, 2016, https://www.vox.com/2016/10/9/13221670/paula-jones-kathleen-willey-bill-clinton-sexual-harassment-accusations; and "Juanita Broaddrick's Case Against Hillary Clinton, Explained," October 9, 2016, https://www.vox.com/2016/10/9/13221340/juanita-broaddrick-hillary-clinton-rape. The most even-handed treatment of Bill Clinton's sex life and how it affected his presidency can be found in John Harris, *The Survivor: Bill Clinton in the White House* (New York: Random House, 2005).

21. Gloria Steinem, "Feminists and the Clinton Question," *New York Times*, March 22, 1998, https://www.nytimes.com/1998/03/22/opinion/feminists-and-the-clinton-question.html. "The President is not guilty of sexual harassment," Steinem wrote in her op-ed. "He is accused of having made a gross, dumb and reckless pass at a supporter during a low point in her life. She pushed him away, she said, and it never happened again." This may be true, but it's not a metric many feminists would find acceptable twenty years later in the age of #MeToo.

22. At the time when this episode was set, the Equal Rights Amendment had passed Congress but was on its way to failing to be ratified by the states.

23. Merriam-Webster, https://www.merriam-webster.com/dictionary/nostalgia.

CHAPTER 6: DOMESTIC FRONT

1. For more on the escalation of Cold War tensions in the early 1980s, see Taylor Downing, *1983: Reagan, Andropov, and a World on the Brink* (New York: Da Capo, 2018).

2. Emmerich made this remark during "*The Americans* Podcast," Season 6, Episode 10, *Slate*, https://slate.com/culture/2018/05/the-americans-insider-podcast-for-episode-610-start.html.

3. Scott Shane and Benjamin Weiser, "Accused Spies Seemed Short on Secrets," *New York Times*, June 29, 2010, https://www.nytimes.com/2010/06/30/world/europe/30spy.html; Adam Epstein, "The Stranger-than-Fiction Story of What Happened to the Real-Life Russian Spies Who Inspired *The Americans*," *Quartz*, March 7, 2017, https://qz.com/926553/what-happened-to-the-real-russian-spies-who-inspired-the-americans/; Jon Levine, "Son of Russian Spies Who Inspired

The Americans Allowed to Stay in Canada," *New York Post*, December 21, 2019, https://nypost.com/2019/12/21/son-of-russian-spies-who-inspired-the-americans-allowed-to-stay-in-canada/.

4. Olivia B. Waxman, "The CIA Officer behind the New Spy Drama *The Americans*," *Time*, January 30, 2013, http://entertainment.time.com/2013/01/30/qa-the-cia-officer-behind-the-new-spy-drama-the-americans/; Laura M. Holson, "The Dark Stuff, Distilled," *New York Times*, March 29, 2013, https://www.nytimes.com/2013/03/31/fashion/joseph-weisberg-uses-his-cia-time-in-the-americans.html.

5. Bill Brioux, "The Americans Debuts on FX Canada January 30," *Toronto Star*, January 30, 2013, https://www.thestar.com/entertainment/television/2013/01/30/the_americans_debuts_on_fx_canada_jan_30.html; Cynthia Littleton, "*The Americans*: Inside Its Six-Season Journey to Critical Stardom and TV History," *Variety*, March 20, 2018, https://variety.com/2018/tv/features/the-americans-final-season-fx-matthew-rhys-keri-russell-1202730301/.

6. Russell's casting has been discussed a number of times; for one example, see her interview with Jimmy Kimmel on May 30, 2018, https://www.youtube.com/watch?v=NWzLscg2NcQ. For an interview in which Thomas compares his roles as John-Boy Walton and Frank Gaad, see Bruce Fretts, "Richard Thomas of 'The Americans' on Agent Gaad's Fate, John-Boy, and Jimmy Carter," *New York Times*, May 18, 2016, https://www.nytimes.com/2016/05/19/arts/television/richard-thomas-of-the-americans-on-agent-gaads-fate-john-boy-and-jimmy-carter.html.

7. Littleton, "Six-Season Journey."

8. These figures were calculated using numbers provided by TV Series Finale, https://tvseriesfinale.com/ (accessed September 4, 2020).

9. Annaliese Griffin, "*The Americans* Is the Most Profound Show About Marriage on Television," *Quartz*, March 29, 2018, https://qz.com/quartzy/1238861/the-americans-is-the-most-profound-show-about-marriage-on-television/; Elise Sandberg, "*The Americans* Co-Creator Says Russian Spy Series Is Really About 'Heartbreaking Marriage Moments,'" *Hollywood Reporter*, August 14, 2018, https://www.hollywoodreporter.com/news/americans-creator-says-russian-spy-series-is-heartbreaking-marriage-moments-1133484; Cynthia Littleton, "'The Americans' Final Season: An Oral History of the FX Drama," *Variety*, March 23, 2018, https://variety.com/2018/tv/news/the-americans-keri-russell-matthew-rhys-final-season-fx-1202734453/.

10. Amy Davidson, "The Secret of *The Americans*," *New Yorker*, May 2, 2013, https://www.newyorker.com/news/amy-davidson/the-secret-of-the-americans.

11. Sarah Archer, "Fifty Shades of Beige: Why *The Americans*' Set Design Is Far Less Simple than It Looks," *Slate*, January 28, 2015, https://slate.com/culture/2015/01/the-americans-season-3-the-hit-shows-set-designers-explain-why-the-shows-sets-are-far-less-simple-than-they-look.html.

12. Emily Nussbaum, "The Finale of 'The Americans' Was Elegant, Potent, and Unforgettable," *New Yorker*, May 31, 2018, https://www.newyorker.com/culture /culture-desk/the-americans-finale-was-elegant-potent-and-unforgettable.

13. For a good reading of this dinner table scene, see Scott Tobias, "*The Americans* Recap: Thanksgiving Day," *Vulture*, May 2, 2018, https://www.vulture.com /2018/05/the-americans-recap-season-6-episode-6-rififi.html.

14. Diderot says this in The Americans Podcast on Apple, S6E10: "START", May 31, 2018, https://podcasts.apple.com/us/podcast/the-americans-podcast/id96 2741924.

15. Emmerich makes these comments in the S6E10 installment of *Slate's* "*The Americans* Podcast."

CHAPTER 7: PROGRAMMING HOPE

1. The diminishing returns of technological revolution in the United States is a major theme of Robert Gordon's *The Rise and Fall of American Growth* (Princeton, NJ: Princeton University Press, 2017).

2. Statistics on initial viewership of the shows is included in the long and informative Wikipedia entry on *Halt and Catch Fire*, which cites (different) sources for the numbers on any given episode. See https://en.wikipedia.org/wiki/List _of_Halt_and_Catch_Fire_episodes, accessed September 4, 2020. Keep in mind, however, that these figures are for initial television viewing, and don't include later streaming, which is where most contemporary viewing takes place.

3. Rick Porter, "'Halt and Catch Fire' Will get a Fourth and Final Season: A Tale of Peak TV," *TV by the Numbers*, October 10, 2016, https://tvbythenumbers.zap2it .com/more-tv-news/halt-and-catch-fire-will-get-a-fourth-and-final-season-a-tale -of-peak-tv/.

4. In 2019, two years after *Halt and Catch Fire* finished its run, *Politico* cited the show as an overlooked gem. See Zack Stanton and Derek Robertson, "No 'Game of Thrones' or 'Veep'? Here's What to Watch Next," *Politico*, May 19, 2019, https:// www.politico.com/magazine/story/2019/05/19/game-of-thrones-recommenda tions-best-tv-shows-politics-netflix-amazon-226928.

5. Lisa Palmer, "'Halt and Catch Fire' Co-Creators Chris Rogers and Chris Cantwell: How We Made It in Hollywood," *Hollywood Reporter*, June 20, 2015, https://www.hollywoodreporter.com/live-feed/halt-catch-fire-creators-chris -803808; Nellie Andreeva, "AMC Orders Period Drama Pilots from Craig Silverstein/Barry Josephson, Mark Johnson," *Deadline*, November 27, 2012, https:// deadline.com/2012/11/amc-orders-period-drama-pilots-from-craig-silverstein barry-josephson-mark-johnson-377847/.

6. Joe Tone, "The Unlikely Engineering of *Halt and Catch Fire*," *Dallas Observer*, May 15, 2014, https://www.dallasobserver.com/film/the-unlikely-engineering-of -halt-and-catch-fire-6432656.

7. The background information on computers is drawn here from Jim Cullen, *A Short History of the Modern Media* (Malden, MA: Wiley Blackwell, 2014), ch. 10.

8. On Babbage, Lovelace, and the development of programming, see Walter Isaacson, *The Innovators: How a Group of Hackers, Geniuses and Geeks Created the Digital Revolution* (New York: Simon & Schuster, 2014), ch. 3.

9. For one account, see Katie Hafner, *Where Wizards Stay Up Late: The Origins of the Internet* (New York: Simon & Schuster, 1996).

10. On the connections between Compaq and *Halt and Catch Fire*, see Jin-Young Sohn, "How Historically Accurate Is 'Halt and Catch Fire'?" *The Take*, August 18, 2016, https://the-take.com/read/how-historically-accurate-is-halt-and -catch-fire; and Brian McCullough, "The Incredible True Story behind AMC's Halt and Catch Fire—How Compaq Cloned IBM and Created and Empire," *Internet History Podcast*, May 26, 2015, http://www.internethistorypodcast.com /2014/05/the-incredible-true-story-behind-amcs-halt-and-catch-fire-how -compaq-cloned-ibm-and-created-an-empire/.

11. James Poniewozik, "How 'Halt and Catch Fire' Made Failure Great," *New York Times*, October 14, 2017, https://www.nytimes.com/2017/10/14/arts/television /halt-and-catch-fire-finale.html.

12. This point is a major theme in Jim Cullen, *The Art of Democracy: A Concise History of Popular Culture*, 2nd ed. (New York: Monthly Review Press, 2002). See in particular the introduction and 137–138.

13. On the process by which this happened, see "A Brief History of the NSF and the Internet," National Science Foundation website, August 13, 2003, https://www .nsf.gov/news/news_summ.jsp?cntn_id=103050.

INDEX

abortion, 30, 135

"Abyssinia, Henry" episode (*M*A*S*H*), 70, 84

Adiarte, Patrick, 79

"Adventure" episode (*Halt and Catch Fire*), 177

Adventures of Ozzie and Harriet, The, 130

advertising: as funding mechanism for TV, 9–10; *Hogan's Heroes* and, 53; *Mad Men* and, 107–121; *M*A*S*H* and, 71

Affleck, Ben, 127

African Americans: in *Halt and Catch Fire*, 181; in *I Spy*, 61; in *Mission Impossible*, 61; in *The Waltons*, 34

"Afterglow" episode (*That '70s Show*), 134

Age of Reform, The (Hofstadter), 12

Albee, Edward, 127

alcoholism, 29

Alda, Alan, 68, 69, 77–78, 81, 85, 89–90, 196n14, 196n18, 196n24

Allen, Woody, 76

All in the Family, 21, 55, 75; early struggles of, 24; as midseason

replacement for *Hogan's Heroes*, 66; ratings, 71

Allman Brothers, 131

All-New Mickey Mouse Club, The, 153

Altman, Michael, 78

Altman, Robert, 74–75, 78

"Amber Waves" episode (*The Americans*), 149, 163

American Dream, 96–97, 190n3; *The Americans* and, 159, 165; King, Jr. and, 19; *Mad Men* and, 94, 96–98, 104, 107–108, 112, 116–118, 120; *M*A*S*H* and, 19, 82

American Movie Classics (AMC), 100; signing of *Halt and Catch Fire*, 172–173; signing of *Mad Men*, 100–101

American Political Tradition, The (Hofstadter), 12

Americans, The, 148–167; "A Little Night Music" episode, 160; "Amber Waves" episode, 149, 163; American Dream and, 159, 165; betrayal of country theme, 156; betrayal of others in, 156–158; biological warfare research theme, 159, 161–162, 164;

Americans, The (cont.)
  Cold War era setting, 148, 150–1521,
  159, 162–165; competing shows, 153;
  "Crossbreed" episode, 155, 162;
  "Darkroom" episode, 161; Davidson's
  review of, 154; "The Day After"
  episode, 159; "Dead Hand" episode,
  149; "The Deal" episode, 149, 163;
  debut of, 153; depictions of sex in,
  154, 158, 163; "Do Mail Robots
  Dream of Electric Sheep" episode,
  156; "Echo" episode, 149, 160;
  evangelical Christianity in, 160–162;
  "Experimental Community of
  Tomorrow" episode, 161; "Glanders"
  episode, 161–162; indoctrination of
  children in, 161–162; "March 8, 1985"
  episode, 149, 152; marital conflicts
  in, 156, 159–160; "Martial Eagle"
  episode, 161; moments of humanity
  in, 157; "Munchkins" episode, 159;
  "New Car" episode, 158; Nussbaum's
  review of, 155; "Persona Non Grata"
  episode, 149; "Pilot" episode, 149,
  156; portrayal of marriage in,
  154–156, 159–160; positive critical
  opinions, 154; racial issues, 165;
  "Rafifi" episode, 164–165; real-life
  espionage roots of, 151–156; spying
  possibilities, 151–156; "START"
  episode, 149; "The Magic of David
  Copperfield V: The Statue of Liberty
  Disappears" episode, 149; "Urban
  Transport Planning" episode, 166;
  violence in, 157–158, 163
"Anastasia" episode (*Boardwalk
  Empire*), 4
Anderson, Paul Thomas, 127
Andreessen, Marc, 180
"And She Was" (Talking Heads), 181

Andy Griffith Show, The, 21, 52, 60
Annie Hall film, 142
"Anniversary, The" episode (*The
  Waltons*), 40
Annual Message to Congress
  (Lincoln, 1862), 45
anti-institutional storylines, of
  M*A*S*H, 80–81
anti-Semitism, 39
Arbus, Allan, 82
Archive of American Television, 80
Arner, Gwen, 30
Arquette, Lewis, 32
Askin, Leon, 54. See also *Hogan's
  Heroes*
Atlantic City, New Jersey, x, 1–4
AuCoin, Kelly, 160
audience profiles: *All in the Family*, 66;
  Halt and Catch Fire, 171; *Hogan's
  Heroes*, 46, 59; *Mad Men*, 101;
  M*A*S*H, 70, 83, 91; *The Waltons*,
  25, 31
Auto Focus film, 66

Babbage, Charles, 173
Baby Boom generation, 5, 21, 146
"Baby Fever" episode (*That '70s
  Show*), 145
"Babylon" episode (*Mad Men*), 106
Banner, John, 44, 45, 51, 53–54, 58,
  193n14. See also *Hogan's Heroes*
"Battle Hymn of the Republic," 1
"Battle of the Sexists" episode (*That
  '70s Show*), 123, 141
Beatles, 20
"Beautiful Mine, A" theme song (*Mad
  Men*), 118–119
Becker, 99–100
Bell, Chris, 128
Benton, Thomas Hart, 19

Bernstein, Melissa, 173
"Better Half, The" episode (*Mad Men*), 115
Beverly Hillbillies, 60
Beverly Hillbillies, The, 21, 23, 60, 66
Bewitched, 60, 119
Beyoncé, 6
"Bicycle, The" episode (*The Waltons*), 17, 31, 35
Bing Crosby Productions, 66
biological warfare research theme (*The Americans*), 159, 161–162, 164
Birth of a Nation, The film (Griffith), 185
Bishé, Kerry, 168, 169, 175–183. See also *Halt and Catch Fire*
black-and-white episodes: *Hogan's Heroes* pilot, 47; *M*A*S*H*, 77; *The Waltons*, 37
blacklisting (Red Scare, 1950s), 65
Black Sabbath, 131
Blade Runner film, 156–157
Bloodworth, Linda, 85
Blundering Generation school, 13
Boardwalk Empire, x, 2–4, 11, 14, 100; "Anastasia" episode, 4; "The Emerald Forest" episode, 4–5; racial issues, 3; set recreation, 189n1
Bohen, Ian, 106
"Bombshells" episode (*M*A*S*H*), 87
Bonaduce, Danny, 131–132
Bonanza, 9, 21
Bondi, Beulah, 27
Boogie Nights film, 127
"Boondoggle, The" episode (*The Waltons*), 34
Boston Globe: article on inappropriateness of *Hogan's Heroes*, 46, 33
Bowie, David, 144
Bozell, L. Brent, 124
Brady Bunch, The, 130

Brady Bunch Movie, The, 127
Brazill, Mark, 128
Breaking Bad, 10, 153, 155, 173
Bridge on the River Kwai, The film, 51
Brie, Alison, 95, 112–113. See also *Mad Men*
Brooks, Mel, 46, 76
Bruce, Lenny, 85
Buono, Cara, 97, 101
Burghoff, Gary, 68, 69, 77, 87
Buscemi, Steve, 4
Bush, George H. W., 43
Bush, George W., 4
BYTE magazine, 175

Caesar, Sid, 76
Caine, Howard, 57. See also *Hogan's Heroes*
Campo 44, 53
"Canadian Road Trip" episode (*That '70s Show*), 123
Cantor, Eddie, 5
Cantwell, Christopher, 172–173, 182. See also *Halt and Catch Fire*
Capra, Frank, 27
"Captive, The" episode (*The Waltons*), 29
Cardellini, Linda, 103
"Carousel, The" episode (*The Waltons*), 40
le Carré, John, 152
Carroll, Beeson, 86
Carsey, Marcy, 127
Carsey-Werner Company, 127
Casablanca film, 54
"Casanova Klink" episode (*Hogan's Heroes*), 55
Castillo, Enrique, 37
Catch-22 film (Nichols), 75
Catch-22 novel (Heller), 75
Catholicism, 39

CBS, 22, 24, 46–47, 53, 66, 71, 75–76, 79

cell phones, 7

Central Intelligence Agency (CIA), 152

Chamberlain, Wilt, 70

Chao, Rosalind, 79

Charlie's Angels film, 131

Chase, David, 100

Cheap Trick, 129

Cheech, Richard, 136

Cheech and Chong, 136

Chilton, Alex, 128

Chong, Tommy, 136

Christianity, 39

"Christmas Comes but Once a Year" episode (*Mad Men*), 97

Christopher, William, 68, 69, 80, 88, 90

Civil War, 12–13, 33, 185

Clary, Robert, 44, 45, 53–54, 58, 193n14, 194n29. See also *Hogan's Heroes*

Clash, 181

"Clearance Sale at the Black Market" episode (*Hogan's Heroes*), 63–64

Clinton, Bill, 91, 138–139

Clinton, Hillary, 138

Clinton-Lewinsky scandal, 138–139

Cocker, Joe, 128

codex, 11, 185

Cold War: ARPANET and, 152; Cuban Missile Crisis, 150; historical background, 59, 64, 150; NATO and, 59; Operation Able Archer, 150, 152; as setting for *The Americans*, 148, 150–1521, 159, 162–165; Strategic Defense Initiative and, 150–151; western shows and, 9. See also *Americans, The*

collective memory: as ever-shifting frontier, 5–6; Great Depression and, 18–19; *Hogans Heroes* and, 66–67; *The Waltons* and, 39, 42

comedy genre, 7, 10, 14. *See also* sitcoms; specific TV shows

comedy shows, 7, 10

Communist Party of the United States, 27

Compaq Computer Corporation, 174

computers: Babbage's designing of, 173; *BYTE* magazine, 175; IBM computers, 107, 174–176; pervasiveness of, 169–170; programming languages, 174; role of Silicon Valley, 168, 173, 179, 182; trajectory in American life, 171; use of "halt and catch fire" term, 174–174; watching television on, 6–7. See also *Halt and Catch Fire*

"Comrades in Arms" episode (*M*A*S*H*), 86

"Conflict, The" episode (*The Waltons*), 17, 26, 33–34, 38

contingency notion, of history, 12–13, 189n5

Cooper, James Fenimore, 74

Corby, Ellen, 16, 17, 30–31, 34, 37, 41. See also *Waltons, The*

Cosby, Bill, 61

Cosby Show, The, 42, 127

Cotler, Kami, 16, 17, 26, 28, 32–33, 38, 41. See also *Waltons, The*

"Courtship, The" episode (*The Waltons*), 40–41

"Cradle, The" episode (*The Waltons*), 17, 30

Crane, Bob, 44, 45, 46, 51, 53, 65, 66, 192n2. See also *Hogan's Heroes*

creative destruction theme, in *Halt and Catch Fire*, 175–180

"Crossbreed" episode (*The Americans*), 155, 162

cross-dressing character, in
  M*A*S*H, 84
Cuban Missile Crisis, 150
Curb Your Enthusiasm, 10

Danson, Ted, 99–100
"Darkroom" episode (*The Americans*),
  161
Darling, Joan, 85
Davidson, Amy, 154
Davis, Ben, 173
Davis, Mackenzie, 168, 169, 175–183.
  See also *Halt and Catch Fire*
Dawson, Richard, 44, 45, 66, 193n10.
  See also *Hogan's Heroes*
"Day After, The" episode (*The
  Americans*), 159
Dayal, Manish, 179
Dazed and Confused (Linklater),
  127
"Dead Hand" episode (*The Americans*),
  149
Deadwood, 10
"Deal, The" episode (*The Americans*),
  149, 163
"Dear Sigmund" episode (*M*A*S*H*),
  90–91
"Dear Uncle Abdul" episode
  (*M*A*S*H*), 80
Decordovier, Jerado, 38
Democratic Leadership Council, 91
DeWitt, Rosemary, 103
Dick, Philip K., 156–157
digital video disc (DVD), 7, 47
DiMaggio, Joe, 70
Dirden, Brandon J., 165
Dixon, Ivan, 33, 45, 53, 60–61, 66.
  See also *Hogan's Heroes*
"Do Androids Dream of Electric
  Sheep?" (Dick), 156–157

"documentary impulse," in photogra-
  phy, 19
"Do Mail Robots Dream of Electric
  Sheep" episode (*The Americans*), 156
domestic life: in *Mad Men*, 113–116; of
  the U.S. in the 1950s, 81; in *The
  Waltons*, 18, 31
"Don't Lie to Me" episode (*That '70s
  Show*), 144
Dr. No film, 52
Dr. Quinn, Medicine Woman, 30
dramatic shows, 7
Drew, Sarah, 118
Duncan, Isadora, 31
Dvorovenko, Irina, 163–164
Dylan, Bob, 20
Dynasty, 30

Echikunwoke, Megalyn, 138
"Echo" episode (*The Americans*), 149, 160
Edwards, Ronnie Claire, 29
egalitarian individualism, 93
Eichmann, Adolf, 54
Eighteenth Amendment (U.S.
  Constitution), 1
Eisenhower, Dwight, 73
"Emerald Forest, The" episode
  (*Boardwalk Empire*), 4–5
Emmerich, Noah, 149, 151, 153, 155–156,
  159, 162, 164–167. See also *Americans,
  The*
Emmy Awards, 100; for *Hogan's Heroes*,
  55; for *Mad Men*, 101; for *The
  Sopranos*, 100; for *The Waltons*, 25, 35
entertainment: appeal of, 3
Entertainment Weekly, 130
Equal Rights Amendment
  (Fourteenth Amendment) (U.S.
  Constitution), 85, 141, 180–181,
  202n22

Esparza, Ernest, III, 38
evangelical Christianity, 160–162
existentialism, 80
"Experimental Community of Tomorrow" episode (*The Americans*), 161
extramarital affair: in *Mad Men*, 102–103; in *M*A*S*H*, 86

"familialism," 25
fantasy genre, 10–11
Farm Security Administration, 19
Farr, Jamie, 68, 69, 84–85, 88–89, 131
Fawcett, Farrah, 144
Federal Republic of Germany, 59
Fein, Bernard, 52–53, 192n1
Felicity, 153
Feminine Mystique, The (Friedan), 112
feminism: in *Mad Men*, 112; second-wave feminism, 138; *That '70s Show* and, 140; third-wave feminism, 112; in *The Waltons*, 20, 29–33, 41
Ferguson, Megan, 103
Fields, Joel, 152–154. See also *Americans, The*; Weisberg, Joe
"Fighter, The" episode (*The Waltons*), 34
"Fire Storm, The" episode (*The Waltons*), 17, 38
flashbacks: in *The Americans*, 157; in *Mad Men*, 103
"Flight" episode (*Mad Men*), 117
"Flood, The" episode (*Mad Men*), 106
FM radio, 20
"Fog, The" episode (*Mad Men*), 109, 117
Foley, Lee Ann, 151–152
Fonda, Henry, 22–24, 190n9
Ford, Gerald, 133
Ford, John, 19
"For Those Who Think Young" episode (*Mad Men*), 106–107

Fourteenth Amendment (Equal Rights Amendment) (U.S. Constitution), 85, 141, 180–181, 202n22
Fox Entertainment, 128
Franklin, Benjamin, 93
Freberg, Stan, 46
Fresh Prince of Bel-Air, The, 130
Friedan, Betty, 112
From Russian with Love film, 52
F Troop, 9
"Fulfillment, The" episode (*The Waltons*), 32
Funny Thing Happened on the Way to the Forum, A, 76
FX network, 151–153

Gaffney, Mo, 142
Game of Thrones, 10–11, 84, 153
Garner, James, 51
Gates, Bill, 173
gay characters: in; in *Halt and Catch Fire*, 181–183; in *Mad Men*, 107, 117–118; in *M*A*S*H*, 83; in *That '70s Show*, 125–126, 138
gay man portrayal, in *M*A*S*H*, 83
Gaynor, Gloria, 136
Geer, Will, 16, 17, 27–28, 38. See also *Waltons, The*
Gelbart, Larry, 76–80
"George" episode (*M*A*S*H*), 83
"Get Fit or Go Fight" episode (*Hogan's Heroes*), 64
"Giant" episode (*Halt and Catch Fire*), 169, 181
Gibson, Mel, 46
Girls, 10
Gish, Annabeth, 178
"Glanders" episode (*The Americans*), 161–162
Golden Globe awards, 101

Goldfinger film, 52
"Gold Violin, The" episode (*Mad Men*), 106
Golubić, Thomas, 181
Gomer Pyle, U.S.M.C., 52
"Goodbye, Farewell, and Amen" episode (*M*A*S*H*), 70, 195n4
"Good Company" episode (*That '70s Show*), 145
Good Times, 137
Gorn, Lev, 149, 155, 160, 163
Gould, Elliot, 74–75
Gould, Jack, 46, 49
Grace, Topher, 122, 123, 125, 128–129, 132–137, 140–145. See also *That '70s Show*
Grapes of Wrath, The movie, 19
Great Depression: Blundering Generation school, 13; economic impact, 18, 189n1; historic proximity of, 18–19; novels of Hamner, Jr., 22; portrayal by *The Waltons* and, 14–15, 26
Great Escape, The film, 51, 53
Green Acres, 21, 66
Griffin, Todd, 128–129
Griffith, D. W., 185
growing pains, *of Halt and Catch Fire*, 180–184
Gunsmoke, 9
Guthrie, Woody, 27
"Guy Walks into an Advertising Agency" episode (*Mad Men*), 95

Haggard, Merle, 34
Halt and Catch Fire, 168–184; "Adventure" episode, 177; AMC's signing of, 172–173; appeal of, 173–174; audience profile, 171; creation of, 172–173; creative destruction theme, 175–180; depiction of the rise of the Internet, 168–184; gay characters in, 181–183; "Giant" episode, 169, 181; growing pains of, 180–184; "I/O" episode, 169; "Limbo" episode, 169, 183; "neXt" episode, 169, 184; overwhelming white cast in, 181; "Play with Friends" episode, 183; racial diversity in, 181–182; rejection by HBO and Showtime, 172; "SETI" episode, 169; sex, sexuality in, 175, 180–181; songs selected for, 181; strong female characters in, 174; suicide in, 179, 184; "Ten of Swords" episode, 169; term (halt and catch fire) derivation, 174–175; underlying optimism in, 183; "Working for the Clampdown" episode, 181; "You Are Not Safe" episode, 169, 184
Hamilton, Lynn, 34–37, 191n24
Hamilton, Melinda Page, 104
Hamilton, Renee, 46
Hamm, Jon, 94, 95, 98–99, 101–120. See also *Mad Men*
Hamner, Earl, Jr., 22–23, 190n5
Hanks, Matthew, 108–109
Happy Days: comparison to *That '70s Show*, 122, 124; ratings comparison, 92
Harper, David W., 16, 17, 35–36, 38, 41. See also *Waltons, The*
Harrison, Lisa, 39
"Hawk's Nightmare" episode (*M*A*S*H*), 82
HBO channel: *Boardwalk Empire* series, x, 2–4, 11, 14, 100; *Deadwood* series, 10; *Game of Thrones* series, 10–11, 153; *Luck* series, 11, 189n3; rejection of *Halt and Catch Fire*, 172; *The Sopranos* series, 4, 10, 110; Weiner's pitch of *Mad Men*, 100

Heathfield, Donald, 151–152
"Heaven Is a Place" (Talking Heads), 181
Heinz, W. C., 72–74
Hendricks, Christina, 95, 100–101, 100–102, 104, 109–111, 117. See also *Mad Men*
Henry, Mike, 86
"Hepatitis" episode (*M*A*S*H*), 86–87
Hernández, Maximiliano, 165
Hesseman, Howard, 137
Hicks, Chuck, 63
Hill, Anita, 138
Hinkleman, Morgan, 182
historical consciousness, of *The Waltons*, 26
Hite, Kathleen, 30
Hitler, Adolf, 38
Hoffman, Dustin, 11
Hofstadter, Richard, 12
Hogan's Heroes, 44–67; *All in the Family* as midseason replacement, 66; "Casanova Klink" episode, 55; choice of shooting pilot in black and white, 47; "Clearance Sale at the Black Market" episode, 63–64; co-creation by Ruddy and Fein, 52–53, 192n1; comparison to *M*A*S*H*, 67, 71; controversy about appropriateness of, 45–47; factory vs. boutique ethos of, 65–67; film-based roots of, 50–54; formula for all episodes, 48–49, 59; "Get Fit or Go Fight" episode, 64; goal of producers for, 48–49; Gould's comments on, 46, 49; influence of spy thrillers, 52; influence on *Inglorious Bastards*, 67; "The Informer" episode, 45; "Is General Hammerschlag Burning?" episode, 45, 62–63; "Klinks Escape" episode, 57; laugh track experiment, 46–47; popularity in Germany, 66; "The Prince of the Phone Company" episode, 45, 61–62; racial issues, 60–63; representation of Nazis in, 46, 49, 53–54, 57–59, 61; "Rockets of Romance" episode, 66; Shandley's comments on, 49, 59; "The Softer They Fall" episode, 63; "The Ultimate Weapon" episode, 60; as veiled anti-war commentary, 14; "Will the Real Col. Klink Please Stand Up?" episode, 57; "The Witness" episode, 65; World War II setting, 45–47, 50–59. See also individual cast members
Holden, William, 51–52
Holocaust mini-series, 56
Holocaust (World War II), 56, 193–194n18, 193n12
Homecoming: A Christmas Story, The (*The Waltons*, prequel movie), 17, 22–24, 27, 34, 190n5
Homecoming, The book (Hamner, Jr.), 22–23
Homecoming, The TV show, 22–24
homosexuality. See gay characters
Hooker, Richard. See Hornberger, Richard
Hope, Bob, 76
Hornberger, Richard, 72–75
Horrocks, Brynn, 103
House of Cards, 153
House Un-American Activities Committee (HUAC), 27
housewives, on *Mad Men*, 103, 112–114
Howard, Ron, 34
"Hunt, The" episode (*The Waltons*), 34

Huss, Toby, 169, 175–177, 182. See also *Halt and Catch Fire*

"Hyde Moves In" episode (*That '70s Show*), 123

IBM computers, 107, 174–176

"I Can See for Miles" episode (*That '70s Show*), 125

"Ice Shack, The" episode (*That '70s Show*), 140

Ice Storm, The film, 127

"Illusion, The" episode (*The Waltons*), 18, 37

I Love Lucy, 10, 47

"I'm Free" episode (*That '70s Show*), 126

Immigration and Naturalization Act (1965), 133

"Informer, The" episode (*Hogan's Heroes*), 45

Inglorious Bastards film (Tarantino), 67

"Innocents, The" episode (*The Waltons*), 18, 32

integrated service digital lines (ISDL), 7

Internet: depiction in *Halt and Catch Fire*, 168–184; early development of, 5; evolution of, 7; transformation of, 169–170; transformative impact on society, 169–170

interracial relationships: in *Mad Men*, 117; in *The Waltons*, 37

"Interview, The" episode (*M*A*S*H*), 70, 77, 82

"In the Street" theme song (*That '70s Show*) (Chilton and Bell), 128–129

intraracial/intergenerational relationships, in *The Waltons*, 37

"I/O" episode (*Halt and Catch Fire*), 169

"Is General Hammerschlag Burning?" episode (*Hogan's Heroes*), 45, 62–63

I Spy, 61

"It's All Over Now" episode (*That '70s Show*), 139

It's a Wonderful Life film (Capra), 27

"I Want You to Want Me" (Cheap Trick), 129

Jeffersons, The, 33, 137

Jethro Tull, 131

Jews: in *The Waltons* episodes, 38–39

Jobs, Steve, 173

Johnson, Dwayne (a.k.a. The Rock), 132

Johnson, Enoch, 2

Johnson, Lyndon, 133

Johnson, Mark, 173

"Joker is Wild, The" episode (*M*A*S*H*), 87

Jones, Claylene, 30

Jones, January, 95, 98–99, 101, 104–105, 107–108, 111–115, 117, 119–121. See also *Mad Men*

Jones, Shirley, 131–132

Judgement at Nuremberg film, 54

Justified, 152

Kartheiser, Vincent, 95, 102–103, 105–106, 108–109, 112–117. See also *Mad Men*

Keaton, Diane, 142

Kellerman, Sally, 75

Kennedy, John F., 22

"Kids Are Alright, The" episode (*That '70s Show*), 140

"Killer Queen" episode (*That '70s Show*), 126

King, Martin Luther, Jr., 19, 105–106

Kinnear, Greg, 66

Kinskey, Leonid, 54

Klemperer, Werner, 44, 45, 53–55193n10193n14. See also *Hogan's Heroes*

"Klink's Escape" episode (*Hogan's Heroes*), 57

Korean War, 66, 68, 70–72, 80

Ku Klux Klan, 4, 155

Kunis, Mila, 122, 123, 126–127, 134, 137–140, 142, 144–145. See also *That '70s Show*

Kutcher, Ashton, 122, 123, 125, 127, 132, 138, 140, 142–144. See also *That '70s Show*

Lacey, Deborah, 113–114

"Lady Lazarus" episode (*Mad Men*), 113

Lambert, Paul, 54, 62

Lange, Dorothea, 19

Langella, Frank, 156

Lardner, Ring, Jr., 74

Larson, Doug, 25–26, 190n16

Last of the Mohicans, The (Cooper), 74

Laverne & Shirley: ratings comparison, 92

Lean, David, 51

Learned, Michael, 16, 17, 23, 27–33, 36, 39, 41. See also *Waltons, The*

Led Zeppelin, 131

Lee, Ang, 127

Lee, Harper, 22

Lee-Sung, Richard, 79

Leonard, Elmore, 152

Leonard, John, 25

"Let's Spend the Night Together" (*That '70s Show*), 132, 137

Lewinsky, Monica, 138–139

liberalism (midcentury), depiction in *M*A*S*H*, 85

libertarian sensibility of *M*A*S*H*, 72

"Limbo" episode (*Halt and Catch Fire*), 169, 183

limitations of television, 8

Lincoln, Abraham, 19, 45

Linklater, Richard, 127

Linville, Larry, 68, 69, 77, 82–83, 87, 196n19

Little, Cleavon, 34

"Little Night Music, A" episode (*The Americans*), 160

Lotz, Caity, 104

Lovelace, Ada, 173

Lucas, George, 20

Luck, HBO series, 11, 189n3

Lucy Show, The, 21

MacArthur, Douglas, 73

Mad Men, 107–121; American Dream and, 94, 96–98, 104, 107–108, 112, 116–118, 120; appeal of, 96; "Babylon" episode, 106; "A Beautiful Mine" theme song, 118–119; "The Better Half" episode, 115; character flashbacks to childhood, 103–105; children in, 113–115, 119–120; "Christmas Comes but Once a Year" episode, 97; comparison with *The Great Gatsby*, 98–99; comparison with *The Waltons*, 15; competing shows, 153; complexity of characters, 102–103; devotion to historical details, 97–08; domestic life in, 113–116, 114–116; Don Draper profile, 99–99; dream margins, 116–118; Emmy and Golden Globe awards, 101; extramarital affairs, 102–103; "Flight" episode, 117; "The Flood" episode, 106, 109, 117; "The Fog" episode, 109; "For Those Who Think

Young" episode, 106–107; gay characters, 107, 117–118; "The Gold Violin" episode, 106; "Guy Walks into an Advertising Agency" episode, 95; housewives on, 103, 112–114; interracial relationships in, 117; "Lady Lazarus" episode, 113; "Maidenform" episode, 95, 115; "New Amsterdam" episode, 105; "The New Girl" episode, 108; "Nixon vs. Kennedy" episode, 105–106; Nussbaum's comment on, 104; "The Other Woman" episode, 95, 110; "Out of Town" episode, 118; "Person to Person" episode, 95, 115, 120; "The Phantom" episode, 111–112; portrayal of vices, 101–102; ratings, 101; secular grace, 118–121; self-made men in, 105, 107; self-made women in, 107; "Severance" episode, 111; sex and sexism, 102–103; "Six Month Leave" episode, 115, 117; "Smoke Gets in Your Eyes" episode, 95, 116; "The Strategy" episode, 109, 115–116; suicide in, 107, 118; "The Suitcase" episode, 95, 108; "Summer Man" episode, 110; "Three Sundays" episode, 109; "Tomorrowland" episode, 111; "Waldorf Stories" episode, 104–105; Weiner's creation of, 96–101, 114, 120–121; "The Wheel" episode, 95, 114; women's work, 94–121. See also specific cast members

"Magic of David Copperfield V: The Statue of Liberty Disappears, The" episode (The Americans), 149

Mahendru, Annet, 155–156

"Maidenform" episode (Mad Men), 95, 115

Malinowski, Bianca, 182

Mandabach, Caryn, 127

Mandel, Johnny, 78

Man from U.N.C.L.E., The, 52

Marc, David, 88

"March 8, 1985" episode (The Americans), 149, 152

Married . . . With Children, 124–125

"Martial Eagle" episode (The Americans), 161

Martindale, Margo, 156

Mary Tyler Moore Show, The, 21, 71, 85–86, 132

MASH: A Novel About Three Army Doctors (Hornberger as Richard Hooker), 72–75

M*A*S*H, 68–93; "Abyssinia, Henry" episode, 70, 84; anti-institutional storylines, 80–81; "Bombshells" episode, 87; choice of Alda as lead, 77–78; as commentary on U.S. civilian life, foreign policy, 71–82; comparison to Hogan's Heroes, 67, 71; "Comrades in Arms" episode, 86; cross-dressing character, 4; "Dear Sigmund" episode, 90–91; "Dear Uncle Abdul" episode, 80; depiction of midcentury liberalism, 85; eleven seasons run for, 71; ethnic profile of cast members, 79; "existential" description of, 81; extramarital affair in, 86; gay characters in, 83; Gelbart's role in the success of, 76–80; "George" episode, 83; "Goodbye, Farewell, and Amen" episode, 70, 195n4; "Hawk's Nightmare" episode, 82; "Hepatitis" episode, 86–87; as historical artifact, 91–92; "The Interview" episode, 70, 77, 82; "The Joker is Wild" episode, 87; Korean

M*A*S*H (cont.)

War setting, 66, 68, 70–72, 80; liberal/libertarian values of, 72, 89, 92; mission to challenge mindless conformity, 83–84; movie version, 72–79; nineteen seventies seasons, 79–91; novel (book) version version, 72–75; "The Nurses" episode, 70, 85–86; "Point of View" episode, 77; portrayal of a gay man in, 83; "Preventative Medicine" episode, 70, 85–86; ratings comparison, 92; Self's role in launching, 75–76, 195n10; "Sometimes You Hear the Bullet" episode, 70, 83–84; "Suicide is Painless" theme song, 78; Vietnam War and, 14; winding down of, 90; "Your Retention Please" episode, 88. *See also* specific cast members

"M*A*S*H: Binding Up the Nation's Wounds" exhibit (Smithsonian Institution's National Museum of American History), 91

mass communication, 6

Masterson, Danny, 122, 123, 125, 130–131, 133–137, 144–145. See also *That '70s Show*

Mayberry R.F.D., 21

McConaughey, Matthew, 127

McDonald, Kelly, 4

McDonough, Elizabeth, 16, 17, 31–32, 37–41. See also *Waltons, The*

McGraw, Melinda, 103

McGreevey, John, 35

McHale's Navy, 52, 76

McNair, Barbara, 62

McNairy, Scoot, 169, 175–182. See also *Halt and Catch Fire*

McQueen, Steve, 51–52

"Medal, The" episode (*The Waltons*), 37

Me Decade, 90, 133

Mein Kampf (Hitler), 38

Meyers, Josh, 143

Microsoft Corporation, 174

Middle, Bette, 131

"Migrant Mother" photograph (Lange), 19

Mission Impossible, 61

Mod Squad, The, 24

Mok, Ivan, 161

Moore, Mary Tyler, 132

Morfaw, Sasha, 181

Morgan, George, 80

Morgan, Harry, 69, 80, 88

Morris, Greg, 61

Morse, Robert, 105

Morse, Samuel F. B., 170

Morse code, 174

Moss, Elisabeth, 95, 101–103, 107–111, 115–117, 120

"Munchkins" episode (*The Americans*), 159

Murphy, Cynthia, 151–152

Murphy, Richard, 151–152

Murray, Joel, 102

Muslims, 39

Nabors, Jim, 52

Nakahara, Kellye, 79

Namath, Joe, 144

Native Americans: in *The Waltons*, 38

Nazi regime: *Judgment at Nuremberg* film, 54; representation in *Hogan's Heroes*, 46, 49, 53–54, 57–58, 61

Netflix, 10, 153

Netscape, 180

Never Have Your Dog Stuffed (Alda), 77–78

"New Amsterdam" episode (*Mad Men*), 105

"New Car" episode (*The Americans*), 158

New Deal, 26–27

"New Girl, The" episode (*Mad Men*), 108

New Left (1960s), 16, 20, 27–28

New Yorker magazine, 154

New York Times: article on inappropriateness of *Hogan's Heroes*, 46; essay on *The Waltons*, 42

New York Yankees, 70

"neXt" episode (*Halt and Catch Fire*), 169, 184

Nichols, Mike, 75

Nielsen ratings, 21, 190n4

Nightingale, Florence, 31

Night (Wiesel), 56

Nineteenth Amendment (U.S. Constitution), 2

Nixon, Richard, 22, 63, 133

"Nixon *vs.* Kennedy" episode (*Mad Men*), 105–106

North Atlantic Treaty Organization (NATO), 59

North Korea, 73

Norton, Judy, 16, 17, 29, 31–32, 37, 41. See also *Waltons, The*

nostalgia, Larson's definition, 25–26, 190n16

nuclear war, 150, 159

"Nurses, The" episode (*M*A*S*H*), 70, 85–86

Nussbaum, Emily, 104, 155

Obergefell v. Hodges, Supreme Court decision (2015), 180–181

"Obsession, The" episode (*The Waltons*), 18, 29

O'Connor, Carrol, 55

O'Connor, John J., 25, 56

O'Hara, Maureen, 22

Old Left (1930s), 16, 20, 27–28

Operation Able Archer (Cold War), 150, 152

Operation Eichmann film, 54

Orange Is the New Black, 10, 132

Ordinary Spy, An (Weisberg), 152–153

Ormond, Julia, 111–112

"Other Woman, The" episode (*Mad Men*), 95, 110

"Out of Town" episode (*Mad Men*), 118

Paar, Bob, 76

Pace, Lee, 169, 175–184. See also *Halt and Catch Fire*

Paley, William, 22–23, 53

Panics of 1819 and 1837 (U.S.), 18

Paré, Jessica, 95, 106–107, 111–112

"Parents Find Out" episode (*That '70s Show*), 141

Parents Television Council (PTC), 124

Partridge Family, The, 131–132

Paulson, Jay, 103

"Peak TV" era, 10, 14, 171

Person, James, 25

"Persona Non Grata" episode (*The Americans*), 149

"Person to Person" episode (*Mad Men*), 120

Petersen, Claire, 30

Petticoat Junction, 66

"Phantom, The" episode (*Mad Men*), 111–112

Philadelphia Warriors, 70

Philip, Karen, 79

Phil Silvers Show, The, 52

"Pilot" episode (*The Americans*), 149, 156

Pitlik, Noam, 55. See also *Hogan's Heroes*

"Play with Friends" episode (*Halt and Catch Fire*), 183

"Point of View" episode (*M*A*S*H*), 77

political incorrectness, of *That '70s Show*, 124

Powell, Richard, 65

Prepon, Laura, 122, 123, 125, 129, 131–132, 135–145. See also *That '70s Show*

"Preventative Medicine" episode (*M*A*S*H*), 70, 85–86

"Prince of the Phone Company, The" episode (*Hogan's Heroes*), 45, 61–62

Producers, The film, 46

Prohibition era, 1–2, 10, 14

"Promise Ring, The" episode (*That '70s Show*), 142

Public Works Administration, 26

Queen, 131

"Quilting, The" episode (*The Waltons*), 17

racial diversity: in *Halt and Catch Fire*, 181–182; in *that '70s Show*, 136–138

racism/racial issues: in *The Americans*, 165; in *Boardwalk Empire*, 3; in *Hogan's Heroes*, 33, 60–63; in *The Jeffersons*, 33, 137; in *That '70s Show*, 124, 126; in *The Waltons*, 33–37, 35–37

"Rafifi" episode (*The Americans*), 164–165

"Ramble On" episode (*That '70s Show*), 135

Ranch, The film, 132

Rand, Ayn, 105

Rapp, Debra Jo, 125

ratings: *All in the Family*, 71; *Happy Days*, 92; *Laverne & Shirley*, 92; *Mad Men*, 101; *The Mary Tyler Moore Show*, 71; *M*A*S*H*, 92; *That '70s Show*, 124

Reagan, Ronald, 4, 72, 91, 150

Reaser, Elizabeth, 103

recording technology, 11

Red Scare (1950s), 65

"Red's Last Day" episode (*That '70s Show*), 129

Reid, Tim, 137

"Relapse, The" episode (*That '70s Show*), 123

religion: *Mad Men* and, 106; *M*A*S*H* and, 72, 81; *The Waltons* and, 39–40

Reynolds, Gene, 66, 76–78, 81, 87, 89, 196n13

Rhys, Matthew, 148, 149, 151, 154–167. See also *Americans, The*

Rice, Elizabeth, 114

Ritter, John, 29

Roberts, Tanya, 142

"Rockets of Romance" episode (*Hogan's Heroes*), 66

Rocky film, 131

Roe v. Wade, 30

Rogers, Christopher, 172–173, 182. See also *Halt and Catch Fire*

Rogers, Wayne, 68, 69, 77–78, 87, 172–173, 182

Roiphe, Anne, 25, 42

Rolling Stones, 131

Ronin, Costa, 149, 155–156, 162, 166

Room 222, 76

Roosevelt, Franklin: New Deal of, 26–27

Roots, 33, 35, 56

"Roots, The" episode (*The Waltons*), 35–36

Roseanne, 127

Ross, Mike, 119

Roth, Peter, 128

Royce, Brenda, 54
Ruddy, Albert S., 52–53, 192n1
Ruptash, Troy, 103–104
Rusler, Morgan, 103
Russell, Kerri, 148, 149, 151, 154–167.
    See also *Americans, The*

Sandburg, Carl, 19
satirical genre, 9, 75
"Scholar, The" episode (*The Waltons*),
    17, 31, 35
Schrader, Paul, 66
Scorsese, Martin, 11, 20
Scott, Eric (Ben Walton, *The Waltons*),
    16, 17, 19, 38, 41, 57. See also *Waltons,
    The*
Searchers, The, 9
second-wave feminism, 138
Self, William, 75–76, 195n10
self-made characters: men, on *Mad
    Men*, 105, 107; women, on *Mad
    Men*, 107
Sellati, Keidrich, 149, 155, 159, 162,
    166–167. See also *Americans,
    The*
Serling, Rod, 22, 190n6
"SETI" episode (*Halt and Catch Fire*),
    169
"Severance" episode (*Mad Men*), 111
sex/sexuality: in *The Americans*, 154,
    158, 163; in *Halt ad Catch Fire*, 175,
    180–181; in *Hogan's Heroes*, 64–65; in
    Mad Men, 102–103; in *That '70s Show*,
    141, 143
Shandley, Robert, 49, 59
Shane, 9
Shevelove, Burt, 76
Shields, Brooke, 140
Shipka, Kiernan, 95, 103, 113–114,
    118–119. See also *Mad Men*

Showrunner Training Program
    (Writer's Guild of America), 172
Siff, Maggie, 103
Silicon Valley, California, 168, 173, 179,
    182
Simpsons, The, 124
sitcoms, 10, 21, 29; *All in the Family*, 21,
    24, 55, 66, 71, 75; *The Andy Griffith
    Show*, 21, 52, 60; *The Beverly Hillbil-
    lies*, 21, 23, 60, 66; description, 60;
    Green Acres, 21, 66; limitations of,
    65–66; *The Mary Tyler Moore Show*,
    21, 71, 85–86, 132; renaissance of, 21;
    Three's Company, 29. See also specific
    sitcoms
"Six Month Leave" episode (*Mad
    Men*), 115, 117
Skaggs, Susanna, 180
Skerritt, Tom, 75
Slate online magazine, 152
Slattery, John, 95, 98, 102, 104–105,
    110–111, 114–117. See also *Mad Men*
slavery, 13, 33–34, 56
Smith, Jaclyn, 144
Smith, Kurtwood, 123, 125–126, 130,
    132–135, 137, 140–142, 144–145.
    See also *That '70s Show*
"Smoke Gets in Your Eyes" episode
    (*Mad Men*), 95, 116
soap operas, 7, 77
Soderbergh, Steven, 11, 189n3
"Softer They Fall, The" episode
    (*Hogan's Heroes*), 63
Sokovikov, Alexander, 163
"Sometimes You Hear the Bullet"
    episode (*M*A*S*H*), 70, 83–84
Sommer, Rich, 113
Sondheim, Stephen, 76
Soo, Jack, 79
Sopranos, The, 4, 10, 100, 110

Southern Baptists, 39
Soviet Union, 64
Spacek, Sissy, 34
Spencer, Abigail, 103
Spencer's Mountain book (Hamner, Jr.), 22, 190n5
Spencer's Mountain film, 22
sports shows, 7
Springsteen, Bruce, 93
Spy Who Came in from the Cold, The (le Carré), 152
Stalag 17 film, 50–51
Stanley, Christopher, 113
Stark, Don, 131
"START" episode (*The Americans*), 149
Star Trek, 117
Star Wars movies, 131
Stevens, Samantha, 119
Stevenson, McLean, 68, 69, 77, 79–80, 84, 87–88
Stiers, David Ogden, 69, 88
Strategic Defense Initiative (a.k.a. "Star Wars"), 150–151
"Strategy, The" episode (*Mad Men*), 109, 115–116
"Stray, The" episode (*The Waltons*), 17, 36
"Street Fighting Man" episode (*That '70s Show*), 123
Sturge, John, 51
suicide: in *Halt and Catch Fire*, 179, 184; in *Mad Men*, 107, 118
"Suicide is Painless" theme song (*M*A*S*H*) (Mandel), 78
"Suitcase, The" episode (*Mad Men*), 95, 108
Suits, 119
"Summer Man" episode (*Mad Men*), 110
Supreme Court, 138

Susman, Todd, 39
Sutherland, Donald, 74
Sutton, Frank, 52
Swit, Loretta, 68, 69, 75, 77, 85–87

"Tailspin, The" episode (*The Waltons*), 38
Talbot, Nita, 64–65
Talking Heads, 181
Tarantino, Quentin, 67
Taylor, Holly, 149, 152, 155, 158–162, 165–167. See also *Americans, The*
"Ten of Swords" episode (*Halt and Catch Fire*), 169
"Thank You" episode (*That '70s Show*), 143
That '70s Show, 127, 132–157; "Afterglow" episode, 134; Albee's comment on, 127; "Baby Fever" episode, 145; "Battle of the Sexists" episode, 123, 141; black characters in, 136–138; "Canadian Road Trip" episode, 123; choosing the show's title, 128; comparison to earlier teen-based sitcoms, 130; comparison to *Happy Days*, 122, 124; comparison to *Married . . . With Children*, 125; description, 15, 122, 123–124, 129–130; "Don't Lie to Me" episode, 144; gay characters in, 125–126, 138; gender relations, 138–146; "Good Company" episode, 145; historical referencing, 131–133; "Hyde Moves In" episode, 123; "I Can See for Miles" episode, 125; "The Ice Shack" episode, 140; "I'm Free" episode, 126; intergenerational cultural cohesion in, 136; "In the Street" theme song, 128–129; "It's All Over Now" episode, 139; "The Kids Are

Alright" episode, 140; "Killer Queen" episode, 126; "Kitty's Birthday (Is That Today?!)" episode, 123, 145; "Let's Spend the Night Together" episode, 132, 137; *Los Angeles Times* review of, 125; millennial's residual affection for, 126–127, 146; nostalgic appeal of, 146–147; offensiveness, political incorrectness of, 124–125; origins/creation of, 127–128; "Parents Find Out" episode, 141; Parents Television Council negative rating of, 124; "The Promise Ring" episode, 142; racial diversity in, 136–138; racism in, 124, 126; "Ramble On" episode, 135; "Red's Last Day" episode, 129; "The Relapse" episode, 123; sex jokes, 125; sexuality in, 126; "Street Fighting Man" episode, 123; "Thank You" episode, 143; Tucker's review of, 130; "The Velvet Rope" episode, 123, 144; "Whole Lotta Love" episode, 133–134; "Who Wants It More?" episode, 145; "You Can't Always Get What You Want" episode, 133

3rd Rock from the Sun, 128

third-wave feminism, 112

33-rpm albums, 20

Thomas, Clarence, 138

Thomas, Danny, 76

Thomas, Richard: in *The Americans*, 149, 153; in *The Waltons*, 16, 17, 24, 26–27, 30–31, 34–35, 38–42. See also *Americans, The*; *Waltons, The*

Three's Company, 29

"Three Sundays" episode (*Mad Men*), 109

"Tiger Rag," 1

To Kill a Mockingbird (Lee), 22

"Tomorrowland" episode (*Mad Men*), 111

Tootsie film, 85

Townshend, Peter, 128

Traffic (music group), 128

Trail of Tears, 38

tribalism, 93

Truman, Harry, 73

Trump, Donald, 4

Tucker, Ken, 130

Tucker, Sophie, 5

Turner, Bonnie, 127–128

Turner, Terry, 127–128

Turner Classic Movies (TCM), 100

Twilight Zone, The, 22, 190n6

"Ultimate Weapon, The" episode (*Hogan's Heroes*), 60

United States (U.S.): American Dream, 19; Great Depression, 5, 13–15, 18–19, 22, 26; Korean War and, 66, 68, 70–72, 80; New Left (1960s), 16, 20, 27–328; Old Left (1930s), 16, 20, 27–328; Panics of 1819 and 1837, 18; special role of television, 6–7; trajectory of computer growth, 171–172; Vietnam War and, 14, 19, 63, 64; war-related collective imagination, 18; World War I and, 29. See also Cold War; World War II

"Unthinkable, The" episode (*The Waltons*), 18, 39

"Urban Transport Planning" episode (*The Americans*), 166

Valderrama, Wilmer, 122, 123, 125–126, 128, 136–138. See also *That '70s Show*

Veep, 10

"Velvet Rope, The" episode (*That '70s Show*), 123, 144

videocassette recorder (VCR), 7

videotaping, 6–7

Vietnam War, 14, 19, 63, 64

"Violated, The" episode (*The Waltons*), 28

violence: in *The Americans*, 157–158, 163; in *Boardwalk Empire*, 14

Von Ryans Express (novel and movie), 52–53

Waite, Ralph (John Walton Sr., *The Waltons*), 16, 17, 23–24, 28–29, 39, 41. See also *Waltons, The*

Waite, Richard, 41

"Waldorf Stories" episode (*Mad Men*), 104–105

Walmsley, Jon (Jason Walton, *The Waltons*), 16, 17, 39, 41. See also *Waltons, The*

Walton Easter, A film, 33

Waltons, The, 17–43; "The Anniversary" episode, 40; "The Bicycle" episode, 17, 31, 35; black-and-white episodes, 37; "The Boondoggle" episode, 34; Bush's comment on, 43; "The Captive" episode, 29; "The Carousel" episode, 40; cast and description, 16; comparison with *Mad Men*, 15; "The Conflict" episode, 17, 26, 33–34, 38; conservative approach, 40–43; "The Courtship" episode, 40–41; "The Cradle" episode, 17, 30; Democrats, Republicans, and, 42–43; demographics in, 34–35; *Detroit News* article, 24, 190n10; as a document of the thirties, forties, seventies, 40; episodes with Jews, 38–39; family considerations, 20–26; fan and cast reunions, 43; feminism and, 20, 29–33, 41; "The Fighter" episode, 34; "The Fire Storm" episode, 17, 38; "The Fulfillment" episode, 32; geographic location, 26; Great Depression setting, 14–15, 26; historical consciousness of, 26; *The Homecoming* (prequel movie), 17, 22–24, 27, 34, 190n5; "The Hunt" episode, 34; "The Illusion" episode, 18, 37; "The Innocents" episode, 18, 32; intergenerational relationships in, 37; interracial relationships in, 37; key episodes, 17–18; Larson's description of, 26; Leonard's praise for, 25; "The Medal" episode, 37; as mythic vision of the ideal family, 42; Native Americans and, 38; nineteen seventy two debut, 92; "The Obsession" episode, 18, 29; O'Connor's praise for, 25; Old Left/New Left authenticity, 27–29; origins of, 20; portrayal of the Great Depression, 15; "The Quilting" episode, 17; racial issues and, 33–37; religion and, 39–40; reunion movies, 24, 30, 32–34, 41, 43, 191n29, 192n36; "The Roots" episode, 35–36; "The Scholar" episode, 17, 31, 35; slow fade of the series, 41; "The Stray" episode, 17, 36; "The Tailspin" episode, 38; television debut of, 22–23, 190n7; "The Unthinkable" episode, 18, 39; uphill battles of, 24–25; "The Violated" episode, 28; *A Walton Easter* film, 33; *A Walton Wedding* film, 34; "The Warrior" episode, 38; World War II and, 32, 37, 41. *See also* individual cast members

Warner Brothers, 9, 23

"Warrior, The" episode (*The Waltons*), 38

Wayne's World film, 127

Weiner, Marten, 114

Weiner, Matthew, 96–101, 114, 120–121

Weisberg, Joe, 152–154. See also
Americans, The; Fields, Joel

Werner, Tom, 127

westerns genre, 8–9, 22

"Wheel, The" episode (*Mad Men*), 95, 114

Whitman, Walt, 93

"Whole Lotta Love" episode (*That '70s Show*), 133–134

"Who Wants It More?" episode (*That '70s Show*), 145

Wiesel, Eli, 56

Wilder, Billy, 50

Williams, Billy Dee, 136

Williamson, Fred, 75

"Will the Real Col. Klink Please Stand Up?" episode (*Hogan's Heroes*), 57

Wilson, Teddy, 34

Winter, Terence, 4, 100. See also
Boardwalk Empire; Sopranos, The

Wire, The, 10

"Witness, The" episode (*Hogan's Heroes*), 65

Wizard of Oz, The (Baum), 5

WKRP in Cincinnati, 137–138

Wolfe, Tom, 90

women's suffrage, x, 2, 10

Women's Temperance League, 1–2

Wood, Grant, 19

Woodside, D. B., 181

"Working for the Clampdown" (Clash), 181

"Working for the Clampdown" episode (*Halt and Catch Fire*), 181

World War I, 29

World War II: Blundering Generation school, 13; Holocaust and, 56, 193–194n18, 193n12; representation of Nazis in *Hogan's Heroes*, 46, 49, 53–54, 57–58, 61; as setting for *Hogan's Heroes*, 45–47, 50–59; *The Waltons* and, 32, 37, 38–39, 41

Wozniak, Steve, 174

Wright, Alison, 149, 157–158, 165

Writer's Guild of America, 172

Yahoo, 180

Yost, Graham, 152

"You Are Not Safe" episode (*Halt and Catch Fire*), 169, 184

"You Can't Always Get What You Want" episode (*That '70s Show*), 133

"Your Retention Please" episode (*M*A*S*H*), 88

ABOUT THE AUTHOR

JIM CULLEN teaches history at the Greenwich Country Day School in Greenwich, Connecticut. He is the author of numerous books, among them *The American Dream: A Short History of an Idea That Shaped a Nation*, *A Short History of the Modern Media*, and *Those Were the Days: Why* All in the Family *Still Matters*. His essays and reviews have appeared in the *Washington Post*, CNN.com, *USA Today*, *Rolling Stone*, and the *American Historical Review*, among other publications. A father of four, Jim lives with his wife, Sarah Lawrence historian Lyde Cullen Sizer, in Hastings-on-Hudson, New York.

Printed and bound by CPI Group (UK) Ltd, Croydon, CR0 4YY

09/06/2025

14685734-0001